THE NEW CAMBRIDGE CO
JOSEPH CONRA

Joseph Conrad's centrality to modern literature *Cambridge Companion to Joseph Conrad* p varied developments in the field of Conrad studies since the publication of *The Cambridge Companion to Joseph Conrad* (1996). The volume's thirteen chapters offer diverse perspectives on emergent areas of interest including canon formation, postcolonialism, gender, critical reception and adaptation. Chapters on Conrad's autobiographical writings, *Heart of Darkness* and 'The Secret Sharer' consider recent trends in literary and cultural studies. A chronology and an updated guide to further reading serve to provide essential orientation to a large and complex field. This volume is the ideal starting point for students new to Conrad's work as well as scholars wishing to keep abreast of current issues.

J. H. Stape, late Senior Research Fellow at St Mary's University, Twickenham, London, taught at universities in Canada, France and Asia. The author of *The Several Lives of Joseph Conrad* (2007) and editor of *The Cambridge Companion to Joseph Conrad* (1996), he edited several of Conrad's texts for *The Cambridge Edition of the Works of Joseph Conrad* and was a co-editor of Conrad's *Collected Letters* (Volumes 7 and 9). He also published on E. M. Forster, William Golding, Thomas Hardy, Frank Harris, Angus Wilson and Virginia Woolf.

A complete list of books in the series is at the back of this book.

THE NEW CAMBRIDGE COMPANION TO JOSEPH CONRAD

THE NEW CAMBRIDGE COMPANION TO
JOSEPH CONRAD

EDITED BY
J. H. STAPE
St Mary's University, Twickenham, London

CAMBRIDGE
UNIVERSITY PRESS

CAMBRIDGE
UNIVERSITY PRESS

32 Avenue of the Americas, New York, NY 10013-2473, USA

Cambridge University Press is part of the University of Cambridge.

It furthers the University's mission by disseminating knowledge in the pursuit of education, learning and research at the highest international levels of excellence.

www.cambridge.org
Information on this title: www.cambridge.org/9781107610378

First published 2015

A catalog record for this publication is available from the British Library.

Library of Congress Cataloging in Publication data
The New Cambridge Companion to Joseph Conrad / edited by
J. H. Stape, St Mary's University.
pages cm. – (Cambridge Companions to Literature)
Includes bibliographical references and index.
ISBN 978-1-107-03530-0 (hardback) – ISBN 978-1-107-61037-8 (paperback)
1. Conrad, Joseph, 1857–1924 – Criticism and interpretation – Handbooks, manuals, etc. I. Stape, J. H. (John Henry) editor of compilation.
PR6005.04Z5693 2014
823′.912–dc23 2014014940

ISBN 978-1-107-03530-0 Hardback
ISBN 978-1-107-61037-8 Paperback

CONTENTS

CONTRIBUTORS

DEBRA ROMANICK BALDWIN, Associate Professor of English at the University of Dallas, has published articles on Conrad in *Conradiana* and *The Conradian* and has contributed to *The Wiley-Blackwell Encyclopedia of Literature* (2010–13). She has also published essays on Saint Augustine, Flannery O'Connor and Primo Levi. She is currently writing a book on narrative solidarity and the problem of universality in Conrad's art.

STEPHEN DONOVAN, Senior Lecturer in English at Uppsala University, Sweden, is the author of *Joseph Conrad and Popular Culture* (Palgrave Macmillan, 2005). He has edited *Under Western Eyes* (Penguin, 2007) and *The Inheritors* (Chatto & Pickering, 2013) and published in *The Conradian*. He is the creator of *Conrad First: The Joseph Conrad Periodicals Archive* (www.conradfirst.net).

ANDREW FRANCIS received his doctorate in English from Trinity College, Cambridge, in 2010 for a thesis on commerce in Conrad's Asian fiction and gained the Diploma in Dutch from Cambridge University in 2011. His work has appeared in *The Conradian*. He is currently writing a book on economics, politics and society in Conrad's Asian fiction, focussing particularly on the Dutch East Indies.

ANDREW GLAZZARD received his doctorate in 2013 from Royal Holloway, University of London, for a thesis on Conrad's use of character types from popular fictional genres. He has written on Conrad as well as the dynamite novel, H. G. Wells and Arthur Conan Doyle, for *The Conradian*, the *Journal for the Study of British Cultures*, *The Wellsian* and *English Literature in Transition, 1880–1920*.

MICHAEL GREANEY, Senior Lecturer in English at Lancaster University, is the author of *Conrad, Language, and Narrative* (Cambridge University Press, 2002) and *Contemporary Fiction and the Uses of Theory* (Palgrave Macmillan, 2006). He is currently completing *The Literature of Sleep: Romanticism to the Present*.

RICHARD J. HAND, Professor of Theatre and Media Drama at the Cardiff School for Creative and Cultural Industries at the University of Glamorgan, is the author of *The Theatre of Joseph Conrad: Reconstructed Fictions* (Palgrave Macmillan, 2005). He has edited *'Victory': The Play and Reviews* in Rodopi's Conrad Studies Series (2009) and co-edited *Joseph Conrad and the Performing Arts* (Ashgate, 2009) and is currently co-editing Conrad's plays for *The Cambridge Edition of the Works of Joseph Conrad*. He is the founding co-editor of the *Journal of Adaptation in Film and Performance*.

DOUGLAS KERR is Professor of English at Hong Kong University. His work on Conrad has appeared in *The Conradian*, *Conradiana*, *Essays in Criticism* and *Clio*. His publications also include *Wilfred Owen's Voices* (Clarendon Press, 1993), *George Orwell* (Northcote House Publishers, 2003) and *Eastern Figures: Orient and Empire in British Writing* (Hong Kong University Press, 2008). He has co-edited *A Century of Travels in China* (Hong Kong University Press, 2007) and three volumes of *Critical Zone: A Forum for Chinese and Western Knowledge* (Hong Kong University Press, 2004, 2006, 2008).

PETER LANCELOT MALLIOS, Associate Professor of English at the University of Maryland, is the author of *Our Conrad: Constituting American Modernity* (Stanford University Press, 2010). He co-edited *Conrad in the Twenty-First Century* (Routledge, 2005) and has introduced and annotated *Almayer's Folly*, *The Secret Agent*, *Under Western Eyes* and *Victory* for the Modern Library (Random House). His work has appeared in *Conradiana* and the *Stanford Humanities Review*.

DAVID MILLER, a director of the London literary agency Rogers, Coleridge, & White, Ltd., studied theology at Cambridge. He has written on Conrad's secretary, Miss Hallowes, and on Conrad's personal life and has published in *The Conradian* and the *Times Literary Supplement*. His short novel *Today* (Atlantic Books, 2011) is set during the last days of Conrad's life.

RICHARD NILAND, Lecturer in English at the University of Strathclyde, Glasgow, is the author of *Conrad and History* (Oxford University Press, 2010) and the editor of Volume 3 of *Joseph Conrad: The Contemporary Reviews* (Cambridge University Press, 2012). He has contributed to *Conrad in Context* (Cambridge University Press, 2009), and his work has appeared in *The Conradian*, the *Polish Review* and the *Journal of Popular Culture*.

ANDREW PURSSELL received his doctorate for a thesis on Conrad at Royal Holloway and Bedford New College, University of London. He has contributed to *Within the Tides* (2012) in *The Cambridge Edition of the Works of Joseph Conrad* and to *Conrad in Context* (Cambridge University Press, 2009). He has published several articles on Conrad in *The Conradian*, reviewed for *English Literature in Transition* and also written and lectured on Graham Greene.

ALLAN H. SIMMONS, Professor of English at St Mary's University, Twickenham, London, is the author of *Heart of Darkness: A Reader's Guide* (Continuum, 2007) and *Joseph Conrad* (Palgrave Macmillan, 2008). As co–general editor of *The Cambridge Edition of the Works of Joseph Conrad* he has co-edited *Tales of Unrest* (2012) and *The Shadow-Line* (2013). The editor of *Conrad in Context* (Cambridge University Press, 2009), he contributed to the *Oxford Reader's Companion to Conrad* (Oxford University Press, 2000) and co-edited *Lord Jim* and *The Nigger of the 'Narcissus' and Other Stories* (Penguin, 2007). He is the general editor of *The Conradian: The Journal of the Joseph Conrad Society* (UK).

J. H. STAPE, late Senior Research Fellow in English at St Mary's University, Twickenham, London, was co–general editor of *The Cambridge Edition of the Works of Joseph Conrad* (2008–14) for which he edited or co-edited *Notes on Life and Letters* (2004), *A Personal Record* (2008), *Last Essays* (2010), *Lord Jim* (2011), *Tales of Unrest* (2012) and *The Shadow-Line* (2013). He edited *The Cambridge Companion to Joseph Conrad* (Cambridge University Press, 1996) and edited Conrad for Oxford World's Classics and Penguin Books. His *The Several Lives of Joseph Conrad* (Heinemann / Knopf, 2007) was translated into Dutch, German, Polish and Spanish. He also published on E. M. Forster, William Golding, Thomas Hardy, Frank Harris, Angus Wilson and Virginia Woolf.

PREFACE

Published in 1996, *The Cambridge Companion to Joseph Conrad* has had a long shelf-life and continues to offer informed insights to the student encountering Conrad in the classroom for the first time or to the scholar who wishes for an erudite and reliable approach to the writer. As the preface to that volume indicated, the aim was to make Conrad's writings more accessible through 'informed appreciation'. *The New Cambridge Companion to Joseph Conrad* complements its predecessor; it brings to the fore areas of concern that have opened up in the nearly twenty years since its publication, aiming to take into account theoretical and hermeneutic perspectives that have come into clearer focus. Whereas the first volume concentrated on the major canonical texts, on offer here are a baker's dozen of essays that engage with the contexts – aesthetic, sociological and historical – out of which these emerged. The essays here endeavour both to show the range of current studies and to suggest future possibilities.

The 'new' element acknowledges advances and shifts in scholarly and pedagogical concern, but there is quite literally more Conrad than ever before available. Introducing his work on the libretto of Tariq O' Regan's opera *Heart of Darkness* (2011), Royal Academician and sometime writer Tom Phillips recollected: 'I first read *Heart of Darkness* at school as a set text, and next read it in university. I discovered that Conrad had, in the interim, added something. On re-reading it after a few years, I found that Conrad had added even more; and now each time I read it, I find that he has made changes'. This is typically the case with a great art: it renews itself with each visit. But the media and forums in which that art is received also change.

Conrad's sustained popular appeal is linked to the fact that his work continues to appear in new guises and in new media, in adaptations that range from the graphic novel to opera and theatre to film to performance installations, while novelists and other writers continue to respond in words to the body of work he produced and, occasionally, if indirectly, to the large body of scholarship on it. The vitality of the Conrad canon, its tendency to shrink and contract, to be revisited and re-envisaged, was a feature of the writer's own day and has, perhaps, gathered pace in our current digital age, when access has altered and 'Conrad' is encountered in several, sometimes shifting, forms – in the original and translation in conventional print, in theatrical or film adaptations or reverberating through the writings of another artist.

Phillips's statement not only reflects how a major work shifts during one's readerly lifetime, but also provides the note for what has happened since the mid-1990s. Conrad has, indeed, 'added something'. *The Collected Letters of Joseph Conrad*, published in nine volumes by Cambridge University Press from 1983 to 2009, are now complete, or temporarily so; caches of letters continue to be discovered in archives and private hands and turn up at auction. Moreover, the information explosion made possible by the Internet means that annotations undertaken in the early 1980s need revision, correction and amplification, with the state of knowledge about Conrad's correspondents, activities and even publications shifting and expanding. The other major scholarly project, at a very early stage in the mid-1990s when *The Cambridge Companion to Joseph Conrad* was making its way to press, is *The Cambridge Edition of the Works of Joseph Conrad* (1990–). This project has variously altered the canon; not only have words, sentences and whole paragraphs been added to the tale Conrad wrote, discovered under accumulated layers of editorial change or transcription error, but as the result of painstaking scholarly investigation, the structure of some of the works has also significantly changed. The text of *Heart of Darkness*, for instance, no longer labours under the quite specific circumstances of its serial publication, which saw it divided into three instalments in *Blackwood's Edinburgh Magazine*. These divisions were carried over into the later book version, published by the same firm. The restored critical text is now a seamless and uninterrupted narrative, delivered without stop and mimicking the fictional occasion whereby Marlow, with rare and distinctively marked pauses, tells his story of nightmare and disillusion.

And there is a great deal more of Conrad – thousands of pages – available as a result of advances in digital technology. *Conrad First: The Joseph Conrad Periodical Archive*, thanks to the Internet (in a fledgling state in 1996), offers Conrad's serial publications in their original contexts, allowing the reader access to texts previously found only in widely scattered archives throughout the world. The founding of this digital archive has both facilitated and encouraged the discovery of 'new' serial texts undreamt of a scholarly generation ago, the study of which promises to alter and complicate our understanding of the contours of Conrad's reputation and reception. As to the latter, Cambridge University Press's publication of the four-volume *Joseph Conrad: The Contemporary Reviews* (2012) offers yet another tool to the student with which to approach the writer, with reviews hitherto mainly available only in major libraries and archives now offering a rich trove of raw materials for revaluating the growth of Conrad's reputation in his own day.

The theoretical approaches, at times somewhat crudely brought to bear in the 1980s and 1990s, have with the passage of time gained in reach, sophistication and subtlety, articulated with less shrillness as elitism has given way to greater readability and reader-friendliness. Feminism and postcolonialism have undergone several transformations, enriched by challenges both from within and without, as the fine-grained work itself has proved stubbornly resistant to easy categorization and pigeon-holing. How we regard it necessarily reflects as much about us as about it; in the maritime and masculinist culture of Conrad's time, he was marketed as a writer of the sea of particular interest to male readers. A recent request for a cover to a book on him alone suggests the shift in paradigm; the illustration was to represent 'colonial adventure', in light of current interest in him as a writer responding to the colonial world. That, of course, is only part of the story, just as his maritime guise – one he objected to as reductive – both assisted and plagued an understanding of him by his contemporaries.

The present collection offers a snapshot (in some fashion a 'selfie') of the current state of Conrad scholarship offering to the student a wide variety of possible approaches and taking in areas that were previously of less concern in the classroom, such as how Conrad was marketed in serials and perceived by his contemporaries. We are still discovering the degree to which a given text being studied has a life – indeed, several lives – one or more in its own time, variously recovered by later readers, and one, or again more accurately more than one, in our time. Advances in scholarship have established how unstable Conrad's texts can be and how political and ideological factors shape the canon widely read. A plethora of reading technologies and historical and aesthetic approaches can fruitfully be brought to bear upon a writer quintessentially chameleon, of multiple national and linguistic identities, at once 'one of us' and a man remote, fixed but unstable, in the late-Victorian and early twentieth-century world.

It is a pleasure to thank Kim Salmons for technical assistance in updating the 'Further Reading' section and to acknowledge Allan H. Simmons's advice on myriad topics.

CHRONOLOGY OF CONRAD'S LIFE

1857	Józef Teodor Konrad Korzeniowski, only child of poet, dramatist, translator and political activist Apollo Korzeniowski and Ewelina (or Ewa), née Bobrowska, born on 3 December in or near Berdichev in the Ukraine
1861	Apollo Korzeniowski arrested and imprisoned in Warsaw for anti-Russian conspiracy
1862	Korzeniowskis exiled to Vologda, northern Russia
1865	Death of Ewa Korzeniowski
1868	Apollo Korzeniowski and his son move to Lemberg (now Lvóv)
1869	Death of Apollo Korzeniowski in Cracow; maternal uncle, Tadeusz Bobrowski, becomes young Korzeniowski's guardian Privately tutored because of ill health, also occasionally attends schools during the next few years
1873	Visits Austria, Germany, Switzerland and northern Italy with his tutor Adam Pulman
1874	Leaves Austrian Poland for Marseilles to become a trainee seaman in the French Merchant Service and works for shippers and bankers Delestang et Fils
1874–7	Passenger and apprentice in the *Mont-Blanc* and 'steward' in the *Saint-Antoine* (to the Caribbean)
1878	Shoots himself in the chest in Marseilles after accumulating gambling debts but escapes serious injury Joins the steamship *Mavis*, his first British ship

	Serves as an ordinary seaman in the *Skimmer of the Sea* (English coastal waters)
1878–80	Ordinary seaman in the *Duke of Sutherland* (to Australia) and in the steamship *Europa* (Mediterranean)
1880	Passes examination for second mate
	Third mate in the *Loch Etive* (to Australia)
1881–4	Second mate in the *Palestine*, *Riversdale* and *Narcissus* (to South-East Asia and India)
1884	Passes examination for first mate
1885–6	Second mate in the *Tilkhurst* (to Singapore and Calcutta)
1886	Becomes a British subject
	Passes examination for master's certificate
1886–7	Second mate in the *Falconhurst* First mate in the *Highland Forest* (to Java); injured on board; hospitalized in Singapore
1887–8	First mate in the steamship *Vidar* (from Singapore to various Netherlands East Indies ports)
1888	Master of the *Otago*, joined in Bangkok, sails to Australia and Mauritius
1889	Resigns captaincy of the *Otago* Settles briefly in London and begins *Almayer's Folly*
1890	Friendship with marriage relation and writer Marguerite Poradowska In the Congo Free State for the Société pour le Commerce du Haut-Congo as second-in-command and, temporarily, captain of the river steamer *Roi des Belges*
1891	Manages the warehouse of Barr, Moering in London
1891–3	First mate in the passenger clipper *Torrens* (to Australia); meets John Galsworthy, among the passengers Visits Bobrowski in the Ukraine
1894	*Almayer's Folly* accepted for publication Meets Edward Garnett, publisher's reader, and Jessie George, his future wife

	Signs on as second mate in the *Adowa* but sails only to France and back; end of his sea career
1895	*Almayer's Folly* published under the pen name 'Joseph Conrad'
1896	*An Outcast of the Islands* published; begins *The Rescue* Marries Jessie George (24 March); honeymoons in Brittany and then settles in Stanford-le-Hope, Essex Becomes acquainted with H. G. Wells and initiates a correspondence with Henry James
1897	Begins friendships with writer and political figure R. B. Cunninghame Graham and with Stephen Crane *The Nigger of the 'Narcissus'* published
1898	Son Borys born *Tales of Unrest* published ('Karain', 'The Idiots', 'An Outpost of Progress', 'The Return', 'The Lagoon') Collaborates with Ford Madox Hueffer (later Ford) and takes over from him lease of The Pent, Postling, Kent
1899	*Heart of Darkness* serialized
1899–1900	*Lord Jim* serialized
1900	J. B. Pinker becomes Conrad's agent
1901	*The Inheritors* (collaboration with Ford) published
1902	*Youth: A Narrative*; and *Two Other Stories* published ('Youth', 'Heart of Darkness', 'The End of the Tether')
1903	*Typhoon and Other Stories* ('Typhoon', 'Amy Foster', 'Falk', 'To-morrow') and *Romance* (collaboration with Ford) published
1904	*Nostromo* serialized and published in book form Jessie Conrad injures her knees, remaining partially disabled for life
1905	Sojourn on Capri *One Day More*, dramatization of 'To-morrow', staged in London
1906	Sojourn in Montpellier Son John born

	The Mirror of the Sea published *The Secret Agent* serialized in the United States
1907	Sojourn in Montpellier and Geneva *The Secret Agent* published in book form Moves to Someries, Luton Hoo, Bedfordshire
1908	*A Set of Six* published ('Gaspar Ruiz', 'The Informer', 'The Brute', 'An Anarchist', 'The Duel', 'Il Conde')
1909	Moves to Aldington, Kent Breaks with Ford
1910	Completes *Under Western Eyes* and suffers a nervous breakdown Moves to Capel House, Orlestone, Kent
1910–11	*Under Western Eyes* serialized and published in book form
1912	*Some Reminiscences* (later *A Personal Record*) and *'Twixt Land and Sea* published ('A Smile of Fortune', 'The Secret Sharer', 'Freya of the Seven Isles') *Chance* serialized in New York
1914	*Chance* published in book form; first financial success Visits Austrian Poland in summer with family; trapped for some weeks by the outbreak of war, then returns to England via Austria and Italy
1915	*Within the Tides* ('The Planter of Malata', 'The Partner', 'The Inn of the Two Witches', 'Because of the Dollars') and *Victory* published
1917	*The Shadow-Line* published
1919	Moves to Spring Grove, near Wye, Kent Basil Macdonald Hastings's dramatization of *Victory* staged in London Moves to Oswalds, Bishopsbourne, near Canterbury *The Arrow of Gold* published
1920	*The Rescue*, begun in 1898, published; writes Author's Notes for Doubleday and Heinemann collected editions
1921	Visits Corsica, doing research for *The Rover* and *Suspense* *Notes on Life and Letters* published; collected editions begin publication

1922 Dramatization of *The Secret Agent* staged in London

1923 Visits the United States to a rapturous reception
The Rover serialized in the United States and published in book form there and in England

1924 Declines a knighthood
Dies of a heart attack at Oswalds on 3 August, aged 66; buried in Roman Catholic section of Canterbury cemetery
The Nature of a Crime (collaboration with Ford) published in book form

1925 *Tales of Hearsay* ('The Warrior's Soul', 'Prince Roman', 'The Tale', 'The Black Mate') and *Suspense* (unfinished) published

1926 *Last Essays*, edited by Richard Curle, published

1928 *The Sisters* (fragment) published

ABBREVIATIONS

Citations to Conrad's writings are to *The Cambridge Edition of the Works of Joseph Conrad* (1990–) when a volume has appeared in it, such citations indicate both page and line number (e.g, 55.15–16). Citations are otherwise to 'Dent's Collected Edition' (1946–55), derived from Doubleday's 'Sun-Dial' texts published in 1920–1.

AF	*Almayer's Folly*
AG	*The Arrow of Gold*
Ch	*Chance*
In	*The Inheritors*
LE	*Last Essays*
LJ	*Lord Jim*
MS	*The Mirror of the Sea*
NLL	*Notes on Life and Letters*
NN	*The Nigger of the 'Narcissus'*
No	*Nostromo*
OI	*An Outcast of the Islands*
PR	*A Personal Record*
Re	*The Rescue*
Ro	*The Rover*
SA	*The Secret Agent*
SL	*The Shadow-Line*
SS	*A Set of Six*
Su	*Suspense*
TH	*Tales of Hearsay*
TLS	*'Twixt Land and Sea*
TOT	*'Typhoon' and Other Tales*
TU	*Tales of Unrest*
UWE	*Under Western Eyes*
Vi	*Victory*
WTT	*Within the Tides*
YHET	*Youth, Heart of Darkness, The End of the Tether*

CR — *Joseph Conrad: The Contemporary Reviews*. General Editors Allan H. Simmons, John G. Peters and J. H. Stape, with Richard Niland, Mary Burgoyne and Katherine Isobel Baxter. 4 vols. Cambridge University Press, 2012

Letters — *The Collected Letters of Joseph Conrad*. General editors Frederick R. Karl and Laurence Davies, with Owen Knowles, Gene M. Moore and J. H. Stape. 9 vols. Cambridge: Cambridge University Press, 1983–2009.

In quotations, unspaced points (...) indicate an ellipsis by the writer, while spaced points (. . .) occur in the work being cited.

I

ANDREW PURSSELL

Making the Conrad Canon

In his 1905 essay 'Books', Conrad ponders the 'secret' of literary longevity: 'the formulas of art are dependent on things variable, unstable and untrustworthy, on human sympathies, on prejudices, on likes and dislikes, on the sense of virtue and the sense of propriety, on beliefs and theories that, indestructible in themselves, always change their form – often in the lifetime of one fleeting generation' (*NLL*, 11.1–6). Conrad would not achieve widespread success until the publication of *Chance* (1913–14), and these remarks can be read as an expression of mild frustration from an author whose popular appeal remained limited and whose most recent novel, *Nostromo* (1904), although later regarded as his undisputed masterpiece, had been coolly received by the critics.[1] Beyond this, Conrad's meditation on the precarious afterlife of the literary text also anticipated the oscillations of popular and critical taste that would continue to mark, and mar, the reputation of his works over the coming decades. Conrad achieved both popular and critical acclaim during his lifetime, but a period of sustained neglect came in the wake of his death in August 1924. This was followed by his dramatic rediscovery and canonization after the Second World War and, in turn, by the gradual recuperation of works excluded from the Conrad canon during the twentieth century's last decades, when the assumptions underlying its formation, and the formations of canons generally, began to be questioned and challenged.

Conrad's nebulous description of 'things variable' carries more than a trace of the 'misty' narrative method identified by his earliest reviewers, such as H. G. Wells, and confirmed by later ones, such as E. M. Forster.[2] However, in gesturing to those systems of valuation and revaluation in which a work is enmeshed on its entry into the literary marketplace, Conrad's 'things variable' is also strikingly attuned to modern theorizations of canon formation. As Barbara Herrnstein Smith has shown, such variables might include the 'innumerable acts of evaluation' performed by those who 'publish the work, purchase, preserve, display, quote, cite, translate, perform, allude to, and imitate it'.[3] They might also encompass 'the highly specialized institutionalized activities of scholars, teachers, and academic or journalistic critics': those who give 'full-dress reviews and explicit rank-orderings, evaluations, and revaluations', who compile anthologies, write introductions, produce department curriculum lists, award literary prizes, and commission and publish articles about certain works; all 'have functions and effects that are significant in the production and maintenance ... of literary value'.[4] More than this, the 'valuational history' of a literary work arguably precedes its publication, beginning in 'the author's either letting the work stand or ripping it up', and even before this, in 'the thousand individual acts of approval and revision, that constitute the entire process of literary composition'.[5] This is especially true of an aspirant writer of 'high' literature such as Conrad, whose third novel, *The Rescue* (1920), begun in 1896, lay abandoned for some twenty years and whose second, *The Sisters*, was abandoned altogether, and whose correspondence – such as the oft-cited letter dismissing 'The Lagoon' (1896) as 'secondhand Conradese' (*Letters*, I, 302) – is interleaved with innumerable judgements on works-in-progress. Similarly, Conrad's later Prefaces (or Author's Notes), several of which are marked by his refusal to reconsider or even remember particular works, offer a corresponding, if playful, public glimpse of the evaluative processes voiced privately in his letters.

The establishment of Conrad's 'literary value', self-evident today in his prevalence in international academe and in literary and popular culture more broadly, might therefore be traced back to the placing of his early short fiction in literary journals rather than popular magazines,[6] and to his early promotion by editors such as W. E. Henley, whose serialization of *The Nigger of the 'Narcissus'* (1897) in the prestigious *New Review* announced Conrad as an author for a 'select, coterie audience'.[7] It might have factored in the award of literary prizes for his early short fiction (such as 1897's *Tales of Unrest*) and of monies by institutions such as the Royal Literary Fund in 1902 and the Royal Bounty Fund in 1905, or the purchasing of his manuscripts by the American collector John Quinn, whereby literary 'value' is more readily measured and monetized. It might even have influenced the early translation of his works into French, which was instrumental in establishing his fame abroad at a time when English 'had not yet reached its planetary hegemony'[8] and which led to the first sustained attempt to write his biography.[9] It might also encompass the early adoption of his works in academe, such as that of *Lord Jim* (1900) for the newly conceived 'Modern Novels' class at Yale in 1902, or the acknowledgement of his influence by contemporary writers and cultural arbiters, such as T. S. Eliot, whose 1925 poem 'The Hollow Men' takes its epigraph ('Mistah Kurtz – he dead') from

Heart of Darkness (1899), not to mention the publication of early surveys of his fiction by Hugh Clifford and Edward Garnett, which marked the first stirrings of Conrad criticism in Britain and abroad, and arguably the first soundings taken of his relation to the Western canon.[10] The interventions of Garnett, who in his role as a publisher's reader at Unwin's had helped place Conrad's fiction and as a reviewer and a critic had helped shape his early reception, are especially integral to the marking and transmission of Conrad's literary value. When the *Youth* volume was published in 1902, it was the title story that drew most of the plaudits until Garnett identified *Heart of Darkness* as 'the high-water mark of the author's talent',[11] and Conrad's subsequent remark to Garnett that 'The ruck takes its tone from you' (*Letters*, II, 468) suggestively underlines the influence of what Stanley Fish calls 'interpretive communities', those groups in a position to decide what is 'literature' and what is not.[12] Conrad's celebrated and controversial novella – the exclusion of the early Marlow narratives from F. R. Leavis's 'great tradition' aside – has regularly been placed at the forefront of Conrad's achievement ever since.

That Conrad was considered 'literature' is also consensually reflected in the appearance towards the end of his life of large-scale collected editions of his works, published by William Heinemann and J. M. Dent & Sons in Britain and by Doubleday, Page & Company in the United States. These editions marked a major stage both in the consolidation of his contemporary reputation and – crucially – in the preservation and transmission of a canon of his works for future generations of readers, with the American 'Sun-Dial' printing providing the *ur*-text of many subsequent popular print editions (including 'Dent's Uniform Edition' of 1923, reissued as 'Dent's Collected Edition' during the 1940s and early 1950s, later a standard text of reference in Conrad studies).[13] These editions were accompanied by a series of prefatory Author's Notes, all of which, excepting those accompanying *Almayer's Folly* (1895) and *The Nigger of the 'Narcissus'* (1897), were produced for Dent's second English edition of his works between 1917 and 1920, when Conrad harboured the (unrealized) ambition of winning the Nobel Prize for Literature. They were conceived as 'a fittingly prepared monument' to a career then nearing its end,[14] and with one eye on the posthumous legacy strived for in 'Books'. By this time, Conrad had achieved the kind of recognition sought after in 'Books', yet he remained aware more than ever that, as in 'Books', this recognition is subject to impermanence, as the Author's Note to *Tales of Unrest* (1897) underscores. In it, Conrad describes retiring his favoured steel pen as a memento of this early foray into short fiction, and the anecdote underlines that Conrad, in the present act of writing the preface, is likewise engaged in an act of memorialization. What happens to the pen – thrown out of the window, along with its ink-encrusted double – is therefore significant. As Vivienne Rundle argues, 'Conrad's anecdote recounts the destruction or devaluing of a memento; it records the transformation *from value to insignificance*'.[15] Thus 'value', once ascribed, can be annulled, and this seems pertinent not only to the current project of memorialization, to which the preface belongs as a whole, but also to his later investiture in English literary studies as a modern 'classic'. As Frank Kermode put it, 'canons are replaced, condemned, or subjected to commentary. In any case, they change.'[16]

When Conrad attained canonical status in the 1940s and 1950s, neither the literary value of the text, nor the 'evaluative authority' of the canon that housed it, needed to be 'affirmed, asserted, or self-justified': 'it was simply assumed'.[17] The interrogative impulse suggested in the title of T. S. Eliot's 1945 essay 'What is a Classic?' did not stretch to a self-questioning of the politics of canon formation. Thus, whereas in his *Anatomy of Criticism* (1957) Northrop Frye could argue the need to 'snip off and throw away' the evaluative practices that he found were irrelevant to 'real criticism',[18] he could also speak, like Eliot, of 'the existing monuments of literature', overlooking that the creation of such monuments was the product of, 'among other things, evaluative practices'.[19] Although Frye might have opposed the rank-ordering of Conrad's works begun in earnest by F. R. Leavis in Britain in the 1940s and continued by Thomas C. Moser and Albert J. Guerard in the United States throughout the 1950s, the underlying assumptions that allowed for such rank-orderings to be made remained untroubled: there could be no prejudicial 'value judgements', but there could, conversely, be 'masterpieces of literature'.[20]

These assumptions remained largely unquestioned until the late twentieth century and the emergence of critical practices such as feminism, deconstruction and postcolonialism, which, underlining the deepening politicization of academe, saw the canon as a 'highly selective instrument'[21] in which were reflected the systems of stratification and exclusion of the culture that produced it.[22] This led to a countermanding emphasis on the study of traditionally excluded authors and works. This debate over canon formation led, in turn, to a revival of the very figure of the author whose 'death' had only recently been announced by poststructuralism in the late 1960s: requiring a representative of a particular constituency or background, the canon became 'concerned, in the first instance, with *authors*, not texts'.[23] Such questions of 'representation' are particularly salient to Conrad given the overwhelming Anglicization of his achievement by a predominantly Anglophone community of critics (though this has been challenged over the years by the concerted attempt to reposition Conrad's French and, in particular, Polish heritages). At the same time, critics such as Kermode, while acknowledging the canon's 'complicit[y] with power',[24] disputed the assumption that it is a 'load-bearing element of the existing power structure, and that by imposing radical change on [it] you can help to dismantle the existing power structure'.[25] The impact of any attempt at discharging the literary canon, like that of the French cannons fired into Africa in *Heart of Darkness*, will always to some degree be lessened by what Kermode calls 'the problem of value'.[26] For although its contents may be challenged and even changed, the canon remains central to the literary critical institution and to literary critical practice, since questions of 'value' remain fundamental to both, just as they do to literary practice more generally.

Leavis's *The Great Tradition* (1948) not only offered the first systematic, full-length construction of a Conrad canon; in addition, it recuperated Conrad to the tradition of the English novel, which for Leavis also included – and somewhat daringly, was *limited* to – Jane Austen, George Eliot and Henry James. At one level then, Leavis's 'great tradition', like later attempts to contest and 'capture' the canon,[27] was itself radical in impulse, offered in reaction, on the one hand, to a contemporary predilection in academe for Victorianism[28] and, on the other, to earlier influential discussions of the Western canon (notably T. S. Eliot's 1921 essay 'Tradition and the Individual Talent') which did not extend beyond poetry and drama. Leavis's 'great tradition' was – like all canons – a construct. It was also, despite the suggestion of longevity implicit in its title, a recent one. Like Garnett, Leavis regretted that the 'vogue' for Conrad during the 1920s had coincided with his 'inferior novels',[29] and that this vogue had quickly been replaced in the 1930s by a period of uncertain stocktaking and comparative neglect. There was much interest in Conrad after his death in 1924, underlined by the publication of a flood of reminiscences by his widow Jessie, Ford Madox Ford and Richard Curle, of volumes of his letters by Garnett and G. Jean-Aubry, and of unpublished novels, collaborations and scattered shorter works and essays, including *The Nature of a Crime* (1924), *Tales of Hearsay* (1925), *Suspense* (1925), *Last Essays* (1926) and *The Sisters* (1928).[30] Yet, in a significant sense, this interest in Conrad after his death had been generated *by* his death, and reflected less the monumentalization of Conrad's achievement than a period of extended obituary. Although these protectors of Conrad's reputation might have deemed him worthy of 'canonical' status, such a status needed to be anchored in, and authorized by, the kind of serious academic scholarship that had yet to emerge (the handful of studies to appear during the period 1930–40, by Granville Hicks, Gustav Morf and Edward Crankshaw, notwithstanding).[31] Rather, Conrad's entry into the canon began with the professionalization of interest in him in Britain and the United

States during the 1940s. This period saw the publication of landmark studies by John Dozier Gordan, M. C. Bradbrook and Morton D. Zabel, paving the way for Conrad's later passage into academe and preparing the ground for Leavis's widely influential and lasting intervention, whereby the conceptual contours of Conrad's 'canonicity' were first laid out.[32]

If Leavis's 'great tradition' was radical in reducing the English canon to four authors (and two women and two 'foreigners' at that), it was also radical in some of its revaluations of Conrad. For example, though *Heart of Darkness* was, 'by common consent, one of Conrad's best things', it was grouped, like most of his short fiction, among his 'minor' works.[33] Leavis felt that the novella's endless positing and withholding of 'significance', echoing Forster's earlier criticism, betrayed not the 'best' of Conrad but rather the worst excesses of 'the magazine-writer'.[34] As several critics have suggested, Leavis's interpretation betrays the mistrust of the empiricist – the classifier who is required to believe in the stability of his classifying categories – of the impressionistic aspects of Conrad's narrative method.[35] Conrad's 'major' works, meanwhile, included his popular breakthrough *Chance* (1913–14), whose success Garnett, among others, had damningly suggested had more to do with its aggressive marketing than with any inherent 'literary value'. Leavis's inclusion of *Chance* captures not only the dichotomy of Conrad as someone who 'desired popularity, yet shunned the writing of a popular novel',[36] but also a problem facing the early constructors of the Conrad canon, where traditionally the 'classic' and the 'popular' are held to be antithetical. This is typified by *Lord Jim*, which, though for most early critics it confirmed Conrad's 'arrival' on its publication in 1900,[37] was simultaneously excluded from and included in the first iterations of the Conrad canon produced in Britain and the United States – a discrepancy born, as Fredric Jameson has suggested, of the novel's straddling, like Conrad's fiction generally, 'of high literature [and] light reading and romance,' 'floating uncertainly between ... "high" culture and mass culture'.[38] Thus, there is the Conrad who wrote the colonial exotic of 'The Lagoon' and 'Karain: A Memory' (1897), which drew early comparisons to popular authors such as H. Rider Haggard, Robert Louis Stevenson and Louis Becke, and, at the same time, the Conrad whose *The Nigger of the 'Narcissus'* (1897), together with the literary manifesto enshrined in its Preface, simultaneously heralded his emergence as an author of 'challenging' fiction.[39] Such a generic straddling is necessarily problematic for the constructors of literary canons, since, as Kermode has argued, a 'classic' definition of what makes an author canonical is that they be 'distinguished from the rabble'.[40]

Conversely, more 'difficult' works, such as *Nostromo*, which eschews the conventions of plot construction, chronology, and narration, were more readily packaged, and consensually regarded, as 'canonical'. Leavis accordingly placed *Nostromo* at the leading edge of a 'major' phase that also comprised *The Secret Agent* (1907), *Under Western Eyes* (1911) and *Victory* (1915), with the partial inclusion of *The Shadow-Line* (1917). Conrad's debut and second novels *Almayer's Folly* (1895) and *An Outcast of the Islands* (1896) and early short fiction such as 'Karain: A Memory' (1897) and 'Youth' (1902), were disregarded as studies in the Kipling-esque Eastern exotic of 'Conrad's earliest vein'.[41] Meanwhile his late works, including *The Arrow of Gold* (1919), *The Rescue* (1920), *The Rover* (1923) and *Suspense* (1925), were deemed collectively the products of a waning ability.

As all of this suggests, Leavis's preference was not just for the middle fiction but also for the novel over the short story. Conrad's short stories may have yielded greater financial rewards than his longer works thanks to the ever-burgeoning popularity of magazines in the late-Victorian and Edwardian literary marketplaces and, later, to the inflated sums paid for his magazine fiction following the publication of *Chance*; however, they were denied a corresponding literary value, and were, with the heavily qualified exception of the novella *Typhoon* (1902), excluded from the Leavis canon.[42] Leavis's generic preference perhaps would not have been recognized by Conrad, all of whose long fictions – apart from *The Sisters* and *The Rescue* – originated as short stories and who believed, moreover, that the 'intrinsic value of a work' had 'nothing to do with its length' (*Letters*, II, 49).[43] At the same time, Conrad's ambition since his unfinished second novel, *The Sisters*, had been to write a novel that would be considered part of the European tradition of the novel, and in *The Great Tradition* this ambition was belatedly realized. Leavis dismissed Conrad's popular reputation as 'the Prose Laureate of the Merchant Service', in a manoeuvre recalling Conrad's resentment at his abiding image as a purveyor of 'sea stuff' (*Letters*, VIII, 130), foregrounding instead the 'great novelist' whose 'great novels' transcended their topographical moorings.[44] He also threw out as irrelevant the longstanding (and for Conrad equally irksome) stress on the writer's 'foreignness': 'Conrad is among the very greatest novelists in the language – or any language'.[45]

Leavis's re-examination of Conrad first appeared as 'Revaluations: Joseph Conrad' in 1941 in *Scrutiny*, the critical journal launched in 1932 together with Q. D. Leavis. If *The Great Tradition* was to prove a widely influential and, for the next thirty years, inescapable work in Conrad criticism, its impact on Conrad studies can be set against the broader impact of the Leavises – together with their contemporaries at Cambridge, I. A. Richards, William Empson and L. C. Knights – on the fashioning of 'English' into a serious discipline in Britain in the years after Conrad's death. Leavis belonged to a group of critics who were trying to give English, then still a relative upstart, the same weight as long-established neighbouring subjects, such as classics and philology. There is a particular logic, then, to the fact that the questions of 'value' surrounding its emergence as a serious discipline should carry over into its object of study – the literary text. Although the type of evaluative criticism practised by Leavis would gradually disappear during coming years, and although the contents – and even the existence – of the canon whose study he prescribed would later be questioned, 'the fact remains that English students in England today are "Leavisites" whether they know it or not, irremediably altered by that historic intervention'.[46] As Terry Eagleton notes, Leavis 'redrew the map of English literature in ways from which criticism has never quite recovered. The main thoroughfares on this map ran through Chaucer, Shakespeare, Jonson, the Jacobeans and Metaphysicals, Bunyan, Pope, Samuel Johnson, Blake, Wordsworth, Keats, Austen, George Eliot, Hopkins, Henry James, Joseph Conrad, T. S. Eliot, and D. H. Lawrence. This *was* English literature.'[47] Leavis was engaged not only in recuperating Conrad to serious academic study, but also in producing a new cartography of English, one of whose principal landmarks was Conrad.

In the 1950s, the American critics Thomas C. Moser and Albert J. Guerard put forward the corresponding, and similarly influential, view that Conrad's late fiction represented a decline after the achievement of his earlier 'major' period, the high points of which were *Lord Jim*, *Nostromo* and *The Secret Agent*. As with Leavis in Britain, they were spurred on by the seemingly moribund state of Conrad criticism in the United States. Guerard argued 'that the large majority of critics in America [at the end of the 1940s] did not read Conrad at all'.[48] By the end of the 1950s, however, Conrad's biographer Jocelyn Baines could be 'self-consciously writing the life of a man whose work was attaining "classic" status',[49] while both Guerard and Moser could agree – with an urgency belying its comparatively recent inclusion in *The Great Tradition* – that 'the time [had] come to drop *Victory* from the Conrad canon' altogether.[50]

As this suggests, Conrad's recovery from the margins of literary criticism in America, and his canonical status there, were by this point assured; what remained was to re-calibrate the canon of his works. Thus works included by Leavis – *Chance*, *Victory* and *The Shadow-Line* – were excluded, and works rejected by Leavis – notably *Heart of Darkness* and *Lord Jim* – were newly incorporated. Meanwhile, the wholesale dismissal of late Conrad and the early Malay novels was countered by the revaluation of his short fiction, with *The Nigger of the 'Narcissus'* (1897) marking the beginning of the 'major' Conrad, and 'The Secret Sharer' (1912) – 'the last first-rate Conrad' – the end.[51] Although the Leavis canon had been replaced, the evaluative and historicizing aspects of his approach were, in effect, retained.[52] Equally, this canon was, like Leavis's, composed not in open concession to its provisionality but, rather, on the assumption that it 'would henceforth be recognized as the valid one'.[53] In other words, it was lined with the presumption that it possessed the same qualities of 'timelessness' and 'universality' as the texts included in it.

These critics, drawing upon and extending similar posthumous appraisals of Conrad by his friends John Galsworthy and Edward Garnett, and more recent critical views, such as that put forward by Douglas Hewitt,[54] together established the evaluative paradigm of 'achievement and decline'. Within this paradigm, much subsequent Conrad criticism would for the most part unquestioningly operate, including Jacques Berthoud's *Joseph Conrad: The Major Phase* (1978), R. A. Gekoski's *Conrad: The Moral World of the Novelist* (1978), Aaron Fogel's *Coercion to Speak* (1985), Suresh Raval's *The Art of Failure* (1986) and Jakob Lothe's *Conrad's Narrative Method* (1989), as well as the major biographies, Bernard C. Meyer's *Joseph Conrad: A Psychoanalytic Biography* (1967) and Frederick R. Karl's *Joseph Conrad: The Three Lives* (1979). That this paradigm should persist and remain prevalent (if no longer uncritically accepted) is because it is itself subject to the same forces as the literary texts on which it offers commentary – the same 'cultural-historical dynamics of endurance' through which a particular text achieves, maintains and preserves 'classic' status, by being 'more frequently read or recited', 'imitated, cited, commented upon, and so forth – in short, culturally re-produced' – than another.[55]

That is not to say there were not challenges to this paradigm. In the 1980s, Gary Geddes, building upon earlier criticism by Morton D. Zabel, John Palmer and Robert Secor, argued that the critics of the 1950s misunderstood Conrad's aesthetic aims in the late fiction through 'their predilection for fictional modes and techniques that were no longer of paramount importance to Conrad' and failed to recognize Conrad's evolving experimentation with the novel form and with new subjects.[56] In the late 1990s, Susan Jones argued that the popular view of Conrad as a male-oriented author who did not represent female experience or subjectivity or cater to women readers is not intrinsic to his fiction as a whole but rather a by-product of canon formation. In particular, the creation of Conrad's 'major phase' under the banner of Modernism during and after the 1950s 'privileged a narrow band of texts that focused on male experience'.[57] As Moser's Mr Jones-like disinclination towards Conrad's women ('the lowest common denominator')[58] suggests, these critics 'promoted those works as modernist in which women feature less prominently, making these texts paradigmatic of his "genius"'.[59] The recent interest in Conrad's continuing engagement with contemporary models of popular fiction and with popular culture more broadly, and the attendant interest in his 'uncanonical' works, has led to a further decentring of the traditional canon.[60]

Chinua Achebe's well-known attack on *Heart of Darkness* during the mid-1970s is, in many ways, also an implicit attack on the received canon of Conrad's works and remains a key intervention for its anticipation of a shift in critical interest during the 1980s and 1990s towards issues of culture, race and colonialism following the appearance of Edward Said's path-breaking *Orientalism* (1978) and of a corresponding interrogation of the problematic relation of the European literary canon to imperialism.[61] In a 1975 address given at the University of Massachusetts, provocatively entitled 'An Image of Africa: Racism in Conrad's *Heart of Darkness*', Achebe argued that the novella reduced Africa 'to the role of props for the break-up of one petty European mind', and that Conrad himself was 'a thoroughgoing racist'. He went on to question the work's position as 'perhaps the most commonly prescribed novel [*sic*] in twentieth-century literature courses in English Departments of American universities'.[62] Achebe's 'most commonly prescribed' gestures to the particular context in which Conrad was being read and studied in the United States at the time, when the psychoanalytical approach of the likes of Moser and Guerard and of later critics, such as Bernard C. Meyer and Paul Kirschner, was prevalent.[63] Moreover, Guerard had written the introduction to the 1950 New American Library edition of *Heart of Darkness*, the psychological approach of which 'de-Africanizes' the novella and ignores the topical and political specificity of its original reception, and, as Robert Hampson notes, this popular cheap edition is likely to have been widely used by the American students taking the courses mentioned by Achebe.[64] In other words, because it approached *Heart of Darkness* from a singularly psychological perspective – and thus *made it* about 'the break-up of one petty European mind' – it is to this American context and a received interpretation of Conrad's novella, as much as the novella itself, that Achebe responds.[65]

In addition, Achebe's 'most commonly prescribed' suggests the academic apparatus through which *Heart of Darkness*, a fixture of anthologies of Conrad ever since the appearance of Zabel's *The Portable Conrad* (1947), had acquired its current canonical value. As Smith underlines, 'the repeated inclusion of a particular work in literary anthologies', and 'its repeated appearance on reading lists' and in university curricula, together 'have the effect of drawing the work into the orbit of attention of a population of particular readers … while at the same time shaping and supplying the very interests in relation to which they will experience the work' and, moreover, experience it 'as valuable'.[66] Such a 'prescription', of course, also grows out from and answers to the practical needs of pedagogy, with Conrad's short fiction supplying the growing post-War student population in the United States with a more readily digestible diet than his novels, as Guerard himself noted.[67] Lastly, Achebe's 'most commonly prescribed' also points to the cultural power invested in the one *doing* the prescribing and to the literary and academic institutions that transmit the culturally appropriate manner of their consumption (or 'true appreciation'), from Garnett's endorsement of *Heart of Darkness* as the keystone of Conrad's literary achievement in 1902 to Moser's arrogation of the category 'Conradian' over half a century later, whereby *Lord Jim* is seen to carry 'that particular magic one thinks of as "Conradian"', while *Under Western Eyes* does not.[68] Achebe underlines that the works in the Conrad canon problematically reflect back upon the cultural circumstances of their production. In so doing, he also indirectly points up the extent to which that canon, *as* a construct, is likewise the product of certain cultural and historical factors.

NOTES

1 *The Times Literary Supplement*, for example, declared the novel a 'critical mistake' (21 October 1904, p. 320).

2 Wells found Conrad's second novel, *An Outcast of the Islands* (1896), 'not so much told as seen intermittently through a haze of sentences' (unsigned review, *Saturday Review*, 16 May 1896, pp. 509–10; *CR*, I, 110). Forster's review of Conrad's *Notes on Life and Letters* (1921) pointedly remarked that 'the secret casket of his genius contains a vapour rather than a jewel' ('The Pride of Mr. Conrad', *The Nation and Athenæum*, 19 March 1921, pp. 881–2).

3 *Contingencies of Value: Alternative Perspectives for Critical Theory* (Cambridge, MA: Harvard University Press, 1988), p. 46.

4 Ibid., p. 46.

5 Ibid., p. 44.

6 Conrad's first short tale, 'The Idiots', was published in *The Savoy* (1896), and his second, 'An Outpost of Progress', in *Cosmopolis* (1897).

7 Susan Jones, *Conrad and Women* (Oxford: Oxford University Press, 1999), p. 12.

8 Mario Curreli, 'Translations' in *Joseph Conrad in Context*, ed. Allan H. Simmons (Cambridge: Cambridge University Press, 2009), p. 100.

9 See G. Jean-Aubry, ed., *Joseph Conrad: Life and Letters*, 2 vols. (London: William Heinemann, 1927).

10 See Hugh Clifford, 'Mr. Joseph Conrad at Home and Abroad', *Singapore Free Press*, 30 August 1898, p. 3; and Edward Garnett, 'Academy Portraits: Mr. Joseph Conrad', *Academy*, 15 October 1898, pp. 82–3. Garnett placed Conrad at the forefront of a Western tradition extending from Horace to Dickens.

11 'Mr. Conrad's New Book', *Academy and Literature*, 6 December 1902, p. 606.

12 Frank Kermode, *History and Value: The Clarendon Lectures and the Northcliffe Lectures 1987* (Oxford: Clarendon Press, 1988), p. 104.
13 As works of scholarly reference, these editions have since been supplanted by the Cambridge Edition of the Works of Joseph Conrad (Cambridge: Cambridge University Press, 1990–).
14 Owen Knowles and Gene M. Moore, *Oxford Reader's Companion to Conrad* (Oxford: Oxford University Press, 2000), p. 26.
15 'Defining Frames: The Prefaces of Henry James and Joseph Conrad', *The Henry James Review* 16, no. 1 (1995), 78.
16 *Pleasure and Change: The Aesthetics of Canon*, ed. Robert Alter (New York: Oxford University Press, 2004), p. 38.
17 Smith, *Contingencies of Value*, p. 24.
18 Quoted in ibid., p. 21.
19 Ibid., p. 21.
20 Northrop Frye, *Anatomy of Criticism: Four Essays* (Princeton, NJ: Princeton University Press, 1957; rpt. Toronto: University of Toronto Press, 2006), pp. 21, 17.
21 Kermode, *History and Value*, p. 115.
22 See especially Pierre Bourdieu, *Distinction: A Social Critique of the Judgement of Taste*, trans. Richard Nice (London: Routledge and Kegan Paul, 1984).
23 Henry Louis Gates, Jr., *Loose Canons: Notes on the Culture Wars* (New York: Oxford University Press, 1992), pp. 181–2. On the death of the author, see Roland Barthes, 'The Death of the Author' (1968), collected in *Image, Music, Text*, trans. Stephen Heath (London: Fontana Press, 1977), pp. 142–8; and Michel Foucault, 'What is an Author?' (1969), collected in *Language, Counter-Memory, Practice: Selected Essays and Interviews*, trans. Donald F. Bouchard (Ithaca, NY: Cornell University Press, 1977), pp. 113–38.
24 Kermode, *History and Value*, p. 115.
25 Ibid., p. 104.
26 Ibid., p. 103.
27 Ibid., p. 114.
28 F. R. Leavis, *The Great Tradition: George Eliot, Henry James, Joseph Conrad* (London: Chatto & Windus, 1948), p. 1.
29 Leavis, *The Great Tradition*, p. 226. In his introduction to *Conrad's Prefaces to his Works*, Garnett commented that Conrad's popularity came with the appearance of 'the least masterly of his novels' (London: J. M. Dent & Sons, 1937, p. 34).
30 See Ford Madox Ford, *Joseph Conrad: A Personal Remembrance* (London: Duckworth, 1924); Jessie Conrad, *Joseph Conrad As I Knew Him* (London: William Heinemann, 1926); Richard Curle, *The Last Twelve Years of Joseph Conrad* (London: Sampson Low, Marston, 1928); Edward Garnett, *Letters from Conrad: 1895 to 1924* (London: Nonesuch Press, 1928); G. Jean-Aubry, ed., *Joseph Conrad: Lettres françaises* (Paris: Gallimard, 1929).
31 See Granville Hicks, 'Conrad After Five Years', *New Republic* 61 (1930), 192–4; Gustav Morf, *The Polish Heritage of Joseph Conrad* (London: Sampson Low, Marston, 1930); Edward Crankshaw, *Joseph Conrad: Some Aspects of the Art of the Novel* (London: John Lane, 1936).

32 See John Dozier Gordan, *Joseph Conrad: The Making of a Novelist* (Cambridge, MA: Harvard University Press, 1940); M. C. Bradbrook, *Joseph Conrad: Poland's English Genius* (Cambridge: Cambridge University Press, 1941); Morton D. Zabel, *Craft and Character: Text, Method and Vocation in Modern Literature* (New York: Viking Press, 1958).
33 Leavis, *The Great Tradition*, p. 174.
34 Ibid., p. 180.
35 See Jones, *Conrad and Women*, p. 25; and Con Coroneos, *Space, Conrad, and Modernity* (Oxford: Oxford University Press, 2002), p. 42.
36 Jones, *Conrad and Women*, p. 12.
37 For a brief survey of Conrad's contemporary critical fortunes, see Allan H. Simmons, 'Critical Responses: Contemporary' in *Joseph Conrad in Context*, ed. Simmons, pp. 59–66.
38 Fredric Jameson, *The Political Unconscious: Narrative as a Socially Symbolic Act* (Ithaca, NY: Cornell University Press, 1981; rpt. Abingdon: Routledge, 2002), p. 191.
39 Conrad himself believed *The Nigger* had 'certain qualities of art that make it a thing apart' (*Letters*, I, 334).
40 *The Classic: Literary Images of Permanence and Change* (London: Faber and Faber, 1975), p. 15. According to Kermode, this definition was first put by the second-century author and grammarian Aulus Gellius: '*Classicus ... scriptor, non proletarius*'.
41 Leavis, *The Great Tradition*, pp. 189–90.
42 For example, Conrad received £20 for the copyright of *Almayer's Folly* in 1895, and half this amount for 'The Lagoon', a story only a tenth its length, in 1896.
43 For a discussion, see Gail Fraser, 'The Short Fiction' in *The Cambridge Companion to Joseph Conrad*, ed. J. H. Stape (Cambridge: Cambridge University Press, 1996; rpt. 2004), pp. 25–44.
44 Leavis, *The Great Tradition*, pp. 17–18.
45 Ibid., p. 226.
46 Terry Eagleton, *Literary Theory: An Introduction*, 2nd edn. (Oxford: Blackwell Publishing, 1983; rpt. 2005), p. 27.
47 Ibid., p. 28.
48 Albert J. Guerard, *Conrad the Novelist* (Cambridge, MA: Harvard University Press, 1958), p. viii.
49 J. H. Stape, 'On Conrad Biography as a Fine Art', *The Conradian* 32, no. 2 (2007), 59.
50 Guerard, *Conrad the Novelist*, p. 275.
51 Thomas C. Moser, *Joseph Conrad: Achievement and Decline* (Cambridge, MA: Harvard University Press, 1957), p. 8.
52 As Kermode underlines, periodization is a familiar operation of canon formation, 'a way of ordering the past' and 'so making it accessible to valuation' (*History and Value*, p. 18).
53 Kermode, *Pleasure and Change*, p. 5.
54 See John Galsworthy, 'Reminiscences of Conrad' (1924), collected in *Castles in Spain and Other Screeds* (London: William Heinemann, 1927); Edward Garnett, ed., *Conrad's Prefaces to his Works* (1937); Douglas Hewitt, *Conrad: A Reassessment* (Cambridge: Bowes & Bowes, 1952).

55 Smith, *Contingencies of Value*, p. 48. For example, M. C. Bradbrook's *Joseph Conrad: England's Polish Genius*, Walter F. Wright's *Romance and Tragedy in Joseph Conrad* (Lincoln: University of Nebraska Press, 1949) and Paul Wiley's *Conrad's Measure of Man* (Madison: University of Wisconsin Press, 1954) had argued Conrad's late fiction did not constitute a decline.

56 *Conrad's Later Novels* (Montreal: McGill-Queen's University Press, 1980), p. 1. See also Morton D. Zabel, 'Joseph Conrad: Chance and Recognition', *Sewanee Review* 53 (1945), 1–22; John A. Palmer, *Joseph Conrad's Fiction: A Study in Literary Growth* (Ithaca, NY: Cornell University Press, 1968); Robert Secor, *The Rhetoric of Shifting Perspectives: Conrad's 'Victory'* (University Park, PA: Pennsylvania University Press, 1971).

57 Jones, *Conrad and Women*, p. 2.

58 Moser, *Achievement and Decline*, p. 2.

59 Jones, *Conrad and Women*, p. 23.

60 See, for instance, Stephen Donovan, *Joseph Conrad and Popular Culture* (Basingstoke: Palgrave Macmillan, 2005).

61 This relation is the subject of Said's follow-up to *Orientalism*, *Culture and Imperialism* (New York: Knopf, 1993)

62 'An Image of Africa: Racism in Conrad's "Heart of Darkness"', *Massachusetts Review* 18 (1977), 782–94; reprinted in *Heart of Darkness*, ed. Robert Kimbrough (New York: Norton, 1988), p. 259.

63 See Bernard C. Meyer, *Joseph Conrad: A Psychoanalytic Biography* (Princeton, NJ: Princeton University Press, 1967) and Paul Kirschner, *Conrad: The Psychologist as Artist* (Edinburgh: Oliver and Boyd, 1968). During this period, Harold Bloom's *The Anxiety of Influence: A Theory of Poetry* (New York: Oxford University Press, 1973), updating Eliot's 'Tradition and the Individual Talent', put forward a psychoanalytical interpretation of the canon.

64 'Joseph Conrad: Postcolonialism and Imperialism', *EurAmerica* 41, no. 1 (2011), 6.

65 For another response, see Cedric Watts, '"A Bloody Racist": About Achebe's View of Conrad', *Yearbook of English Studies* 13 (1983), 196–209. Such qualifications and counter-responses are themselves one of the hallmarks of 'canonicity', as Smith has pointed out: 'When the value of a work is seen as unquestionable, those of its features that would, in a non-canonical work, be found alienating' are 'repressed or rationalized' (*Contingencies of Value*, p. 49).

66 Smith, *Contingencies of Value*, p. 46.

67 Guerard, *Conrad the Novelist*, p. xiii. Eagleton notes a corresponding preference for poetry by the American New Critics at this time, for similarly practical reasons (*Literary Theory*, p. 43).

68 Moser, *Achievement and Decline*, p. 2.

2

ALLAN H. SIMMONS

Reading *Heart of Darkness*

The phrase 'heart of darkness' has become a journalistic byword for atrocity, used even by those who have not read Conrad's best-known story, with the novella serving as a template for monomania, exploitative imperialism and the abuse of power. Indeed, the tale has acquired the status of a modern myth addressing the nature of evil, in which Marlow's voyage upriver is fashioned, in Albert J. Guerard's phrase, as a 'night journey into the unconscious'.[1] The text draws on Conrad's own experiences in 1890 as an employee of the Société Anonyme Belge pour le Commerce du Haut-Congo in the Congo Free State of Leopold II, King of the Belgians. Conrad confessed to Lady Ottoline Morrell in September 1913 that he had never recovered from the six months he spent in Africa, and his first biographer attributed his decision to become a writer to the poor health he brought home from the Congo.[2] The Congo inspired a journal, 'The Congo Diary', two tales, 'An Outpost of Progress' (1897) and *Heart of Darkness* (1899), and the essay 'Geography and Some Explorers' (1924) and provoked some of the writer's most trenchant comments on Western colonialism, in his letters. One of the most shocking aspects of *Heart of Darkness* is how little of its content Conrad had to invent. Neither Africa nor the Congo Free State is actually named in the narrative, but, from the first, the novella's reception has been linked to its historical and political setting: the late nineteenth century's 'Scramble for Africa'.

The centre of the novella and the object of Marlow's quest is Kurtz, to whom 'All Europe contributed' (95.10). But there is also a sense in which all European literature went into the making of *Heart of Darkness*, a generically multi-faceted fiction – part travelogue, part colonial adventure, a modern psychological drama and political satire, and an autobiography and Gothic fantasy, with *Ur*-texts ranging from the Bible (Marlow's opening words come from Psalm 74) to Dante and Virgil. Its frame of reference is both historical, in its appeal to the Roman conquest of Britain for a parallel, and contemporary, in the use it makes of the 'Scramble for Africa'.[3] The compendium of Western cultural references out of which the work emerges indicates the audacious scale on which it was conceived; fittingly, its range of creative sources has been complemented by numerous critical approaches. Conrad's most famous fiction has become a staple of the undergraduate seminar, in which it figures as a key text in the development of literary Modernism, signalling the break with nineteenth-century realism and ushering in Modernist experimentation. More recently, it has become a 'site of contestation' in critical theory courses, in which angles as diverse as psychoanalysis, New Historicism and, in the wake of the Nigerian novelist Chinua Achebe's polemical attack, postcolonialism have been used to interpret it.[4]

The text is not reducible to its sources, although to read it without knowing them would be to receive it in impoverished form; nor can a single interpretive approach hope to encompass it. Rather, each attempt has revealed something but not everything about the text. As if to mirror the work's enduring fascination to would-be interpreters, it continues to be reinvented in other genres, including film, opera, puppet shows and graphic novels.[5] Such an afterlife confirms that there are many ways of addressing great art and proves the fertility of a text that so signally articulated the anxieties of its age.

I

Conrad began drafting what he first called *The Heart of Darkness* (its original serial title) in mid-December 1898. This moment in his writing career is significant. With his first two novels, *Almayer's Folly* (1895) and *An Outcast of the Islands* (1896), behind him, Conrad embarked on what would eventually become *The Rescue* (1920). Reflecting his growing confidence in himself as an author, he interrupted work on it as new creative possibilities presented themselves. A week after the publication of *An Outcast*, Conrad acknowledged that 'The literary profession is ... my sole means of support' (*Letters*, I, 266), tacitly confessing that he had abandoned any idea of returning to the sea to earn his livelihood. His developing commitment to the craft of fiction is articulated in the practical advice he gave to another aspirant author and ex-seaman, Edward Noble (1857–1941), only six months after the publication of *Almayer's Folly*. Conrad encouraged Noble to 'treat events only as illustrative of human sensation – as the outward sign of inward feelings', claiming that a writer's imagination 'should be used to create human souls; to disclose human hearts' (28 October 1895; *Letters*, I, 252–3). In order to accomplish this, Noble was enjoined to 'cultivate your poetic faculty':

> You must give yourself up to your emotions (no easy task) you must squeeze out of yourself every sensation, every thought, every image – mercilessly,

> without reserve and without remorse; you must search the darkest corners of your heart, the most remote recesses of your brain; – you must search them for the image, for the glamour, for the right expression.

The counsel to Noble concludes with this observation upon literary perspective: 'You have many stories by you. Rewrite some of them from an inward point of view. In that point of view anything may be made interesting'. Such advice, ranging from the relationship between incident and character to the necessity of correct expression – Conrad would later confess to being 'haunted, mercilessly haunted by the *necessity* of style' (*Letters*, II, 50) – and the creative possibilities afforded by point of view, constitutes a general briefing to the would-be author while simultaneously identifying literary Modernism's central preoccupations, with its emphasis on form and subjectivity.

Conrad's Preface to *The Nigger of the 'Narcissus'* (1897), a more formal statement of his aesthetics, has come to be regarded as his artistic manifesto, containing as it does the celebrated claim: 'My task which I am trying to achieve is, by the power of the written word to make you hear, to make you feel – it is, before all, to make you *see*' (x). The Preface's emphasis on the rhythmic and poetic qualities of prose, to 'the perfect blending of form and substance' and 'the shape and ring of sentences' (ix), offers insight into a key feature of Modernism. In the 1890s, the boundaries between prose and poetry were becoming increasingly blurred under the influence of Continental writers like Baudelaire and Rimbaud – Baudelaire's posthumously published *Le Spleen de Paris* (1869) was intended to be called *Petits poèmes en prose*[6] – and, at home, Walter Pater and Oscar Wilde. This blurring provides a stylistic expression of the iconoclasm associated with modern literature, as writers were enjoined by Ezra Pound to 'Make it new'. Conrad was strident in his sense of himself as a Modern; in a letter to his publisher in 1902, the year of the publication of *Heart of Darkness* in book-form, he distanced himself from Thackeray, Walter Scott and George Eliot saying: 'I am *modern*, and I would rather recall Wagner the musician and Rodin the Sculptor' (*Letters*, II, 418). Closer to home, obvious clues to Conrad's developing poetics may be found in his reading: Edward Garnett's *An Imaged World: Poems in Prose* (1894) and Turgenev's *Dream Tales and Prose Poems* (1897) in Constance Garnett's translation.[7]

Conrad's modernity helped to focus the lens through which we view and understand modern literature. What follows will examine *Heart of Darkness* as an expression of Conrad's poetics, showing as well how their demands have required developing appropriate analytical tools. While the necessary attention to fine detail involves concentrating on selective aspects of the text, this sample will convey something of the stylistic intricacies that articulate its ideological concerns and underpin the narrative's enduring richness.

II

Conrad began writing *The Heart of Darkness* at a moment when his sense of himself as an author was being strengthened and when, despite his protestations to the contrary, his first novels were being favourably received by the critics. It first appeared in *Blackwood's Edinburgh Magazine* in three monthly instalments from February to April 1899. Later, the three-part structure was retained, but the title was revised, when the novella was published by Blackwood's in book-form in *Youth: A Narrative and Two Other Stories* (1902).

To begin with, the tale is circular, opening and closing on the *Nellie* in the Thames estuary. Within this overall shape are other gestures towards circularity: Marlow's quest begins and ends in Europe; his journey upriver to find Kurtz is reversed in his journey down river. The very occasion of telling the tale is associated with the circular rhythm of the ebb and flow of the tide; Marlow recounts his experiences while waiting for the flowing tide to turn and thus allow the *Nellie* to be carried down river for a pleasure cruise. When he concludes, the Director announces 'We have lost the first of the ebb' (126.11–12), suggesting not only that the tale is symbolically told between the turning of the tide but also that it has distracted this group of friends, experienced sailors all, from noticing that the tide has turned.

Structural symmetry is sustained through such devices as repetitions and parallels – four of the first five paragraphs conclude with a reference to the 'brooding gloom' that hovers over London; Marlow's tale of nineteenth-century imperialism is prefaced by an account of Roman imperialism – but there is nothing consolatory about the echoes they provoke: The menacing London 'gloom' anticipates the 'darkness' that Marlow encounters in the tale, suggesting that the latter is coterminous with the former. The message behind the comparison – a stark truth for the contemporary British readership – is that all empires rise and fall. The very paean to Britain's maritime history is undermined by a subtle collocation of legend and reality. The ship's names provide a clue: Alongside Sir Francis Drake's *Golden Hind* we find Sir John Franklin's *Erebus* (the name of the primordial deity personifying darkness) and *Terror*. Similarly proleptic are the two knights themselves: Drake associated with plunder and Franklin with his failed search for the Northwest Passage involving suspicions of cannibalism.[8] The challenge to colonialism persists even in the fine construction of sentences and paragraphs – in, for instance, the simple ordering of information (the nation's representatives had set out for the unknown world 'bearing the sword, and often the torch' (45.4–5)) and, as playfully, in the paragraph break that invokes the age's great truism, 'The sun will never set on the British empire', only to debunk it: 'The dreams of men, the seed of commonwealths, the germs of empires. ¶ The sun set' (45.7–10).

The anonymous first-person narrator who introduces Marlow's tale is also given the novella's last word, completing the frame, as it were. But as the frame-narrator anticipates the story to follow in both mood and method, any structural sense of closure is revealed as illusory, even ironic; Marlow's tale cannot be contained. We should take seriously the seemingly flippant remark: 'we knew we were fated, before the ebb began to run, to hear about one of Marlow's inconclusive experiences' (47.31–33). Form is at odds with content; the frame's structural elegance provides a damning comment on the moral dereliction and turpitude described within. To evoke Samuel Beckett's description of Marcel Proust's narrative method, 'The whiskey bears a grudge against the decanter.'[9] In this vein, Kurtz's presence lingers long after he has been buried 'in a muddy hole' (117.32), haunting Marlow's interview with the Intended, Marlow's memory and, ultimately, the reader.

Marlow's narration begins, as does Classical epic, *in medias res*: '"And this also," said Marlow suddenly, "has been one of the dark places of the earth"' (45.17–18). The opening phrase, with its emphasis on continuation (*And* this *also*) implies that he is either developing an idea whose origins we have not heard or responding to someone else's words. In this tale about the dark truths of human nature, the interplay between the stated and the implied, indeed between the sayable and the unsayable, is elevated to a stylistic virtue. The technique by which this will be accommodated is then identified, in the frame-narrator's description of Marlow's storytelling method:

> The yarns of seamen have an effective simplicity, the whole meaning of which lies within the shell of a cracked nut. But … Marlow was not typical (if his propensity to spin yarns be excepted) and to him the meaning of an episode was not inside like a kernel but outside, enveloping the tale which brought it out only as a glow brings out a haze, in the likeness of one of these misty halos that, sometimes, are made visible by the spectral illumination of moonshine. (45.33–40)

This metaphorically dense description is a triumph of suggestiveness under the guise of trying to be precise, and as such it enacts the very definition it provides. 'Meaning' is not inherent but 'outside, enveloping'; and the impalpability of this 'outside' is developed by the accretion of abstract images – 'glow', 'haze', 'misty halos', 'spectral illumination' and 'moonshine' – and qualifications: 'only as', 'in the likeness', 'sometimes'. According to the narrator, then, the meaning in Marlow's tale inheres not in the tale itself but rather in the prevailing impression or atmosphere that it arouses in the reader. In his correspondence, Conrad stressed the active and collaborative role demanded of the interpreter: 'one writes only half the book; the other half is with the reader' (*Letters*, II, 370).

This sense that literature communicates via feeling rather than reason extends the claim in the Preface to *The Nigger of the 'Narcissus'* that art appeals to temperament. The added claim that the meaning depends on a lingering impression provides insight into the artistic method of *Heart of Darkness*. Fittingly for a narrative whose action is set in a tropical forest and is so perceived in shadow – a fact compounded by the river mists through which the steamboat sails and the dream-like quality of some of the sequences – Conrad's methods are characterized by a suggestiveness that in part originates in painterly Impressionism. From the abandoned and decaying European machinery at the first station, which emblematizes the abandoned and decaying civilized Western values, to the river journey into the jungle, which is reconfigured as both a journey into the psyche and, with its emphasis on navigation and interruption, a literal expression of the narration itself, Marlow's narrative transforms correspondences and juxtapositions into a structural principle. To begin with, the narrative is marked by repetitions and returns. Individual words – 'darkness', 'ivory' or 'Kurtz' – echo insistently throughout, performing the same rhythmic function as rhyme in poetry while conferring and sustaining a widespread sense of obsession: the European colonialists' greed, Marlow's fascination with Kurtz. Conradian narrative demands, then, the close attention usually reserved for poetry. However audacious its grand themes – the collapse of the civilized self, the challenge to European imperialism – to reduce *Heart of Darkness* to a series of nuclear statements about life is to ignore the poetic character that defines it as literature.

From the outset, incidents are invested with symbolic weight. Marlow's encounter with the two silent women, 'feverishly' (51.20) knitting black wool in the outer room of the Company offices, leaves him 'with an eerie feeling' that gestures beyond the specific moment to a Classical context freighted with additional interpretive significance: 'She seemed uncanny and fateful. Often far away there I thought of these two, guarding the door of Darkness' (51.31–33). In like manner, the reader is prompted to recognize the latent meanings in Kurtz's painting, seen at the Central Station: 'a small sketch in oils on a panel representing a woman draped and blindfolded carrying a lighted torch. The background was sombre – almost black. The movement of the woman was stately and the effect of the torchlight on the face was sinister' (67.21–25). The iconography in Kurtz's sketch, which summons up the contemporary Symbolist painting *Hope* (1885) by G. F. Watts, in which a blindfolded female figure sits playing a broken lyre, can be seen as providing a commentary on the colonial venture, where whatever light is being carried into the darkness is obscured.[10] To Marlow, 'It was just robbery with violence, aggravated murder on a great scale, and men going at it blind' (47.15–16). The image itself recalls and synthesizes other such images and ideas; for instance, the lighted torch is most obviously an extension of the fire that has destroyed a shed filled with trade goods in the compound outside and which has occasioned such brutal treatment of the African that 'the wilderness without a sound took him to its bosom again' (66.3–4). The image also looks back to that primal fire stolen by Prometheus, 'the torch' of civilization, the 'spark from the sacred fire', that is preceded by 'the sword', in the frame narration (45.4–6). In this manner, meaning in *Heart of Darkness* is discovered through gradual, subtle and intricate accretion and shared reference; the description of the woman's movement as 'stately' anticipates the description of Kurtz's African mistress, 'stately in her deliberate progress' (107.26). Similarly, the descriptor 'draped' will be applied to her and to the columns in the Intended's house (122.10), at a moment when Marlow recalls Kurtz as 'draped nobly in the folds of a gorgeous eloquence' (121.22–23). In November 1898, while working on *The Rescue*, which he would interrupt a month later to begin *Heart of Darkness*, Conrad wrote of his progress that he was 'dreamily dreaming how fine it could be if the thought did not escape, if the expression did not hide underground, if the idea had a substance and words a magic power, if the invisible could be snared into a shape' (*Letters*, II, 119). It is precisely through assiduous attention to style and composition, as demonstrated in such sequences as Kurtz's sketch, that this narrative succeeds in its struggle to snare 'the invisible' into shape.

Marlow's is an oral narration; he *tells* the story that we *read*. His first-person narrative, characterized both by the authenticity of bearing witness to the events being described and by the necessary limitations of subjective vision, imitates the qualities of a spoken report, founded upon memory and subject to interruption and digression. Shaped by recollection, the narrative is freed from the demands of linear chronology and, while broadly following events as they occurred, Marlow is able to disrupt the time-sequence – for instance, when he pauses, then appears to lose his thread and gesture into the future: 'He was silent for a long time. ¶ … "I laid the ghost of his gifts at last with a lie," he began, suddenly.… "Girl! What? Did I mention a girl?"' (93.21–22). His narration combines the intimacy of an 'I' speaking to 'you' with the testament of first-hand experience. A refutation of nineteenth-century omniscient narration, first-person narrative celebrates the improvisational possibilities of telling a tale in which the ordering of information is subject to the processes of recollection, and certainty is replaced by impression and speculation.

Using first-person narration also collapses the distinction between the present (in which the tale is told) and the past (in which the events being described took place). A well-documented technique for achieving this effect is what Ian Watt christened 'delayed decoding',[11] whereby the listener-reader is invited to understand or 'decode' the unfolding events in Marlow's narrative at the same rate as he does. When his steamboat comes under attack on the journey between the Central and Inner Stations, Marlow's first impression is: 'Sticks, little sticks, were flying about, thick; they were whizzing before my nose, dropping below me, striking behind me against my pilot-house' (89.21–23). He then revises this initial impression: 'Arrows by Jove! We were being shot at' (89.26–27). However brief, his confusion is sufficient to recreate in the reading experience Marlow's perception of the moment. In this way, story and storytelling are intimately connected, and the reader shares the shock of recognition with the force of immediacy.

In addition to interpretive conundrums, there is also a schizophrenic quality to the narration. Marlow is clearly obsessed with communication, as when he strains for the exact word – 'the bewildering, the illuminating, the most exalted and most contemptible, the pulsating stream of light or the deceitful flow from the heart of an impenetrable darkness' (92.21–24) – but this compulsion is matched by a reluctance to reveal all; at the core of the tale about Kurtz lie 'unspeakable rites' (95.18), left deliberately undetailed so as to invite the reader's imaginative capacity to become engaged. In this way, Marlow resembles Coleridge's Ancient Mariner, fated to recount a traumatic experience that is not fully understood and, in effect, appealing to his friends (and enlisting the reader) to help him understand his encounter with Kurtz at 'the farthest point of navigation and the culminating point of [his] experience' (47.40–48.1).

The occasion of telling is dramatized, as Marlow occasionally pauses to address his audience, and they, in turn, occasionally interrupt him. Such reminders cast readers in the role of a second-degree audience, listening over the shoulders of the audience on the *Nellie*, as it were, and looking to them for guidance as to how to respond. For his part, Marlow, 'no more to us than a voice', appeals to his audience – 'Do you see him? Do you see the story? Do you see anything?' (70.2–3) – and comments self-consciously on both his story's progress and, paradoxically, the impossibility of adequately communicating it: 'it is impossible to convey the life-sensation of any given epoch of one's existence – that which makes its truth, its meaning – its subtle and penetrating essence. It is impossible. We live, as we dream – alone …' (70.10–13).

One consequence of this emphasis on orality is that the reader is invited to listen to the 'ring of sentences'. When we do, the poetry of Conrad's prose becomes apparent. Much is made of the fact that Conrad wrote in his third language, after Polish and French, yet his English is marked by an audible lyricism – witness the sibilance in the sentence 'On silvery sandbanks hippos and alligators sunned themselves side by side' (77.11–12) – and by rhetorical balance: 'Their talk, however, was the talk of sordid buccaneers. It was reckless without hardihood, greedy without audacity and cruel without courage. There was not an atom of foresight or of serious intention in the whole batch of them, and they did not seem aware these things are wanted for the work of the world' (73.28–33). In this description of the Eldorado Exploring Expedition the parallel adjectival structure – reckless / hardihood, greedy / audacity, cruel / courage – attracts attention; the second adjective in each pair contains more syllables than the first, giving emphasis to what these adventurers are 'without'. Such devices – repetition, alliteration, internal rhyme – suggest a fine ear for effect, and this elegant rhythmic structure passes its own critical comment on the feckless venture it describes.

III

The narrative of *Heart of Darkness* is famed for its indirectness. Conrad cautioned a friend that 'the idea is so wrapped up in secondary notions that You – even You! – may miss it!' (*Letters*, II, 157). Not only does Marlow punctuate his account with modalizing locutions that ensure suggestiveness – in forms such as 'perhaps', 'as if', 'seemed' and 'like' – but the emphasis also falls on the intangible rather than the factual, a method that has tripped up (and frustrated) some commentators insisting upon realist protocols in a text that consistently undercuts and even mocks them. For instance, when the jungle's stillness is described as 'the stillness of an implacable force brooding over an inscrutable intention' (77.22–23), the sense of strangeness is productive, giving the narrative a metaphysical dimension while implying as much about Marlow's perceiving consciousness as about the world he perceives.

One fertile consequence of this narrating style, with its stress on suggestiveness and indirection, is a polyphony of competing voices capable of sustaining a range of attitudes. The novella is set in Africa during the era of European imperialism, and its language and frame of reference can sometimes be jarring to the present-day reader. But the racist vocabulary is part of the point; Marlow is acutely of his age, and he does not seek to excuse himself, as his own sardonic admission proves: 'After all, I also was a part of the great cause of these high and just proceedings' (57.20–21). Against this, however, his sympathies and judgements prove that he transcends the crude colonial attitudes that motivate his contemporaries. Thus, *Heart of Darkness* is at the confluence of the colonial and postcolonial worlds; of its historical moment, it also transcends it. To take a single example of how this works in practice, here is Marlow's description of the fireman aboard his steamboat:

> And between whiles I had to look after the savage who was fireman. He was an improved specimen; he could fire up a vertical boiler. He was there below me and, upon my word, to look at him was as edifying as seeing a dog in a parody of breeches and a feather hat, walking on his hind legs. A few months of training had done for that really fine chap. He squinted at the steam-gauge and at the water gauge with an evident effort of intrepidity – and he had filed teeth too, the poor devil, and the wool of his pate shaved into queer patterns and three ornamental scars on each of his cheeks. He ought to have been clapping his hands and stamping his feet on the bank – instead of which he was hard at work, a thrall to strange witchcraft, full of improving knowledge. He was useful because he had been instructed; and what he knew was this – that should the water in that transparent thing disappear, the evil spirit inside the boiler would get angry through the greatness of his thirst and take a terrible vengeance. So he sweated and fired up and watched the glass fearfully (with an impromptu charm, made of rags, tied to his arm and a piece of polished bone as big as a watch stuck flatways through his lower lip), while the wooded banks slipped past us slowly, the shore noise was left behind, the interminable miles of silence – and we crept on, towards Kurtz.
>
> (80.20–81.1)

The casual racism here is obvious; the African is a 'savage', implying that Europeans, by contrast, are 'civilized'; European mechanization and science (in which terminology the fireman is a 'specimen') is juxtaposed with 'witchcraft and 'superstition'; and the exotic portrait of the African is clearly designed to render him as 'Other'. But qualifying ideas coexist as well. The description of the fireman as 'a dog in breeches with a feather hat' recalls Dr Samuel Johnson's comment about women preachers: 'A woman's preaching is like a dog's walking on his hinder legs. It is not done well; but you are surprised to find it done at all.'[12] Two comparably crude codes of diminution, gendered and cultural, are thus brought into correspondence as Marlow's image invites us to question Western judgement. Even though the fireman can only perceive the alien Western technology required to run the steamboat as witchcraft and superstition, he none the less accomplishes his tasks, inviting the reader to ask to what degree science functions as Western 'witchcraft'. And, finally, the tone of Marlow's comments clearly suggests where his sympathies lie: When he claims that 'A few months of training had done for that really fine chap', he traces African ruination to European contact. Furthermore, in the claim 'He ought to have been clapping his hands and stamping his feet on the bank, instead of which he was hard at work, a thrall to strange witchcraft, full of improving knowledge', Marlow appeals to the discourse of morality ('ought') to indicate that this contact has reduced rather than elevated the man, rendering ironic the phrase 'improving knowledge'. In this way, Marlow's narrative acquires double authority, both reflecting and transcending its age.

The tropical forest against which the action is cast evokes in Marlow images of 'the earliest beginnings of the world, when vegetation rioted on the earth and the big trees were kings' (77.5–7). Contextually, these 'Trees, trees, millions of trees, massive, immense, running up high' (78.30–31) perhaps recall the opening lines of Dante's *Inferno*: 'Half way along the road we have to go, / I found myself obscured in a great forest, / Bewildered, and I knew I had lost my way.' The setting offers an image of energy to set against the sterility that characterizes the 'pilgrims' or the Intended. Importantly, when Kurtz's African mistress is first viewed, in a description whose paradoxes – 'wild' / 'gorgeous', 'proudly' / 'barbarous', 'savage and superb, wild-eyed and magnificent' (107) – imply that she evades definition by Marlow, she appears as a *genius loci*: 'the colossal body of the fecund and mysterious life seemed to look at her, pensive, as though it had been looking at the image of its own tenebrous and passionate soul' (107.27–30). The setting is also politicized, serving as an inimical space resistant to the European presence: 'The high stillness confronted these two figures [the Manager and his uncle] with its ominous patience, waiting for the passing away of a fantastic invasion' (76.26–28). As Marlow journeys upriver, the setting is steadily reconstituted as an expression of uncontrollable forces. At the same time, he throws himself into the practical work of piloting the steamer to escape the nightmarishly hypnotic sensations conjured up by the journey: 'When you have to attend to things of that sort, to the mere incidents of the surface, the reality – the reality, I tell you – fades. The inner truth is hidden – luckily, luckily' (77.32–35). Such ideas combine to recast the jungle, from external environment to an image of innerness, reconfiguring Marlow's upriver voyage as a voyage into the self.

The transformation of background into foreground, and the productive implications of this for interpretation, centre on the figure of the totemic European, Kurtz. First, he is identified with the object of his obsession; his head, 'patted' by the wilderness, has come to resemble 'an ivory ball' (93.30–31). Then, within the tale's symbolic register, the wilderness, invaded by him, invades Kurtz in turn: 'It had taken him, loved him, embraced him, got into his veins, consumed his flesh and sealed his soul to its own by the inconceivable ceremonies of some devilish initiation' (93. 32–35). The African wilderness is, by these terms, less a geographical place than a symbolic space, reflecting and accommodating European dreams of wealth and power. If Africa is transformed into a function of European fantasy, it also resists and transcends such fantasies. The metaphorical richness of the narrative and the narration's rhetorical insistence facilitate such substitutions; as Marlow claims in *Lord Jim*, 'the power of sentences has nothing to do with their sense or the logic of their construction' (61.35–36).

Marlow's is a journey of disillusion; the further he travels upriver, the less he believes that the European presence in Africa is motivated by anything other than sordid greed backed by brute force and outright cruelty. As successive experiences reveal the degree to which European civilized values have collapsed, so Kurtz represents Marlow's only hope of rescuing his belief in sustainable moral values. His insistence that the river carries him 'towards Kurtz – exclusively' (78.39) acquires a note of desperation. If Kurtz can somehow have retained his humanity, the actions of other Company agents can be cast into relief. Of course, the Accountant's claim, early in the narrative, that Kurtz 'Sends in as much ivory as all the others put together' (60.26–27) means that the reader does not hold out much hope – and, with human heads on stakes ornamenting his hut, the 'remarkable' Mr Kurtz turns out to be an extremist even more morally derelict than his fellows. Whatever hopes that Marlow entertained about Kurtz disappear, and with them, seemingly, goes the broader belief that morality is absolute rather than relative.

But then, in a supreme moment of reversal that continues to vex readers, Kurtz famously declaims 'The horror! The horror!' (117.14). Marlow conceives this judgement, wrung out of Kurtz at 'that supreme moment of complete knowledge' (117.11), as 'his final burst of sincerity' and 'an affirmation, a moral victory paid for by innumerable defeats' (114.3, 118.31–32). According to Marlow, Kurtz has retained the capacity to judge his actions – and found them wanting – and in this judgement has proclaimed his worth and separateness from the rest of the Europeans, blind or indifferent to their motivations and failings. With his verdict on Kurtz – 'his soul was mad' – Marlow also identifies the journey undertaken in the novella as an odyssey of self-discovery: 'being alone in the wilderness it had looked within itself and by Heavens! I tell you, it had gone mad. I had – for my sins I suppose – to go through the ordeal of looking into it myself' (113.39–114.2). Through Kurtz, Marlow comes to understand something of the extremes of human nature beyond the purview of his lived experience, allowing him to confess:

'It is his extremity that I seem to have lived through' (118.23–24). In this identification, teller and tale, narrator and subject, become fused, as the narrative, like a Klein bottle or a Möbius strip, disorients the reader, conveying something of Marlow's own experience at the level of Conrad's narrative poetics.

The reaction to Marlow's tale by his audience is ambivalent. Initially, nobody moves; then the Director announces that the tide has turned. It is left to the frame-narrator to close the narrative: 'The offing was barred by a black bank of clouds and the tranquil waterway leading to the uttermost ends of the earth flowed sombre under and overcast sky – seemed to lead into the heart of an immense darkness' (126.13–16). The description initially points beyond the tale to the setting and the weather, allowing the atmospheric setting to act as commentary. But the post-positioned clause, introduced by the modalizing locution 'seemed', not only ensures open-endedness (did it, or didn't it 'lead'?) but, in a final gesture of circularity and recurrence, also ensures that the novella ends by returning us to the journey's beginnings. This voyage of discovery refuses a consolatory conclusion; instead, the aesthetics demand further confrontation with unsettling truths about the collapsed European self, from which there is no return. The phrase ensures that Marlow's story cannot be contained within the frame, while the addition of the descriptor 'immense' (more French than English in its inflection) ensures that the tale ends on an emphatic note of linguistic ambiguity and sibilance, poetically conjuring up the snake/river that had fascinated Marlow to begin with (48) and in whose coils we, like him, are still inextricably caught.

NOTES

1 Albert J. Guerard, *Conrad the Novelist* (Cambridge, MA: Harvard University Press, 1958), p. 39.
2 Martin Ray, comp., *Joseph Conrad: Memories and Impressions: An Annotated Bibliography* (Amsterdam: Rodopi, 2007), p. 112; G. Jean-Aubry, ed., *Joseph Conrad: Life and Letters* (London: William Heinemann, 1927), I, 141–2.
3 For more on the novella's rich allusiveness, see Cedric Watts *Conrad's 'Heart of Darkness': A Critical and Contextual Discussion* (1977; rpt. Amsterdam: Rodopi, 2012), and Owen Knowles, 'Explanatory Notes', *Youth, Heart of Darkness, The End of the Tether* (Cambridge: Cambridge University Press, 2010), pp. 439–55.
4 See Chinua Achebe, 'An Image of Africa: Racism in Conrad's "Heart of Darkness"', *Massachusetts Review* 18 (1977), 782–94; reprinted in Achebe's *Hopes and Impediments: Selected Essays* (London: Anchor Books, 1989), pp. 1–20.
5 Examples include Francis Ford Coppola's film *Apocalypse Now* (1979), Tarik O'Regan's opera *Heart of Darkness* (2012), and Tom Tirabosco and Christian Perrissin's graphic novel *Kongo* (2013).

6 To his publisher, Baudelaire outlined his ideal as 'a poetic prose, musical though rhythmless and rhymeless, flexible yet strong enough to identify with the lyrical impulse of the soul, the ebbs and flows of reverie, the pangs of conscience' (quoted in *London Review of Books*, 21 February 2013, p. 33).

7 Conrad to Edward Garnett, [8 January 1895] (*Letters*, I, 198, 360). Significantly, Garnett's admiration for the manuscript of *An Outcast of the Islands* included its 'poetical passages' (*Letters from Conrad: 1895 to 1924* (London: Nonesuch Press, 1928), p. xiii).

8 Sir Philip Sidney remarked of Drake, 'about the world he hath been, and rich he is returned' (to Robert Sidney, 18 October 1580) in *Sir Philip Sidney: Selected Prose and Poetry*, ed. Robert Kimbrough (Madison: University of Wisconsin Press, 1983), p. 95. Reports of the Franklin expedition's outcome began to surface in late 1854; see, for example, 'The Fate of Sir John Franklin', *Daily News*, 23 October 1854, p. 4, which includes testimony from Dr John Rae of the Hudson's Bay Company.

9 Samuel Beckett, *Proust / Three Dialogues* (London: Calder & Boyars, 1970), pp. 21–2.

10 Conrad mentions 'poor Watts' in a letter written a day after the painter's death (to R. B. Cunninghame Graham, 2 July 1904 (*Letters*, III, 149)).

11 Ian Watt, *Conrad in the Nineteenth Century* (London: Chatto & Windus, 1980), pp. 175–6.

12 James Boswell, *The Life of Samuel Johnson, LL.D.*, ed. Percy Fitzgerald (1791; rpt. London: George Allen & Unwin, 1924), I, 285.

3

RICHARD NILAND

The Political Novels

From the awakening of Kaspar Almayer in *Almayer's Folly* (1895) to the ocular emphasis of *Under Western Eyes* (1911), Conrad's fiction is concerned with a capacity for political vision. In the major novels, a number of specific political forms are identifiable: *Under Western Eyes* challenges Russian autocracy and its oppositional movements; *Nostromo* (1904) examines the politics and economics of imperialism in the development of Latin America; and *The Secret Agent* (1907) glances at the various forms of revolutionary thought that entered politics in nineteenth-century Europe after their long theoretical gestation. While Conrad's work is concerned with existing reality and moral contradictions, frequently, and in a reversal of the Marxist formula that 'explains the formation of ideas from material practice' rather than explaining 'practice from the idea',[1] Conrad is interested in the 'descent' of political ideas into the arena of practical political application. In his political essay 'Autocracy and War' (1905), he lamented the 'degradation of the ideas of freedom and justice' inherent in the implementation of political ideals, writing that 'it is the fate of any idea to lose its royal form and power, to lose its "virtue" the moment it descends from its solitary throne to work its will amongst the people' (*NLL*, 73.18, 73.13–16). This notion is repeated in *Nostromo*, a novel concerned with the material realities and transformational powers of capitalism and economics, where Conrad writes of 'something inherent in the necessities of successful action which carried with it the moral degradation of the idea' (*No*, 521).

So, where does Conrad's work stand in relation to such political thought? As Laurence Davies has noted, owing to Conrad's pervasive irony and the 'irreconcilable antagonisms' inherent in his life and art, 'Whoever wants to claim Conrad for some favourite stance or cause will easily find the necessary evidence.'[2] The best-known contemporary political Conrad is the one who has emerged as a critic of imperialism through the central position of *Heart of Darkness* in twentieth-century literature. At the same time, the recurring view of Conrad's conservative politics is outlined by Terry Eagleton, who sees the writer possessed of 'an unthinking respect for authority and tradition' alongside 'his hatred of socialism, his disgust with democracy, and his patronizing attitude to the common people'.[3]

Conrad wrote at a time when, as the rather impercipient narrator of *Under Western Eyes* observes, 'A devotion to Church and Throne is not in itself a criminal sentiment; to prefer the will of one to the will of many does not argue the possession of a black heart or prove congenital idiocy' (233.38–234.1). Eagleton offers a reformulation of the views of a 1916 essay on 'Democracy in Modern Fiction' that insisted that Conrad was not 'a true leader of democracy,' but rather a 'Bourbon, who never forgot any of his inherited prejudices'.[4] Among these was a sense of political failure, the 'cruel futility of things' (*No*, 364), related to his childhood in the Ukraine and Austrian Poland and his familial experience of the politics of Russian imperialism. Allied to this was his later, acquired experience of British domestic politics and his encounter with a range of European imperialisms. Accordingly, pessimism informs his most overtly political fiction in that order and progress hide violence and repression while ideals of change and improvement founder on the rocks of an unfeeling cosmos and an incorrigibly divided human nature.

Nostromo

Responding to the recent American victory in the Spanish-American War (1898) and the United States' instrumental role in the secession of Panama from Colombia in 1903, *Nostromo* (1904) explores a political and cultural landscape where military force is associated with 'the natural order of things' (393). While offering a somewhat 'Occidental' portrait of a 'S[outh] American state in general' (*Letters*, III, 175), Costaguana is nevertheless a country where, in Martin Decoud's view, 'everything merely rational fails' (315), thereby evoking the polarities of Hegel's famous reflection on the political in *The Philosophy of Right* (1820): 'What is rational is actual and what is actual is rational'.[5] If, as Jürgen Habermas notes, 'Hegel inaugurated the discourse of modernity',[6] then this is a discourse taken up and interrogated by Conrad's political novels. The dubious necessity of interpreting and moulding the rational to accommodate the intransigent demands of the actual colours the politics of *Nostromo*, as the Hegelian dichotomy of rationality and realism presents itself in the 'conviction of practical necessity, stronger than any abstract political doctrine' (142). As a result, political labels have a 'nightmarish meaning in this country. Liberty, democracy, patriotism, government – all of them have a flavour of folly and murder' (408); and politics is subordinate to the actual and 'subtle force' of capitalism, manifested in the exploitation of the San Tomé mine. The mine overrides political aspirations, such as Charles Gould's idealism, destroying his hope that the Gould Concession can serve a 'better justice' (84).

As the natives of Costaguana are shoved 'out of the way of the San Tomé silver escort going to the sea' (114), *Nostromo* offers a complex vision of the 'brazen-faced scramble for a constantly diminishing quantity of booty' (115–16) that informs *Heart of Darkness* and Conrad's late essay 'Geography and Some Explorers' (1924), where he wrote that 'the discovery of America was the occasion of the greatest outburst of reckless cruelty and greed known to history' (*LE*, 4.37–39). In these works, colonialism launches a modernity founded on imperial adventure and exploitation. In addition to being a 'captain of industry' implicated in 'imperial democracy' (405), Gould is an 'adventurer in Costaguana' with an 'adventurer's easy morality' (365) whose conscience is ultimately corrupted. *Nostromo* explores the varied consequences of the alliance of the 'fanatical spirit' of moral absolutism with the development of material interests, in which 'the magnitude, the importance of the task' dwarves 'all merely humane considerations' (439). One view of the origins of this corruptibility is offered by Martin Decoud, who sceptically characterizes politics as a shifting response to the contingent in which political conviction is a 'particular view of our personal advantage either practical or emotional' (189). The politics of incorruptibility, which feature in relation to Gould's development, Nostromo's character and the nature of the silver, evoke the spectre of noble or revolutionary ideals, their transformation and their degradation, embodied by Robespierre and Saint-Just in the French revolutionary tradition, a subject Conrad also explores in 'Autocracy and War' and in *Under Western Eyes*. In the latter, Razumov embodies a political passivism in which 'nothing can be changed – neither happiness nor misery. They can only be displaced at the cost of corrupted consciences and broken lives' (201.25–27).

In its involved Modernist chronology, *Nostromo* encourages an abstruse understanding of political and historical development, illustrating how revolutions 'distort time' and how the 'turmoil of revolutionary events prompts people to disconnect one moment from the next'.[7] Behind this confusion, *Nostromo* also recounts identifiable stages of history in Costaguana that have seen both the earlier colonial traditions of ecclesiastical courts and the later arrival of modern trade and infrastructure. By the novel's close, Marxist socialism presents itself as an emerging political force. For the present, though, the historical evolution of imperialism ensures that Costaguana's postcolonial independence is nearing an end, with Sulaco 'on the point of being invaded by all the world' (150). With its focus on the United States' role in the politics of Latin America, the future development of geo-political power in the twentieth century is 'chillingly scripted' in *Nostromo*.[8] The Californian entrepreneur Holroyd is the embodiment of the principles of the Monroe Doctrine (1823) and the Roosevelt Corollary (1904) of United States entitlement in Latin American politics and the new 'manifest destiny' of the American role in global politics. He also stands as an inflated incarnation of the Protestant work ethic outlined by Max Weber, 'one of the constituents of the modern capitalist spirit',[9] especially with the narrative's focus on economic exploitation and development, the endowment of churches and the 'Protestant invasion of Sulaco organized by the Holroyd Missionary Fund' (509).

Civilization, which in Conrad's work is often a masked barbarism, is viewed with scepticism as a process of rationalization not wholly removed from that outlined in the political thought of Marx and Weber; and the 'material apparatus of perfected civilization' ushers in the 'stereotyped conveniences of modern life' (96). With its emphasis on Costaguana's transformation, *Nostromo* resonates with Weber's notion of the disenchantment of modernity. A sense of pastoral, imaginative and aesthetic loss is illustrated in Charles and Emilia Gould's conflicting attitudes to the country's landscape. With her aesthetic sensibility, Emilia's artistic creations offer a vision of the untouched beauty of the country as a 'hanging garden above the rocks of the gorge'. In his focus on the 'clearing of the wilderness' (106) and the destruction of obstacles to the mine's success, her husband embodies the nineteenth-century classical liberal 'anti-esthetic of neglect', as outlined by Mary Louise Pratt,[10] in which South America's various natural and social panoramas offer not an opportunity for the type of perorations that open *Nostromo* but rather a distinct sense of lack in relation to social and economic potential. However, Emilia Gould's reflections on the development of Costaguana do not go unquestioned. The romantic vision of noble nature and humanity derived from Rousseau is ironized alongside modern history's atrocities:

> At no time of the world's history have men been at a loss how to inflict mental and bodily anguish upon their fellow-creatures. This aptitude came to them in the growing complexity of their passions and the early refinement of their ingenuity. But it may safely be said that primeval man did not go to the trouble of inventing tortures. He was indolent and pure of heart. He brained his neighbour ferociously with a stone axe from necessity and without malice.
>
> (373)

While capitalism and civilization bring uniformity and disenchantment, the Weberian enchanted garden is revealed to be a 'paradise of snakes' (105). Modernity does not replace purity with barbarity – it merely represents an advance in dissimulation and ingenuity over primitive men, who were 'more artless in their recognition of success as the only standard of morality' (386).

If Protestantism offers a capacious cloak for concealing the rapacious development of economic interests, Catholicism contributes to a less appealing manner of enchantment by sustaining the political ignorance of the Indios, who, according to Decoud, 'know nothing either of reason or politics' (181). Such ignorance can be extended to the Blanco faction and Captain Mitchell, who has a 'strange ignorance of the real forces at work around him' (136), and others who believe themselves to be in control of political events. Father Roman actively discourages the people, mere 'ignorant sinners', from 'inquiring into the magnitude of the earth, with its countries and populations altogether beyond your understanding' (104) revealing a 'paternal scorn' (399) for the Indios. This view of Catholic and indigenous submission is, however, mirrored in the descriptions of the new force of capitalism, whose vast historical workings render upheaval inevitable and determined. The narrative's panoramic vistas of the landscape and people dwarfed within it encourage a conservative view of historical change and the immensity of forces that direct human affairs. In this respect, as Susan Sontag notes, such rhetoric indicates that 'sufferings and misfortunes are too vast, too irrevocable, too epic to be changed by any local political intervention. With a subject conceived on this scale, compassion can only flounder and 'make abstract'.[11] *Nostromo* echoes Conrad's 1897 letter to R. B. Cunninghame Graham that speaks of the universe knitting the fabric of human destiny, creating 'time, space, pain, death, corruption, despair and all the illusions – and nothing matters' (*Letters*, I, 425) This indifference notably informs Decoud's suicide, as the Golfo Placido's 'glittering surface remained untroubled' (501) by the fall of his silver-weighted body.

Nostromo pays detailed attention not only to the economic realities controlling the politics and society of Costaguana, but also to the architectural structures and institutions of civil society, such as trade, printing and journalism, from which emerge ideas that will shape the political future. With the deposed dictator Ribiera taking shelter in the Oceanic Steam Navigation (O.S.N.) Company's offices, the novel draws attention to the varied sites of politics in Sulaco. Captain Mitchell is concerned with the O.S.N. buildings, the railway and the 'protection of the Company's property' (14) from the 'crazy mob' (13) that emerges in the revolution, while Viola defends his private property and family from the crowd. The subjects of family and public sites of capital, such as the infrastructure of the port and railway, are focal points for an exploration of the politics of modernity. More precisely, from the description of the Aristocratic Club of Sulaco (98) to the Holroyd building in San Francisco (143), the novel enters the various portals that influence power. This includes the private spaces of home and family, which emerge as fiercely contested sites of the political.

Indeed, the political tide of Costaguana rises and falls in the Gould drawing-room, and the majestic natural forces that overlook Sulaco are linked to the domestic forces of politics. In his domestic relations, Charles Gould is 'the most anxious and deferential of dictators' (62), and his actions in the Casa Gould reflect on the emerging tumultuous politics of Sulaco. It is in the interstitial spaces and increasing silences of the Casa Gould that the politics of the country as a whole is given a shape. Decoud's speculative plan for the political development of Sulaco emerges from a drawing-room conversation, primarily a method for Decoud to advance his love for Antonia Avellanos. The emphasis on the Casa Gould and the empty spaces it harbours replicates Costaguana's fate, as Emilia, in the 'degradation of her young ideal,' ends up 'all alone in the Treasure House of the World' (443), with the Casa Gould a microcosm of the macrocosmic structures of politics.

In *The Political Unconscious*, Fredric Jameson asserted that 'it is inconceivable that a Latin American novelist' could have produced such a work as *Nostromo*,[12] given that Conrad's novel draws from a deep well of traditional Anglo-Saxon views of the Latin race. While *Nostromo* certainly draws upon the conventional rhetoric of contemporary coverage of Latin American politics, Costaguana's authenticity, one attested to by Latin American writers such as Jorge Luis Borges, derives from a finely pitched use of numerous references to the history of nineteenth-century Latin America (such as the careers of Bolivar, De Rosas and Juarez), especially the emergence of national independence movements and economic and political liberalism. In his reading and exchanges with Cunninghame Graham, who travelled widely in South America, Conrad engaged with a rich tradition of Latin American ideas that make a layered historical portrait of the internal politics of nineteenth-century Latin America as much a part of the novel's achievement as its global political prescience. However, ultimately, Conrad's Costaguana occupies a fictional space between historical realities. Robert Hampson has elaborated on Conrad's fiction as the creation of an 'alternative space' that, 'with its depth of historical awareness and emphasis on local specificities, heterogeneity, and difference, provides a continuingly effective antidote' to the 'monolithic mapping' of empire.[13] In its aesthetic plenitude, *Nostromo* opens a space for investigating political certainties, historical developments and actions that lead to moral solitude, promoting Conrad's view that fiction is 'nearer truth' than history (*NLL*, 19.12).

The Secret Agent

Reflecting on the political revolutionaries and idealists of nineteenth-century Soho, Russian exile Alexander Herzen (1812–70), editor and publisher of the political newspaper *The Bell* (1857–67), which evokes the 'rousing titles' (9.23) sold by Mr Verloc, noted 'the chaos of ideas and theories in these specimens of every kind of moral formation and reformation, of every protest, every Utopia, every disillusionment, and every hope, who meet in the alleys, eating-houses and beer-shops of Leicester Square and the adjoining back streets'.[14] On one level, this ineffectual and 'wretched population of foreigners ... a miserable, poverty-stricken, harassed population who set all the powerful monarchs of Europe trembling except the Queen of England' (2), forms the backdrop to *The Secret Agent* (1907). On another level, the novel draws on the climate of the 'dynamite outrages in London' (6.2) by the Irish Republican Brotherhood in the 1880s and the sensational, and sensationalized through journalism and popular fiction, late-nineteenth century world of anarchist deeds in Europe, such as Auguste Vaillant's bomb attack on the French Chamber of Deputies in 1893 and, of course, Martial Bourdin's accidental outrage of self-destruction at the Greenwich Observatory in February 1894.

The Secret Agent, with its references to various forms of butchery, links cannibalism and the political. A 'monstrous town' and a 'cruel devourer of the world's light' (6.31, 6.32), London holds the cannibalistic feast that is family, society and politics, with Conrad juxtaposing domestic politics in the familial sense to the larger scene of the national domestic politics of Britain. From the Verloc's 'domestic drama' (168.2) in the oppressive closeness of Brett Street to the 'wider space of Whitehall' (121.31), the narrative explores both London's impoverished districts and 'the precincts of the House which is *the* House, *par excellence*, in the minds of many millions of men' (162.7–9). In a novel that, like Mr Vladimir, revels in 'discovering droll connections between incongruous ideas' (20.39–40), such connections rely upon the author's 'ironic method,' which allows Conrad 'to say all I felt I would have to say in scorn as well as in pity' (7.29). As Linda Hutcheon notes, 'irony can and does function tactically in the service of a wide range of political positions, legitimating or undercutting a wide variety of interests'.[15] In *The Secret Agent*, Conradian irony ensures that the typically 'janiform' nature of Conrad's work is present.[16] Such duality appears in the Professor's understanding that revolution and legality are 'counter moves in the same game' (58.17–18) and in Stevie's 'immoderate compassion' and 'innocent but pitiless rage' (130.24–25), which are as 'indissolubly joined and connected as the reverse and obverse side of a medal' (130.23–24). However, exploring the consequences of Mr Vladimir's insistence upon a 'purely destructive' deed (30.11), the penetrating regard of Conrad's irony also exemplifies what Walter Benjamin describes as 'The Destructive Character'. Not unlike Stein's 'destructive element' in *Lord Jim*, this destructive character reveals 'an insuperable mistrust of the course of things and a readiness at all times to recognize that everything can go wrong,' seeing 'nothing permanent. But for this very reason he sees ways everywhere'.[17]

Such narratorial percipience in *The Secret Agent* is contrasted with the determination of various characters to remain 'in the dark' (6.15) and to avoid, as Sir Ethelred does, 'details' (106.7), an attitude crystallized in Winnie's fatal 'belief that things did not stand being looked into' (137.14–15). Concurrently, objects given full scrutiny become illegible, with the geometrical patterns that recur in the novel pointing beyond the irreconcilability of binary antagonisms to the cyclical and multiple concerns of modernity. Stevie's mutilated body, a 'heap of mixed things', evokes a Cubist painting, a broken 'heap of nameless fragments' (71.9, 7l.19–20), while the materiality of London becomes obscured through elemental impenetrability. The novel's burgeoning Modernism explores the 'sudden holes in space and time' (69.24) that characterize both the topography of the novel's London and the chronological jumps and ironic foreshadowings of its narrative structure.

As in *Nostromo*, which noted the credulity of a public delivered over to 'the wiles of swindlers and to the pitiless enthusiasms of leaders inspired by visions of a high destiny' (420), in his 1920 Author's Note to *The Secret Agent*, Conrad condemns anarchism in all its manifestations, 'doctrine, action, mentality', as a 'half crazy pose as of a brazen cheat exploiting the poignant miseries and passionate credulities of a mankind always so tragically eager for self-destruction' (5.3–5). The novel ironically addresses 'all shades of revolutionary opinion' (26.3). Such irony is never far from the surface of this rather aquatic tale when Sir Ethelred, a pillar of the establishment, is accused of being the harbinger of 'social revolution' (112.20) because of his Bill for the Nationalization of Fisheries. Among Conrad's anarchists, each a parody of an influential historical figure such as Mikhail Bakunin (1814–76) or Prince Peter Kropotkin (1842–1921), Michaelis expounds a broadly Marxist interpretation of history that sees 'Capitalism doomed in its cradle' (43.2–3). The Professor embodies the individualist anarchism of Max Stirner's *The Ego and Its Own* (1845) and the nihilistic anarchism expressed in Sergei Nechayev's *Catechism of a Revolutionary* (1869), both of which, *avant la lettre*, sought a Nietzschean 'disintegration of the old morality' (60.38). The only breakdown of this morality in the novel is a gruesomely inverted one, as Stevie falls victim to the hollow 'doctrine' of Verloc's 'supreme wisdom and goodness inculcated by two anxious women'

(178.26–27). The Professor's view of Nietzschean *ressentiment* insists that the 'theology' of the weak 'has invented hell for the strong' (227.8–9). For the narrator, though, the Professor's extremism has its origins in his own history of vanity and thwarted ambition, the result of 'personal impulses disguised into creeds' (66.29). This Conradian 'irrationalism',[18] recurs in *Victory* (1915), where 'the use of reason is to justify the obscure desires that move our conduct, impulses, passions, prejudices and follies, and also our fears' (83).

In Conrad's political novels, a belief in practical political panaceas constitutes an extreme form of political naivety. Stevie's 'symbolic longing' to take both the malnourished cabman and his suffering horse to bed is understood by the narrator as 'impossible' but 'not mad'. Unfortunately, 'To be taken into a bed of compassion was the supreme remedy, with only the one disadvantage of being difficult of application on a large scale' (129.29–31). In this respect, Stevie's understanding of possibility is more enlightened than the anarchists, who focus on the laws of historical evolution. In the final view of Michaelis, as related by the Professor, the ticket-of-leave apostle's political thinking, which 'has no logic' and reveals a 'poverty of reasoning', has become a reformulation of Stevie's powerless compassion: 'He is elaborating now the idea of a world planned out like an immense and nice hospital, with gardens and flowers, in which the strong are to devote themselves to the nursing of the weak' (225.33–35). An emphasis on simplicity and childishness related to political aspirations recurs in *Under Western Eyes*. When Razumov produces his political confession, 'his neat writing lost its character altogether – became unsteady, almost childish', whereas for the narrator and the Western European sensibility, 'all ideas of political plots and conspiracies seem childish' (*UWE*, 57.15–16, 90.4–5).

Mr. Vladimir asserts that 'Murder is always with us. It is almost an institution' (31.5–6), and *The Secret Agent* analyzes a number of institutions of modernity. Foremost among these is the family, as the novel investigates 'the reticent decencies of this home life, nestling in a shady street behind a shop where the sun never shone' (194.26–27). According to Richard Sennett, in the nineteenth century, the family was 'an idealized refuge, a world all its own, with a higher moral value than the public realm'. Indeed, as the family 'became a refuge from the terrors of society, it gradually became also a moral yardstick with which to measure the public realm of the capital city'.[19] *The Secret Agent* overturns this understanding of private and public. While Verloc periodically looks upon Winnie as an embodiment of the 'sacredness of domestic peace', as well as his 'chief possession' (137.41, 137.39), domestic harmony and the home in the novel become a 'cold, black, wet, muddy, inhospitable accumulation of bricks, slates, and stones, things in themselves unlovely and unfriendly to man' (48.8–10). Unsurprisingly for a London novel, *The Secret Agent* owes a debt to Dickens, especially his treatment of family, fathers and children. In addition to the 'volatile and revolutionary' Toodles (162.9), who descends from the similarly titled character in *Dombey and Son* (1848), Conrad overturns the sentimental and morbid affection of Mr Dombey for his doomed son Paul by treating the horrific consequences of Stevie's inculcated belief in Verloc's fatherly '*good*' (135.23). As a 'SIMPLE TALE OF THE XIX CENTURY' (2.6), *The Secret Agent* also draws on Émile Zola's Naturalist writings on such matters as the domestic violence, murder and hereditary disturbances of *Thérèse Raquin* (1867), reinforcing a view of latent violence in human conduct. Traditional sites of domesticity and security are pathways to the ultimate end. Mrs Verloc's charity cottage, 'by the exiguity of its dimensions and the simplicity of its accommodation, might well have been devised in kindness as a place of training for the still more straitened circumstances of the grave' (123.39–124.2). Indeed, the very embraces of familial affection acquire an ominous and grotesque colouring, as when it is 'uncertain whether he [Verloc] meant to strangle or to embrace his wife' (149.20–21). For Winnie, the 'seven years of life' (206.17) of her marriage mirror Inspector Heat's sense of '"Seven years hard"' (74.25–26) of incarceration, as the symbol of idealized married union lies 'dropped in a dust-bin' (161.12), just as the anarchists' philosophies of history are consigned to the dust-bin of history.

Under Western Eyes

In a 1912 review of E. A. Vizetelly's *The Anarchists: Their Faith and Their Record* (1912), Sydney Waterlow asked 'How much, in such crimes, is to be put down to madness? How much to desire for fame swollen to a fantastic bulk in the twilight between madness and sanity? How much to sober conviction? For light on such questions it is still to novelists like Dostoievsky and Mr. Joseph Conrad that we must turn'.[20] *Under Western Eyes* (1911) saw Conrad examine betrayal, political commitment and conspiratorial revolutionary opposition in Russian society and politics, where Razumov faces 'the hazards of a furious strife between equally ferocious antagonisms' (243.33–34). Ambivalent about Russia and particular strands of Russian literature because of his Polish heritage, the Russian character, in Conrad's view, possessed a 'propensity of lifting every problem from the plane of the understandable by means of some sort of mystic expression' (86.18–19). Dostoevsky's work perfectly embodied an Eastern obscurantism that focussed on 'damned souls knocking themselves to pieces in the stuffy darkness of mystical contradictions' (*NLL*, 41.24–25). *Under Western Eyes* unveils

Conrad's own understanding of 'the very essence of things Russian' (*Letters*, IV, 14), which he had already elaborated on in 'Autocracy and War' (1905), treating Russia's 1905 defeat in the Russo-Japanese War. With its Faustian imagery of ghosts, apparitions and devils, *Under Western Eyes* contends, along with 'Autocracy and War', that 'spectral' (*NLL*, 77.29) Russia totters on the edge of a nihilistic abyss in the event of political transformation.

Not unlike the larger natural and urban vistas of *Nostromo* and *The Secret Agent*, in *Under Western Eyes* Razumov sees 'an immense wintry Russia which somehow his view could embrace in all its enormous expanse as if it were a map' (57.36–37). Along with this broad focus, localized attention is given to St Petersburg, Geneva, the private settings of Razumov's rooms, the Haldins' apartment in Geneva and the Château Borel that houses domestic rituals and abuses and the plotting of political conspiracy. *Under Western Eyes* couples a treatment of 'mental and political unrest' in Russia with a focus on 'normal, practical, everyday life' (16.28–29) led by Razumov. This everyday life is characterized by Razumov's isolation and the lack of a 'moral bond' (36.24) between him and anyone else, least of all Victor Haldin, who keeps alive a 'false idea' of revolution that contradicts 'the secular logic of human development' (79.2, 79. 5–6). Razumov is without the familial environment so central and so disruptive to *The Secret Agent*, as 'no home influences had shaped his opinions or his feelings' (16.34–35). Believing the 'only ties I have in the world are social' (53.16–17), his future is accordingly bound up with 'the sphere of public life' (52.8), as he seeks to become a 'great reforming servant' (231.21) of the Russian state. Significantly, though, in *Under Western Eyes*, the politics of Russia is characterized by no healthy division between private and public, and the narrator discovers that the 'real drama of autocracy is not played on the great stage of politics' (258.1–2).

As with *The Secret Agent*, *Under Western Eyes* interrogates the contiguous private, social and political spaces of modernity. According to Agnes Heller, the influential Hegelian tradition of political philosophy isolates 'three spheres of activity in the modern world' that constitute the 'three ethical powers in modernity';[21] namely, the family, civil society and the state. Conrad's writing, which in his early career he deliberately described as '*modern*' (*Letters*, II, 418), challenges an ethical reading of these forces by interrogating their internal workings and their interrelationship. Contrasted with the freedom of civic discourse in the West, embodied by the work of an 'enterprising correspondent' (90.30) for the London's *Evening Standard*, who reveals Haldin's involvement in the assassination of Mr de P—, the conflated public, private and political arenas of Russian life are dominated by autocracy: 'Whenever two Russians come together, the shadow of autocracy is with them, tinging their thoughts, their views, their most intimate feelings, their private life, their public utterances – haunting the secret of their silences' (88.21–24). The actions of all Russians are influenced by 'a hereditary and personal knowledge of the means by which a historical autocracy represses ideas, guards its power and defends its existence' (27.13–15). Sophia Antonovna becomes a revolutionist because of her familial experience of state politics and the experience of her father, who was a victim of 'the great social iniquity of the system resting on unrequited toil and unpitied sufferings' (202.26–28). Echoing the view of religion expressed in *Nostromo*, Sophia Antonovna's early experience of the Church was one 'where the priests of the system exhorted such unconsidered vermin as I to resignation' (202.34–35). On the other hand, autocracy has ensured that the subject of class politics, philosophized over at length by the anarchists of *The Secret Agent*, takes on a stark simplicity in Russia. For the forward momentum of revolutionary history in *Under Western Eyes*, the most pressing problem lies in the form of the Romanovs: 'there is only one class in Russia which must be extirpated. Only one. And that class consists of only one family' (173.8–10).

Given the importance of Russian nihilism to the writings of Turgenev and Dostoevsky, it is fitting that Razumov is warned about involvement with 'Nihilists'. *Under Western Eyes* examines the political choices facing those who confront autocracy. Without autocracy, Russia, as Conrad stated in 'Autocracy and War', was '*le néant*' (*NLL*, 79.13), a 'nothing' or 'blank'. While Haldin's appearance in his rooms represents 'Fatality' (70.30.) for Razumov, Haldin, who regards himself as a harbinger of freedom and justice, quickly embodies a European and Russian tradition of nihilism to Razumov's thinking. Nietzsche's famous description of nihilism as 'the uncanniest of all guests'[22] is evoked through the spectral nature of Razumov's visions of Haldin reclined on the snows of St Petersburg, but Haldin also nihilistically threatens to destroy the foundation upon which Razumov can build his 'sane ambitions' (6.31). For the narrator, Razumov's politics are those of a man of 'conservative convictions diluted in a vague liberalism natural to the ardour of his age' (58.29–30). Given Conrad's interest in the legacy of the French Revolution, it is significant that this event has been understood politically as the 'first great historical experience of the void underlying established structures, and therefore of the possibility of the tabula rasa and radical transformation'.[23] In the Russia of *Under Western Eyes*, Razumov regards the potential transformations of Haldin's radical politics as nothing less than a journey to the abyss. He consequently engages in a reforming defence of the autocratic tradition, asserting that he is no 'moss-grown reactionary' (34.39). In the face of the overthrow of existing structures, Razumov submits to autocracy's 'overpowering logic'

(33.26) and experiences a 'longing for power to hurt and destroy' (32.1), thereby meeting first-hand the compromising reality of Weber's influential view in 'Politics as a Vocation' (1919) that in the pursuit of political ends, 'the essential means is violence'.[24] Razumov's belief in his own 'independent thinking' assures that he sees himself 'more free than any social democratic revolution could ever make me' (81.20–21).

This emphasis on freedom and solitude is important in relation to Rousseau, whose ideas figure in the novel. Razumov's acts of writing evoke the philosopher's celebrated *Confessions* but also, in part, the emotional self-indulgence associated with Rousseau's autobiography, as Razumov is as certain of his uniqueness as the Genevan thinker: 'Not one of them is capable of feeling and thinking as deeply as I can. How many of them could accomplish an act of conscience?' (37.11–12). The novel also probes the questions of political power and sovereignty that occupied Rousseau's political philosophy, addressing whether politics should express the 'conflicting aspirations of a people' or 'a will strong and one' (33.22). In his estimation of the people, which employs a condemnatory rhetoric of idleness and sloth, Razumov embraces Rousseau's idea of the 'natural innocence of a brute' with a contrasting ideology regarding such innocence, like *The Secret Agent*, as unfit for political responsibility: 'just try to give these children the power and stature of men and see what they will be like' (176.27–29). Peter Ivanovitch becomes a parody of Rousseau's noble savage in the narrator's account of his journey to exile and freedom. Adopting *The Secret Agent*'s ironic focus on duality, there are 'two human beings indissolubly joined' in the great feminist, the 'civilised man, the enthusiast of advanced humanitarian ideals' and the 'stealthy, primeval savage' (99.29, 99.30–32), the latter of which has an unfortunate habit of emerging in his dealings with Tekla. Ultimately, for her, Peter Ivanovitch is 'the greatest genius of the century' as well as 'the most inconsiderate man living' (117.9–10).

The statue of Rousseau in Geneva sits on 'a perfection of puerile neatness' (223.1), and Rousseau's democratic thinking is implicated in the evolution of political liberties that have created what the novel regards as the 'marvellous banality' (221.24) of modernity. For Razumov, Geneva's public spaces and freedoms are 'the very perfection of mediocrity attained at last after centuries of toil and culture' (159.1–2). Contrasted with the oppressive interaction of family and state life in autocratic Russia is the experience of open society in Switzerland, 'whose fate was made secure from the cradle to the grave by the perfected mechanism of democratic institutions' (138.16–17). In place of such mundane political certainties, Natalia Haldin, for the narrator, embodies the Russian mysticism that has 'scorn for all the practical forms of political liberty known to the Western world' (86.20–21), as she believes that 'Russians shall find some better form of national freedom than an artificial conflict of parties' (87.28–29). Ultimately, the public security possible under democratic institutions is not realizable under autocratic structures, and Natalia returns to Russia to live between the oppressive spaces of the broken Russian family and the tyranny of the autocratic state, 'sharing her compassionate labours between the horrors of overcrowded jails and the heartrending misery of bereaved homes' (286.27–28).

Throughout *Nostromo*, *The Secret Agent* and *Under Western Eyes*, Conrad's irony ensures that absolute readings of his novels' politics are, happily, elusive. Scornful of fixed ideas and possessed of a scepticism that Conrad regarded as 'the tonic of minds, the tonic of life, the agent of truth' (*Letters*, II, 359), Conrad's political novels offer the spectacle of realists, idealists and dreamers who participate in the unceasing drama of passing victories and permanent defeats. Even his most nefarious characters are allowed moments of Conradian insight, such as Peter Ivanovitch, who observes in a telling manner that 'The man who says that he has no illusions has at least that one' (161.26–27). In a challenging interpretive suggestion to Conrad's readers, the narrator of *Under Western Eyes*, in one of his many reflections on the art of writing, asserts that a novelist's 'own belief is made sufficiently manifest by a telling phrase, a poetic image, the accent of emotion' (128.31–32). In such phrases, images and accents, Conrad's political beliefs lie veiled in the pages of his elaborate fictions, the product, he states in the Preface to *The Nigger of the 'Narcissus,'* of the artist's encounter with the world, his descent into himself and his appeal to temperament.

NOTES

1 Karl Marx and Friedrich Engels, *Basic Writings on Politics and Philosophy*, ed. Lewis S. Feuer (Glasgow: Fontana, 1976), p. 298.
2 Laurence Davies, '"The Thing Which Was Not" and The Thing That Is Also: Conrad's Ironic Shadowing', *Conrad in the Twenty-First Century: Contemporary Approaches and Perspectives*, ed. Carola M. Kaplan, Peter Lancelot Mallios and Andrea White (London: Routledge, 2005), p. 230.
3 Terry Eagleton, *The English Novel: An Introduction* (Oxford: Wiley-Blackwell, 2004), pp. 234, 233.
4 Mary Ogden White, 'Democracy in Modern Fiction', *Bulletin of the American Library Association* 10, no. 4 (July 1916), 134.
5 G. W. F. Hegel, *Hegel's Philosophy of Right*, trans. T. M. Knox (Oxford: Clarendon Press, 1952), p. 10.
6 Jürgen Habermas, *The Philosophical Discourse of Modernity* (Oxford: Polity Press, 1987), p. 51.
7 Richard Sennett, *The Fall of Public Man* (London: Faber & Faber, 1986), p. 226.
8 'Introduction', *Conrad in the Twenty-First Century*, p. xiv.

9 Max Weber, *Selections in Translation*, ed. W. G. Runciman and trans. Eric Matthews (Cambridge: Cambridge University Press, 1994), p. 169.
10 Mary Louise Pratt, *Imperial Eyes: Travel Writing and Transculturation* (London: Routledge, 2008), p. 147.
11 Susan Sontag, *Regarding the Pain of Others* (New York: Picador, 2003), p. 79.
12 Fredric Jameson, *The Political Unconscious: Narrative as a Socially Symbolic Act* (London: Methuen, 1981), p. 270.
13 Robert Hampson, 'Conrad's Heterotopic Fiction: Composite Maps, Superimposed Sites, and Impossible Spaces', *Conrad in the Twenty-First Century*, pp. 127, 122.
14 Alexander Herzen, *My Past and Thoughts*, trans. Constance Garnett (London: Chatto & Windus, 1926), V, 2.
15 Linda Hutcheon, *Irony's Edge: The Theory and Politics of Irony* (London: Routledge, 1994), p. 10.
16 Cedric Watts, *A Preface to Conrad* (Harlow: Longman, 1993), p. 55.
17 Walter Benjamin, *Reflections: Essays, Aphorisms, Autobiographical Writings*, trans. Edmund Jephcott (New York: Schocken Books, 1986), p. 302.
18 Eagleton, *The English Novel*, p. 235.
19 Sennett, *The Fall of Public Man*, p. 20.
20 Sydney Waterlow, Review of E. A. Vizetelly's *The Anarchists, Their Faith and Their Record*, *International Journal of Ethics* 23, no. 1 (October 1912), 119.
21 Agnes Heller, *A Theory of Modernity* (Oxford: Blackwell, 1999), p. 23.
22 Shane Weller, *Modernism and Nihilism* (Basingstoke: Palgrave Macmillan, 2011), p. 34.
23 Andrew Gibson, quoted in Weller, *Modernism and Nihilism*, p. 17.
24 Weber, *Selections in Translation*, p. 218.

4

DOUGLAS KERR

Approaching Conrad through Theory: 'The Secret Sharer'

The theoretical turn in criticism, as everyone knows, began to make itself felt in Anglo-American literary studies some fifty years ago and has profoundly shaped critical practice and language in the ensuing decades. It has left a decisive mark, too, on the institutions of literary criticism and education. Yet at the height of the ideological and methodological struggles that this revolution entailed, the proponents of 'theory' enjoyed taunting their more traditionally minded opponents by pointing out that their methods were just as underpinned by theory as the work of the most up-to-date poststructuralist. This was quite right. Every enquiry in the humanities rests upon a theory about the object of enquiry and a set of principles that governs the method of enquiry, whether this theory and these principles are articulated or assumed *a priori*. An approach to Conrad's novels that sees them as lightly disguised reports on Conrad's own adventures and moods, or one that assesses them as vehicles for moral instruction, is just as theory-driven as a reading of their heteroglossia or one that mines the novels for instances of the social construction of sexualities.

From the start, readers have been approaching Conrad through theory. When Sir Hugh Clifford chided Conrad for not knowing much about life in the Malay Archipelago, his criticism was based on a theory of fictional representation. The early reviewers who hailed Conrad as 'the Kipling of the Seas' were deploying a theory of intertextuality. And those who grumbled that his later novels were not as good as his earlier ones were making a judgement informed by an idea, perhaps refined over a lifetime of reading, of what literature 'should' be.

So 'approaching Conrad through theory' may seem to amount to no more or less than 'approaching Conrad'. Still, the decades since the 1960s have put into the hands of readers a particularly varied, sophisticated and powerful set of critical modalities – some mutually contradictory – and this state of affairs has produced a rich critical literature that can help students release a wealth of satisfying, provocative and perhaps unsuspected potentialities in the Conradian text. It has also fostered a self-consciousness about the grounds of literary criticism that can now be taken for granted in most students of literature. This discussion will set out to sketch what some of these modalities are and what they entail. Theory is not something to be chosen from a catalogue and then applied to a literary text, like a paint colour. The reader has a duty to be responsible to the text, and sometimes this will require us to wait patiently for the text to reveal what kinds of critical attention it will respond to (willingly or not). There is something slightly artificial about using a text to illustrate different critical approaches, but it does seem worthwhile to explore the relevance of theory-based approaches to a reading of Conrad's work.

If we are to lift these critical theories out of the realm of abstraction and put them to work as criticism, we will need a point of focus. Here that will be 'The Secret Sharer', a story Conrad wrote at the end of 1909 – taking a break from wrestling with the novel that would become *Under Western Eyes* – and included in the collection *'Twixt Land and Sea*, published in 1912. It is a tale in which a ship's captain who has just taken up his first command gives refuge to an officer from another ship, a man named Leggatt, who has killed a crewman and escaped by swimming from his own vessel. The young captain, feeling a strange affinity for the fugitive whom he calls his 'double', conceals Leggatt in his own cabin, keeping this a secret from his crew, and eventually enables him to escape by swimming to an island, just as the wind rises and the captain's ship begins its own voyage. The captain narrates the story.

Criticism tends to lag behind creative work, and it could be argued that the theory revolution of the twentieth century was a belated attempt to rise to the challenge of the great Modernist writers, the contemporaries of Conrad and the generation that followed. Conrad himself has provoked some of the most distinguished work of leading critical practitioners as varied as the Marxist Fredric Jameson, the deconstructionist J. Hillis Miller and the postcolonial humanist Edward Said.[1] New critical languages seem to have been required to account for modern literature, with its fascination with forms of subjectivity and the unconscious, its often broken rhythms and inorganic structures, its rehearsal of a crisis of authority in many forms, its ambiguous relation to history and tradition, its linguistic estrangement, its obscurities which seem to cry out for interpretation. In this sense, 'theory' is a response to Modernism.

The features just listed can be found in Conrad's work – in fact, we can find all of them in 'The Secret Sharer' – but there are aspects of Conrad's case that make certain critical modalities especially appropriate. The recurrence in his stories of certain psychological patterns and relationships has, from the start, attracted criticism attentive to the psychology of both his characters and their author. The predominantly masculine world of Conrad, typically a world of action remote from domestic life, has often put the question of gender at or near the centre of recent critical studies of his work. The foregrounding of storytelling itself in so many of Conrad's tales has drawn critics interested in structure, voice and narrative, in questions of testimony and truth and in how readers respond to stories. Conrad's early professional experience as a sailor, in the traffic of empire and trade around the globe, which provided him so much of the narrative capital for his fiction, has made him inevitably an important and controversial figure in colonial discourse analysis and postcolonial studies, and for students of politics, history and geography. A work like *Heart of Darkness* – probably the world's most taught literary text – stands at the intersection of virtually all the most important approaches in the current study of literature.

It is convenient to group the principal critical modalities according to their main object of attention, so we will talk about those that focus on the author, those that focus on textuality and those most interested in the literary work's relation to history. Conrad's fiction has attracted criticism from all three orientations.

Author

Much early work on Conrad was author-based, resting on a theory that saw literature as, above all, an expression of the individual writer's experience, character and intention. This kind of critical reading was probably the norm in the first half of the twentieth century, as it had been in the nineteenth, and it was the target of one of the early assaults in the 'theory wars', Roland Barthes' 1968 essay 'The Death of the Author'.[2] Author-based criticism seemed particularly suited to Conrad's novels, many of them explicitly taking their starting point from events in the writer's adventurous early life. Conrad claimed he was no good at making things up and told an American interviewer in 1923 that he simply wrote 'in retrospect of what he saw and learned during the first 35 years of his life'.[3] Biographers and biographical critics have traced the origins of many tales to episodes in Conrad's career, and the completion of the *Collected Letters* in nine volumes has afforded insight into what was in the author's mind as he struggled with his writing.

Psychological criticism often finds a key to Conrad's fiction in his early life in what, by way of shorthand, is called 'Poland' (that country at the time being divided into three and absent from the map of Europe, with Conrad spending, in fact, little time in what we now think of as 'Poland'). His father's literary activities and devotion to the lost cause of Polish nationalism, the family's consequent internal exile to Russia, his mother's early death and then his father's and, later, the young Conrad's decision to abandon his homeland and go to sea can all be seen as providing the emotional raw materials from which Conrad fashioned a body of work that returns obsessively to questions of loyalty and betrayal, romantic idealism and its defeat, the need to cling faithfully to a given set of values and a doubt that any values, in the end, have a solid foundation. From his life as a seaman, visiting far flung ports and oceans, and later a ship's officer, derives the recurrence in his stories of questions of command and responsibility, the relation between men at close quarters, and all the political and ethnographic and communicative issues attending on the encounter between different cultures on unequal terms. The novels and tales are not a straightforward, autobiographical record of his experience, of course – nor, for that matter, are his autobiographical writings, such as *A Personal Record* – but a stern repudiation of the figure of the originary author, as Barthes advocated in 1968, would be to miss an important aspect of the work. Conrad's relation to the world of Marlow and Lord Jim is different in quality from that of J. R. R. Tolkien to the world of Bilbo Baggins. The murder that triggers the plot of 'The Secret Sharer' had its precedent in a widely reported crime aboard the *Cutty Sark* in Eastern waters in 1880. And like the captain in 'The Secret Sharer', in 1888 Conrad began a voyage from the Gulf of Siam on his first command, the *Otago*.

A psychologically oriented, author-based approach was taken by Albert J. Guerard, whose still valuable *Conrad the Novelist* (1958) mines the tales for fictionalized examples of 'the un-English genre of the spiritual autobiography'.[4] Borrowing from the theory of archetypes associated with C. G. Jung, Guerard found some of Conrad's major conflicts and anxieties shadowed in a number of his first-person narrative tales, including 'The Secret Sharer'. These, argues Guerard, enact a 'night journey', a voyage through psychic darkness that dramatizes a kind of introspection, a test of the self driven by insecurity and doubt: 'We cannot achieve wholesome integration of the personality until we have made the archetypal journey into the self' (31). Guerard sees the fugitive who is a double as presenting a challenge for the captain in 'The Secret Sharer', confronting him with guilty aspects of himself that he must manage or dispose of before he can continue the journey of life. In teasing out this dark plot from the unconscious of the story, Guerard emphasizes the tale's inward and psychological aspects and seems ready to identify the narrator with the author in a way that students are often warned against. However, his approach convincingly relates this tale to a number of preoccupations and patterns that are to be found throughout Conrad's fiction.

A more conventionally Freudian psychoanalytical reading of Conrad can find a strong basis in the clearly Oedipal feelings of the novelist for his father.[5] In the end Conrad turned his back on Poland and his father's political beliefs, language and even name (Korzeniowski), but at some psychic cost. His father was a figure of stern authority – and a precursor as writer – who set impossibly high standards for his son and deprived him of his mother, resulting in the kind of unacknowledged resentment, melancholy and self-doubt that Freud had discussed in the case of Shakespeare's father-haunted Prince Hamlet. This is a state of mind that might help to explain the apparently irrational anxieties of the young captain in 'The Secret Sharer' about his own fitness for command among older and more experienced men. Does the decisive and virile intruder Leggatt correspond to the captain's dream of manliness – 'that ideal conception of one's own personality every man sets up for himself secretly', as the story has it (*TLS*, 83.8–10) – the kind of man he would like to be? Or, as Daniel R. Schwarz has suggested, perhaps Leggatt is unbalanced in opposite ways to the captain, 'a man of unrestrained id and under-developed superego', driven by his reckless desires and careless of authority, whereas the captain is hyperconscious and so unsure of himself that he can't *do* anything. The captain then learns from Leggatt how to act instinctively, and thus 'his adult ego is created by appeasing the contradictory demands of the id and the superego',[6] a mature balancing act between instinctive action and prudent reserve.

Schwarz historicizes the psychological plot by seeing it as dramatizing a *modern* split between mind and instinct: this is not simply a drama of the private life of an individual (author or character) but an episode in the psychology of modernity. Lacanian psychoanalysis is another way to move the insights of Freud out of the bedroom and into the world of society and politics. Lacan supposes psychic development to entail the eviction of the child from the imaginary – a pre-linguistic state of mind in which no clear distinction is felt to exist between subject and object, child and mother – into the more austere realm of the symbolic order, a place of law, language, difference and the curtailment of desire. The point of transition between the imaginary and symbolic order is the mirror phase in which the child contemplates its own image and begins to form an apparently unified ego.

Lacanian criticism can find much in 'The Secret Sharer' to ponder: the hesitation of the captain at the threshold of the (professional) maturity of command; his eagerness to identify with his double or mirror image and his final separation from him as he enters a new phase of his life; his nervousness in the presence of threatening and whiskery authorities such as Captain Archbold and his own first mate (Leggatt, the double, is also a 'mate'); his desire for insertion into the patriarchal order of command and his simultaneous compulsion to flout its most basic rules by harbouring a radical transgressor; the strange doubleness of his speech, participating out loud in the official discourse of seamanship and captaincy (the Lacanian 'word of the Father') with the crew and Archbold, while carrying on an illicit dialogue, out of sight and in whispers, with the secret young outlaw who reminds him of himself. Josiane Paccaud finds in the tale a story of 'the subject's accession to the symbolic after inner divisiveness and the unbridgeable gap between desire and its impossible object, between signifier and signified, between the speaking "I" and the psychic self, have been acknowledged'.[7] Speaking of desire, this story is also one of the most explicit instances in Conrad of the recurring theme of male bonding, and it has significant sexual connotations, from the rescue of the naked Leggatt to his sharing of the captain's bed. There is an unacknowledged but unmistakable undercurrent of homoerotic feeling in Conrad's fiction, and this is sometimes traced, by a certain kind of biographical critic, to the author's unconscious homoerotic attachment to a father lost in childhood.

Textuality

The theory revolution was related to the academic professionalization of literary criticism, and, like any professionalization, it soon began to produce a stream of specialist technical language and protocols. This was entailed by a perceived need to concentrate on 'the literary' as the object of enquiry – what made literature different from other discourses – and this turned out to be largely a propensity for figurative language (symbol, metaphor, metonymy) and an unusual degree of textual organization, so that the form of the literary text was understood to be an essential part of its meaning or theme, not just a container or vehicle for it. Once again, this critical formalism was particularly rewarding as an approach to modern writing but might equally be seen as a response to the challenges that writing posed. Conrad has certainly proved a suitable object for formalist enquiry, particularly in the discipline of narratology. His fiction was soon noted for its fondness for the tropes or devices of the 'unreliable narrator', where we cannot be sure the storyteller knows the truth of his story or really wants to disclose it, and of 'delayed decoding', a phrase coined by Ian Watt to describe disorienting moments in a narrative where a subjective impression is narrated, but its cause or meaning is withheld for a while.[8] Both devices 'foreground' or draw attention to the subjectivity of literary representation.

Realism – in fiction or drama, painting or photography – is a style of representation that tends to conceal its own artifice, presenting its object or story as if it 'really' and naturally 'just happened', or happened to be there.

In many ways, Conrad is a product of the great realist tradition of the nineteenth-century European novel, but he is modern in the way he foregrounds the formal qualities of his stories, not concealing their processes and devices but drawing attention to them. We can see this, for example, in the way memory is not simply a storehouse of past events, but often an uncertain and sometimes painful *activity*, for his remembering narrators. We can see it in his use of unreliable and multiple storytellers, in the way that scenes of narrating – spoken or written – often become part of his stories, and in the way gaps, digressions and resumptions in the chronology of events keep reminding us that a story is something that is made, more like a machine under construction than a flower to be picked, fully formed by nature.

Narratology busies itself with uncovering the role of structures or patterns established through narrative method, and the implications of these things for thematic effect: that is, narratologists study the rhetoric of storytelling. How is a narrative text structured; how does it begin and move through time and where does it end; through what voice or voices is it delivered; what perspectives does it stage; which characters are accorded interiority so that we can see what they are thinking and which are estranged so that we only see from the outside what they do and say; how fast does it move; what does it concentrate on; what is it unwilling or unable to tell us? Novels like *Lord Jim* or *Nostromo* are textual machines of enormous complexity and richness. By Conrad's standards, 'The Secret Sharer' seems a quite straightforward narrative. It has a single narrator (the captain), a single plot, few characters; and it moves swiftly through the events of its simple story from beginning to end.

As its theme of doubleness might lead us to expect, a major feature of the tale's narrative method is its use of various forms of likeness, complement and contrast. These doublings, which have been schematically represented by Cedric Watts,[9] are combined with the principle of suspense, to produce a well-formed symmetrical narrative driving towards a strong conclusion and closure with Leggatt's escape. Indeed, so shipshape is the story's structure that it leads the narratologist Jakob Lothe to worry that its neatness and economy actually blur the moral or ethical issues it raises (64–71). After all, Leggatt is getting away with murder, and the captain is an accessory after the fact. Leggatt makes an exciting escape, but the moral ambiguity of his mirror relationship with the narrator remains largely unresolved.

In a personal narrative, as Lothe observes, 'the absence of a stable, correcting position of authorial authority presents difficult problems of interpretation'.[10] This is no doubt just why Conrad was drawn to personal, sometimes multiple narration, for the essaying of authority in many forms is one of his recurring themes. In a first-person narrative, we see and understand events as the narrator sees and understands them: other forms of vision and understanding are excluded in the structure in which this narration creates events. Deconstructive criticism sees its task as recovering those excluded stories. Deconstruction is a practice of sceptical reading. For deconstruction, all narrators are unreliable, and all acts of speech depend on something being silenced. Speech depends on difference; a thing is alive because not dead, feminine in that it is not masculine, a *tree* in that we recognize its difference from a *tray*. Every structure is framed through acts of exclusion, but, deconstructionists aver, the excluded always returns to unsettle it. Having its meaning by virtue of its difference from something it does not name, every text is haunted by its own contradiction. Strictly speaking, one never deconstructs a text but shows how the text has already deconstructed itself.

Highly sceptical about the reliability of the captain-narrator of 'The Secret Sharer', Brian Richardson sees his insistence on identifying with Leggatt, and his eagerness to lend him a sympathetic ear, assure him of his understanding and excuse his crime as very suspicious.[11] The captain's fussing over Leggatt, and his romantic identification and bonding with him, ensure that we have little more than his interpretation of Leggatt's narrative, 'itself internally consistent but unable to account for the numerous anomalies, elisions, and contradictions that surround it' (314). For all we know, Leggatt could actually be a murderous and lying thug, but the narrator is unwilling to admit this possibility into his story. Rash, credulous and egotistical, the captain – as Richardson reads him – is a comic figure, the subject of a subtle, ironic drama of self-deception and misprision that is an instance of Conrad's mockery of the dangers of reading too much romantic fiction (with its childish semi-supernatural theme of doubles) (318). He is a thoroughly unreliable narrator and by no means to be identified as a surrogate for his author, or a vehicle for that author's doubts and anguish.

Richardson's reading sets out to uncover what the tale (or its narrator) has passed over in silence. His is not really a deconstructive reading, however, for he is arguing that the interpretive bias of the captain's story is a deliberate strategy, Conrad's Modernist mockery of romantic gullibility. Deconstruction finds contradictions in a text that are intrinsic, even unconscious. If one were putting together a deconstructive reading of 'The Secret Sharer', one might start with Captain Archbold (if that, indeed, is his name).

Archbold is the captain of the *Sephora*, from which Leggatt has escaped, and he visits the narrator's ship in his search for the fugitive. The narrator gives a highly unflattering description of Archbold and is barely polite to him, interrupting him, hardly listening, even pretending to be deaf. In his loyalty to Leggatt, the narrator portrays Archbold as a muddled old fool and an incompetent captain; we should not take him seriously. Yet if one listens, through the noise of the captain's derisive narration, to what Archbold is reported as actually saying, he seems to have qualities of maturity, responsibility and good sense that the narrator himself lacks. The narrator is obscurely aware of being assessed by Archbold and found wanting, as well he might be. He is unable to see in Archbold a model of the commander he aspires to be – legitimate in his authority, careful of his command, resolute but risk-averse in his leadership. Anxious for a role model, to embody the ideal conception of his own personality, has the captain identified the wrong secret sharer? In a face-to-face tableau that recalls the intimate exchanges between the narrator and Leggatt, the two ship's captains sit opposite each other. Which is the ignorant fool? 'And as I gazed at him certainly not prepared for anything original on his part, he advanced his head close to mine and thrust his tongue out at me so suddenly that I couldn't help staring back' (*TLS*, 100.30–33). Archbold's mimicry of the face of the strangled crewman doubles as an uninterpreted gesture of mockery of the captain who cannot see the model of captaincy that is staring him in the face.

Genre is another dimension of textuality. Fictions exemplify, and may combine, existing paradigms that are pre-set, as it were, with certain conventions and habits and horizons of expectation. Genre theory asserts that such paradigms may play as important a role as the author's individual intention in determining both the nature and the meaning of a text. Conrad made his name as a writer of adventure tales in exotic locations, and 'The Secret Sharer', with its tropical setting and exciting narrative climax, in some respects marks Conrad's return to this sort of tale. It participates too in the genre of romantic introspection and its subgenre of masculine maturation – a compressed *Bildungsroman*, concerned as this genre is with the hero's struggles to discover his identity, grow up and find his proper place in his community or society.

Other genres jostle to be heard in the rich discursive mix of the tale's textuality, and help to give it that essential novelistic quality M. M. Bakhtin described as heteroglossia, even though it has only a single narrator.[12] There is a distinct note of Gothic in the dreamlike night atmosphere, the discovery of the apparently headless body of the murderer floating in the water and in all the talk about uncanny and ghostly doubling. In the undignified hide-and-seek in the captain's quarters, there is even an incongruous accent of bedroom farce. The admixture of the voice of farce to the generic polyphony of the tale might act as a check on our inclination to romanticize the relationship between the captain and the fugitive. Farce is an under-explored weapon in Conrad's generic armoury. It can be an unsettling presence even at life-and-death moments, such as the murder of Carlier in 'An Outpost of Progress' or of Verloc in *The Secret Agent*.

Finally, a text can be in dialogue not only with a genre but also with other particular texts. The long list of intertextual relatives of 'The Secret Sharer' includes Conrad's other first-person stories (notably, the Marlow-narrated tales like 'Youth' and *Heart of Darkness* as well as the yet-to-be-written *The Shadow-Line*), romantic fictions centring on a 'double', such as Maupassant's 'Le Horla', adventure stories for boys about perils surmounted by flood and field, the textbooks on seamanship Conrad studied for his master's certificate and so on. Gérard Genette has shown how these intertextual relationships contribute to the meaning of a literary text.[13] One of the most interesting of intertexts for 'The Secret Sharer' is *Under Western Eyes*, the novel Conrad interrupted in December 1909 to write this tale.

History

Critical technologies with a historical orientation – including the often overlapping Marxist, postcolonial and new historicist approaches – attend to the represented world of the literary text, and its relation to the play of historical forces at the time of its events or composition. Texts are interrogated for their symptomatology and criticism of the work of such forces. Marxism has always regarded literature, such as novels, as part of the superstructure raised upon and expressing the base of economic relations and the struggle between classes. It has seen it as either valuable, inasmuch as it can help to exemplify the stresses and tendencies of the historical process, or, all too often, an example of 'false consciousness', concealing the real truth of history (this is the way Fredric Jameson (206–80) reads the romance elements of *Lord Jim*). Historicist critical theory urges attention especially to the changing meanings in literary discourse of class, gender and race or ethnicity.

Again, Conrad's fiction seems particularly inviting to historical criticism, and it will be clear that even in dealing with author-based or textual criticism, as we have done here, we have already been engaging with the stories as historical texts. In particular, Conrad lived in and wrote about the great century of modern imperialism, and its expressions in trade, colonialism and cultural encounter from the Caribbean to the Malay Peninsula and from the time of Napoleon to the Great War. The world we inhabit today was formed out of that era and its aftermath – a postcolonial, global world. Conrad is one of the most valuable of reporters of empire, whether one regards him as a critic of or – as the late Chinua Achebe famously asserted – an apologist for the phenomenon.

Achebe reacted with anger to what he saw as the racist representation of Africa and Africans in *Heart of Darkness*.[14] He argued that the criticism of the Europeans in that tale should not disguise or excuse what he saw as its demeaning portrayal of black people. Achebe was among the first to mount what would later be called a postcolonial critique of canonical Western literature, drawing attention to its complicity with racism, violence and oppression, and its reinforcement of a view of the world coloured by the aggression and arrogance of the imperial powers, even when it might seem to have no overt political agenda – a modality that Edward Said was to term 'latent Orientalism'.[15] The other face of postcolonialism is the promotion or rediscovery of indigenous expressions and traditions, resistant discourse and the forging of new national identities.

The action of 'The Secret Sharer' is set in the Gulf of Siam, but contains no Siamese or Cambodian characters, aboard or ashore, a fact that, postcolonial critics might say, speaks for itself. Siam (present-day Thailand) was one of the very few Asian nations never at any time formally controlled by a Western power, but the French colonial territory of Cambodge also had a coastline on the Gulf. In this story, this ambiguous space with its shifting sandbanks is appropriated as the picturesque backdrop for an exclusively English drama. In his opening description, the narrator is at pains to survey the scene commandingly, while emptying both sea and visible land of any signs of a living indigenous presence. This could be seen as an example of the trope of *terra nullius*, with which travel writers and particularly explorers are wont to give the impression that the territory they traverse is empty of all but themselves.

The narrator describes the islands on the east side of the Gulf as 'Unknown to trade, to travel, almost to geography', virtually off the human map, though, he concedes, 'There must be villages' upon them (112.9–11). The islands can provide a refuge for the fugitive Leggatt and therefore a solution to a European problem. Although he has effectively stripped these Asian shores of any human agency – dehumanizing them, in fact, as Achebe felt that Marlow dehumanized the Africans in *Heart of Darkness* – the narrator has not, perhaps, completely erased their capacity for resistance or threat to this Western incursion. As he sails perilously close to the southern hill of the island of Koh-ring in the darkness, it seems to hang over the ship like a towering fragment of the night itself, a Wordsworthian instance of the terrifying sublime: 'On that enormous mass of blackness there was not a gleam to be seen, not a sound to be heard. It was gliding irresistibly towards us and yet seemed already within reach of the hand' (116.26–28). The reversal of agency in this sentence (because, of course, it is actually the ship that is gliding towards the island) seems to intuit the possibility of an irresistible postcolonial resurgence.

The *Sephora* is bringing coal from Liverpool. We are not told what cargo the narrator's ship carries, only that she is headed back to England after a long voyage. How can we best replace 'The Secret Sharer' in the history of Victorian commerce, infrastructure, the professions? These sailors are not military or administrative personnel but are doing the business of empire along the trade routes of the world. What sort of Englishmen were engaged in this service, and what was required of them? It is a perennial Conrad theme, implicating both gender and ethnicity. And, just as he recorded, with some melancholy, the supersession of sailing ships by steamships, so in 'The Secret Sharer' we can see dramatized, and perhaps romanticized, a change in the nature of service at sea that is of some moment in the history of Britain and her empire.

We find the captain at the moment of the formation of his identity as a master. What kind of a ship's officer will he be? Leggatt provides him with one model, Archbold with another. Leggatt is dashing, intuitive and brave, a romantic and athletic individualist with a heroic self-conception. He is prepared, in Nietzschean spirit, to break the law and not regret it. He tells the captain that he is unafraid of punishment, but would disdain explaining himself 'to an old fellow in a wig and twelve respectable tradesmen' (111.2) He is a gentleman, the son of a Norfolk clergyman (like the hugely heroic Horatio Nelson), and (like the captain himself) a *Conway* boy, who has trained for command at the nautical equivalent of an English public school. He got his berth as mate of the *Sephora* through family influence.

Archbold has none of Leggatt's glamour or his eloquence. He is of a lower class, unprepossessing appearance and respectable and probably pious habits (teetotal, wife on board), a career sailor of thirty-seven years' service. When Leggatt kills a man on board his ship, Archbold plays by the book, imprisoning him so as to deliver him to justice in an English port. Here we can see Conrad deviating significantly from the original case, or anecdote, on which Leggatt's story is based. For after John Anderson, alias Sidney Smith, killed a man on board the famous and romantic clipper *Cutty Sark* during a stormy passage, his captain, the celebrated J. S. Wallace, allowed him to escape and swim to an American ship. Days later, Captain Wallace committed suicide, walking off his ship into shark-infested waters.[16] The prosaic Archbold would be quite incapable of either of these melodramatic actions.

In this case we can, in the manner of New Historicist criticism, both acknowledge that the past only comes to us mediated through texts and read the literary text as producing history. 'The novel is a discursive event. It does not *reflect* history. It *is* history.'[17] The *Cutty Sark* story, subject at the time of much sensational journalistic copy,[18] casts Wallace as a dashing, tragic, even mysterious figure. The *Sephora*'s captain in Conrad's story is a humdrum professional, reliable, predictable, law-abiding but far from romantic. He is a modern sailor for a bureaucratic age. 'The Secret Sharer' has a historical self-consciousness that sees clearly which way the wind was blowing for the swashbuckling gentlemen-heroes of an earlier phase of empire. The tale resolves itself, as stories so often do under the optic of New Historicism, into a pattern of subversion and containment. Leggatt's transgression is a romantic challenge to the order of things, but his escape only confirms that the future belongs to the likes of the prosaic Archbold. The captain's secret aiding of Leggatt is itself a gesture of subversion of the rule-bound modern profession but, at the same time, an acknowledgement of its authority. Archbold returns to his command. Leggatt is seen at the end swimming off, with a last romantic flourish, into legend or at least into history.

The author gratefully acknowledges assistance from the Hong Kong Research Grants Council, GRF project HKU 745009H.

NOTES

1 See Jameson's *The Political Unconscious: Narrative as a Socially Symbolic Act* (London: Methuen, 1981); J. Hillis Miller's *Poets of Reality: Six Twentieth-Century Writers* (Cambridge, MA: Belknap Press of Harvard University Press, 1966) and *Fiction and Repetition: Seven English Novels* (Cambridge, MA: Harvard University Press, 1982); and almost all of Said's literary-critical works from *Joseph Conrad and the Fiction of Autobiography* (Cambridge, MA: Harvard University Press, 1966) to *On Late Style: Music and Literature against the Grain* (New York: Pantheon Books, 2006).

2 Roland Barthes, 'The Death of the Author', *Image/Music/Text*, trans. Stephen Heath (New York: Hill & Wang, 1977), pp. 142–8.

3 Martin Ray, ed. *Joseph Conrad: Interviews and Recollections* (Basingstoke: Macmillan, 1990), p. 189.

4 Albert J. Guerard, *Conrad the Novelist* (Cambridge, MA: Harvard University Press, 1958), p. 12.

5 Barbara Johnson and Marjorie Garber, 'Secret Sharing: Reading Conrad Psychoanalytically', *College English* 49, no. 6 (1987), 631–2.

6 Daniel R. Schwarz, *Rereading Conrad* (Columbia: University of Missouri Press, 2001), p. 157.

7 Josiane Paccaud, 'Under the Other's Eyes: Conrad's "The Secret Sharer"', *The Conradian* 12, no. 1 (1987), 62.

8 Ian Watt, *Conrad in the Nineteenth Century* (Berkeley: University of California Press, 1979), pp. 175–6.

9 Cedric Watts, 'The Mirror-Tale: An Ethico-Structural Analysis of Conrad's "The Secret Sharer"', *Critical Quarterly* 19 (1977), 29.
10 Jakob Lothe, *Conrad's Narrative Method* (Oxford: Clarendon Press, 1989), p. 71.
11 Brian Richardson, 'Construing Conrad's "The Secret Sharer": Suppressed Narratives, Subaltern Reception, and the Act of Interpretation', *Studies in the Novel* 33, no. 3 (2001), 306–21.
12 M. M. Bakhtin, *The Dialogic Imagination: Four Essays by M. M. Bakhtin*, ed. Michael Holquist and trans. Caryl Emerson and Michael Holquist (Austin: University of Texas Press, 1981), pp. 301–31.
13 Gérard Genette, *Palimpsests: Literature in the Second Degree*, trans. Channa Newman and Claude Doubinsky (Lincoln: University of Nebraska Press, 1997).
14 Chinua Achebe, 'An Image of Africa: Racism in Conrad's *Heart of Darkness*', *Hopes and Impediments: Selected Essays* (New York: Doubleday, 1989).
15 Edward W. Said, *Orientalism* (Harmondsworth: Penguin, 1985), p. 206.
16 [Jacques Berthoud], 'Introduction', *Twixt Land and Sea: Tales*, ed. J. A. Berthoud, Laura L. Davis and S. W. Reid (Cambridge: Cambridge University Press, 2008), p. xxxvii.
17 Claire Colebrook, *New Literary Histories: New Historicism and Contemporary Criticism* (Manchester: Manchester University Press, 1997), p. 38.
18 Norman Sherry, *Conrad's Eastern World* (Cambridge: Cambridge University Press, 1966), pp. 253–69.

5

ANDREW GLAZZARD

Letters and Autobiographical Writings

I

In 1906, Conrad experienced something of a literary triumph. His new book, *The Mirror of the Sea*, brought letters of congratulation from the day's literary lions, including John Galsworthy, Henry James and the semi-reclusive Rudyard Kipling, and the press on both sides of the Atlantic praised it almost unanimously, with reviewers remarking on its narrative skill, abundance of metaphor, eloquence, atmosphere and originality of vision. The *Morning Post* opined that Conrad had 'achieved something remarkably noteworthy – more noteworthy even than his remarkable novel "Lord Jim"', while the *Spectator*'s notice found chapters within the book that 'reach at times a poetry which is almost sublime' (*CR*, II, 288, 303). Perhaps the most adulatory of a remarkable run of notices was that in the *Glasgow News*, which lauded Conrad as the first writer 'in the history of the world' who was in combination 'the experienced seaman, the thinker of sincere and subtle vision, and the artist with the faculty and the will to express what had been seen and felt'; his new work, the reviewer continued, was 'the greatest book ever written' about its subject (*CR*, II, 291–2).

That this was *The Mirror of the Sea*, a collection of sketches on the theme of sailors and sailing, might strike today's reader as anomalous. The author, whose list by this point included *Heart of Darkness* (1899), *Lord Jim* (1900) and *Nostromo* (1904) and who, in 1906, was hard at work on *The Secret Agent*, would surely be valued by his contemporaries for technically innovative, politically penetrating and psychologically insightful fictions and not for a vaguely autobiographical collection on a nautical theme. The acclaim might strike us as all the more unexpected in light of the work's origins and publishing history. It comprises fifteen episodes divided into forty-nine sections; the first episodes were written and published in newspapers and journals in early 1904 while Conrad struggled not only with completing *Nostromo* but also with his finances following the collapse of his bank.[1] Conrad's self-deprecation in a letter to H. G. Wells appears to confirm that what he called 'a series of sea sketches' was little more than a source of ready cash during a financially precarious period: 'This must *save* me. I've discovered that I can dictate that sort of bosh without effort at the rate of 3000 words in four hours. Fact! The only thing now is to sell it to a paper and then make a book of the rubbish. Hang!' (*Letters*, III, 111–12). As the first sketches were bought up by both heavyweight periodicals such as *Blackwood's Edinburgh Magazine* and the mass-circulation *Daily Mail*, Conrad produced more of them in two further intensive bursts in 1904 and 1905, revising and adding to the corpus (and tagging onto it a piece written for the centenary of Trafalgar) for its publication as a volume in October 1906.[2]

It is tempting to dismiss *The Mirror of the Sea* as little more than the belletristic off-cuts of a financially strained author and its reception as a quirk of Edwardian literary taste. This would, however, miss the significance of the work itself and what it tells us about Conrad's approach to the craft – or, perhaps, the business – of literature. Indeed, *The Mirror of the Sea* and Conrad's other ostensibly autobiographical and semi-autobiographical writings – 'The Congo Diary', *A Personal Record*, his letters and his prefaces to his collected edition – may all in different ways challenge our assumptions about fact and fiction, about what is 'literature' and what is not, about the separation of 'the art and the life', of 'life and letters'.[3] Uneven though it may be – perhaps inevitably, given the circumstances of its production and publication – *The Mirror*, now long out of critical favour, is in many ways a remarkable work, and some of those contemporary reviews were as incisive as they were adulatory. R. A. Scott-James in the *Daily News*, for example, detected psychological and philosophical dimensions to its descriptive passages and saw the absence of novelistic requirements as having liberated the author from convention:

> The narrative is the least part of this book. Though stories and anecdotes of persons come up in every section, each fact is made important in proportion to its effect upon the mind. Above all, it must be noted that Mr. Conrad is not a mere 'descriptive writer'. He is essentially creative in that he has learnt to apply the modern spirit of self-consciousness to the panorama of nature; he is doing in art what the transcendental idealists are doing in philosophy, teaching us to see material things as part of an all-embracing spiritual unity.
>
> (*CR*, II, 269–72)

The book's sub-title, *Memories and Impressions*, suggests that this work seeks to recreate for the reader the effects of scenes and experiences upon the mind, the emotions and the senses; that is precisely what Scott-James found, executed with such skill that ships, weather systems and even the sea itself all began to acquire human characteristics.[4]

In the eyes of contemporary reviewers, then, *The Mirror of the Sea* was more than a collection of descriptive sketches and semi-autobiographical musings; it was the result of the application of the fiction writer's highly developed skills to personal experience and should not, therefore, be seen as distinct from his fiction. The *Outlook*'s reviewer, for example, asked which of *The Mirror* and *Typhoon* deserved to be called the more imaginative work, commenting that in both 'the boundaries between fact and fiction are crossed and recrossed' (*CR*, II, 275). The porosity of these boundaries has, indeed, been a persistent concern of writing about Conrad – he commented himself, in public and private, on the first-hand actuality of his fiction. Almayer, the *Narcissus*, the Congo of *Heart of Darkness*, the events of *The Shadow-Line* are just a selection of people, places and events that he acknowledged as grounded in his life and experiences. Biographers and critics have since assembled a formidable body of work showing the correspondences between Conrad's life and fiction, addressing also the disparities between the autobiographical writings and documented facts. Such enquiries have shown that, even where Conrad purports to be telling the truth as 'Joseph Conrad', author and former master mariner, he is often doing no such thing. He invents, embellishes, distorts and leaves out inconvenient facts. For a writer who frequently disavowed the ability to imagine and invent – writing in the Author's Note to his first collection of short stories that the 'sustained invention of a really telling lie demands a talent which I do not possess' (*TU*, 6.35–37) – his own ostensibly 'truthful' writing shows a pronounced tendency towards fiction.

The Mirror offers a particularly powerful example. The penultimate sketch is entitled 'The *Tremolino*', the name of a *balancelle* (a small Mediterranean sailing boat) owned by a Marseilles syndicate that included Conrad, aged around twenty at the time (1877–8). The key to the story told in 'The *Tremolino*' is the syndicate's involvement in gun-running for the Carlists, supporters of Don Carlos (1848–1909), Duke of Madrid and pretender to the Spanish throne, and one side in the Third Carlist War (1872–6). Among the cast in the drama that unfolds is Dominic Cervoni, the *Tremolino*'s Corsican captain, based on a merchant seamen with whom Conrad had served during the mid-1870s. Dominic's romantic yet uncanny presence is conjured through metonymy and synecdoche: 'with those massive moustaches and his remorseless eyes set off by the shadow of the deep hood, he looked piratical and monkish and darkly initiated into the most awful mysteries of the sea'.[5] 'Astute and ruthless', adventurous and rebellious, Cervoni exemplifies the Conradian heroic rebel – he has been taken for the original of Nostromo[6] – and the story has a villain too in Dominic's nephew, Cesar. No punches are pulled in the presentation of the latter:

> His parchment skin, showing dead white on his cranium through the thin wisps of dirty brown hair, seemed to be glued directly and tightly upon his big bones. … An utterly, hopelessly depraved nature was expressed in physical terms. … You imagined him clammily cold to the touch, like a snake. The slightest reproof, the most mild and justifiable remonstrance, would be met by a resentful glare and an evil shrinking of his thin dry upper lip, a snarl of hate to which he generally added the agreeable sound of the grinding teeth.
>
> (*MS*, 165–6)

With such an extraordinary crew aboard, the *Tremolino* sets off on what proves to be its final voyage. The sharp-eyed narrator (we might call him 'Conrad') notices another vessel apparently in pursuit, evidently a coastguard vessel, and its position suggests prior knowledge of the *Tremolino*'s departure. A chase ensues as Dominic comes to terms with the realization he has been betrayed, and this means he has only one course of action available: 'A mysterious, remorseless whisper came from within the motionless black hood at my side. … "She must be killed" (*MS*, 176). 'She', of course, is the *Tremolino*, and the act of nautical murder is entrusted to the narrator, who has also discovered that his secret hoard of ten thousand francs in gold is missing. Following Dominic's instructions, he bears onto the tiller to drive the *Tremolino* onto the rocks.

As she breaks apart, with a mighty blow Dominic consigns his traitorous nephew to the waters of the Mediterannean, and the stolen gold does the rest; Cesar drowns. Is this fact or fiction? The most honest answer may be that it is both – or neither. We can be sure that this is not accurate, objective autobiography. Aside from the heavily literary presentation of the episode – the personification of the boat, the melodramatic plot, the strong character lines – what are ostensibly facts have been revealed to be either unlikely or wholly inaccurate. Carlism was a spent force and the Third Carlist War was over by the time Conrad could have taken part in these events; the real-life César Cervoni, despite the coincidence of names, was not the real-life Dominique Cervoni's nephew, and he most certainly did not drown with stolen gold about his waist, as he outlived Conrad. Despite extensive archival searching, no ship named the *Tremolino* has been traced.[7] *The Mirror of the Sea*, then, as some of its reviewers realized, reflects its author working across boundaries – of genre, of memory and imagination, of fact and fiction.

II

In the history of its writing and publication, *A Personal Record* (1912) could hardly be more different from *The Mirror of the Sea*. Where the earlier work was composed mostly of short pieces written for a range of periodicals including mass-publication newspapers, *A Personal Record* began life as *Some Reminiscences* (1908–09), a serial written for the highbrow audience targeted by Conrad's friend and sometime collaborator Ford Madox Hueffer (later Ford). Ford intended the *English Review* to provide a vehicle for the kind of writing that would not or could not find favour in mainstream publications. In 1909, he told Arnold Bennett that he was 'running a philanthropic institution for the benefit of the better letters', and its 'definite design', he later wrote in a memoir, was to give 'imaginative literature a chance in England'.[8] Ford also recalled that his most urgent motive in 1908 was 'to provide some money for Conrad by printing the *Personal Record*'.[9] The *English Review* is therefore an important development in literary Modernism, as it sought to provide a refuge for non-commercial literary writing at a time when the social and economic forces that shaped the literary marketplace threatened, in the eyes of some purist practitioners, to limit originality and innovation.[10] This context invites us to see *Some Reminiscences* as an experimental work directed to an elite audience, transforming the conventional autobiography or memoir as completely as *Lord Jim* had transformed the novel of adventure.

Sure enough, when published in book form in 1912, *Some Reminiscences* (*A Personal Record* was its original title in the United States and, from 1916, in the United Kingdom) prompted a notably varied reaction from reviewers, in contrast with the almost universal panegyrics that greeted *The Mirror*. Many reviews noted the work's 'reticence', some with disappointment, others, such as a pleased reviewer in *Punch*, commending Conrad's lack of egotism (*CR*, III, 108). Some found its form exasperating, such as the *Nation*'s anonymous reviewer: 'In the whole fascinating library of confession, we suppose there was never a volume so wild in its disorder. … If a ship put to sea like this, the cargo would all be on deck or hanging overboard, the passengers would be stowed in the rigging, the crew in the hold; she would usually sail stern foremost, and would reach her destination by going wrong way round the world' (*CR*, III, 54–5). The work's a-chronological and Impressionist complexities, its associative structure and its digressions on Polish history and Conrad's ancestry drew as much praise as censure; the *Birmingham Daily Post* observed that 'Mr. Conrad starts his latest book at the end, and then works back to the beginning', but this notably simplified the work's complexity, to which the *Outlook*'s reviewer paid a witty and vivid tribute to this 'fragmentary and incomplete and irresistible work of pure literature' in one of the most perceptive notices:

> It is quite unlike any biography that ever was written. Its discursiveness, the chronological chaos of it, are hardly to be described. … The narrative, always

> on an easy conversational note, sways gently onward ... doubling and twisting like a very lazy eel, moving backwards, sideways, or ahead, creating for us an unbroken succession of those unforgettable pictures in words which are the distinguishing thing about Mr. Conrad's works of genius.
>
> (*CR*, III, 50)

As finally constituted by Conrad, *A Personal Record* begins with an Author's Note he added in 1919, followed by 'A Familiar Preface' (written in 1911), before reprinting, with minor revisions, the seven parts of *Some Reminiscences*.[11] Even before we have reached the reminiscences themselves, Conrad has delayed the reader by inserting two prefaces that discuss the reception of the memoirs and anticipate what is to come, warning us against any expectation of a linear narrative: 'I fear that trying to be conversational I have only managed to be unduly discursive' (*APR*, 17.27–28). Once the reminiscences are underway, the discursiveness becomes immediately apparent; Part I opens with the writing of the tenth chapter of *Almayer's Folly* on board the S.S. *Adowa* in Rouen (why not the first chapter?), takes in a digression on the ship's owners, the ill-fated Franco-Canadian Transport Company, and develops this into an anecdote about Captain Froud of the London Shipmaster's Society. Before the first part has concluded, the reader has visited Conrad's furnished rooms in a Pimlico square (the unnamed Bessborough Gardens) where he began *Almayer's Folly*; Cracow (unnamed) or possibly the Ukraine where the young Conrad is looking at a map of Africa; the interior of the Congo; a cabin on board a ship heading for Australia (the unnamed *Torrens*); Berlin's Friedrichstraße Bahnhof (railway station); an hotel in Warsaw; an inn near a Ukrainian railway station; and, finally, Kazimierówka (unnamed), the nearby estate belonging to his maternal uncle, Tadeusz Bobrowski (also anonymous).

Throughout, Conrad recalls memories not only of events (giving the instalment a complex time-scheme ranging from the 1860s to the 1890s) but also of characters and scenes in *Almayer's Folly*, so that the 'Malayan Isles' – more specifically, the Berau region of north-east Borneo – becomes yet another locale in this disjointed odyssey, to say nothing of other fictional locations alluded to – the Rouen of Flaubert's *Madame Bovary* and the Scotland of Walter Scott's *The Bride of Lammermoor*. While this intricate discursiveness baffled some contemporary readers, recent critics have tended to emphasize the methodological and narratological commonalities in Conrad's fiction and memoir, and the latter's modernity; H. Porter Abbott reads *A Personal Record* as a distinctively Modernist account of self-transformation, reflecting on the enigmas of human agency and radically departing from Victorian norms of life-writing.[12] Douglas Kerr, who highlights its lack of linearity as a distinctively Conradian way of making progress, identifies its apparent inability to narrate the primal act of writing – the writing of the first words of *Almayer's Folly* in Pimlico – as a narrative lacuna akin to Lord Jim's inability to narrate the experience of jumping from the *Patna*. *A Personal Record* is a story about writing in which remarkably little writing gets done.[13]

Indeed, if we turn from its extraordinary formal qualities to its themes, that of not writing proves to be one of the most prominent. The opening scene in Rouen is a scene of interruption, in which the *Adowa*'s third officer intrudes like Coleridge's Man from Porlock and the vision of a Malayan sunset that Conrad's muse has invoked is lost. Later, in Part V, Conrad recalls summoning into existence *Nostromo*'s Republic of Costaguana – an imaginative ordeal that he associates with Jacob's wrestling with a figure later revealed to be God (Genesis xxii.22–32) and then with 'a desperate fray' leaving scores of dead pages on the battlefield – only for this immense act of creativity to be destroyed by the intrusion of a Kentish neighbour, 'the general's daughter': 'The whole world of Costaguana … had come down crashing about my ears' (*APR*, 92.18–28). As if this were not bad enough, the young lady goes on to comment that sitting in a study writing stories all day must be 'perfectly delightful' (94.3); fresh from his God-wrestling exploits, the author is forced to observe the social niceties of entertaining a guest while his creation lies in metaphorical ruins. On one level, these episodes are part of the myth-making enterprise of *A Personal Record*, which refreshes the Romantic image of the artist as an isolated and unworldly hero in mystical communication with forces beyond him. On another level, however, the mystification of the act of writing in these episodes might be read as partly ironic, undermined by humour and hyperbole, which, in the case of the general's daughter, prompts an extended sally poking fun at a nineteenth-century method of language-teaching and a comic scene involving two sparring dogs. Moreover, the theme and the form come together in an implicit critique of this mythic Romantic hero-writer. *A Personal Record* frequently foregrounds the writer's environment as in itself productive, both in the recollections of past acts of writing and in the memoir itself, which weaves its anarchic way through memories, events and people that intrude and distract but also inspire. Almayer is the prime example, distracting Józef Korzeniowski the sailor from the task of unloading a pony onto a Bornean wharf but inspiring Joseph Conrad the writer to immortalize Almayer in prose.

III

If *The Mirror* and *A Personal Record* highlight the difficulties of separating fact from fiction, truth from artifice, we might expect Conrad's personal correspondence to offer a haven of autobiographical simplicity. Here, we might expect, we will find the man without literary qualities, revealing himself – his circumstances, his opinions, his relationships, his aspirations, his reactions – unmediated by the established or the experimental techniques of imaginative literature. The letters would, we might assume, provide a scholarly resource and biographical raw material while offering little, in their own right, to the reader or student of literature.

It is undeniable that the letters are a scholarly and biographical treasure trove. Begun in 1983, the publication of the nine-volume *Collected Letters*, was completed in 2008; scholars are still coming to terms with the scale, depth and richness of what it offers in terms of understanding Conrad's life, mind and art, his relationships, and, of equal importance, the times in which he lived. In terms of literary history alone, Conrad's 1,200 letters to his agent (and later friend) J. B. Pinker from 1899 to the latter's death in 1922 stand alongside Anthony Trollope's *Autobiography* (1883) and Arnold Bennett's *Journals* (1932–3) as among the most privileged insights we have into the professional writer's world – insights that challenge the Romantic myth, partly endorsed by Conrad, as we have seen in *A Personal Record*, of the writer as isolated genius, hewing words out of seemingly intractable rock or communing in almost mystical fashion with the scenes and people of his imaginary worlds.

Although in his letters to Pinker he does not abandon metaphors of inspiration, toil and pain, Conrad's self-mythologizing is tempered by observations on the hard, practical facts of making a living from his pen. Who reads *Blackwood's Edinburgh Magazine*? How influential in literature is the chemicals magnate Sir Alfred Mond? How many words can be written in a calendar year? Which is the most energetic publishing house as regards publicity – Dent's or Methuen's? What are the risks and benefits of newspaper syndication? Is it a good idea or not to provide an author's photograph? In answering – as well as asking – questions such as these, we see Conrad's skill and commitment to managing his position in the literary marketplace. Although he undoubtedly became dependent on Pinker for financial as well as literary services – almost embarrassingly so when, for example, tetchily requesting Pinker to pay his fuel bills or to provide him with writing-paper or a replacement ink pen – Conrad was far from being an ingénue in the literary marketplace.[14] This is evident, for instance, in his insistent instructions to his literary agent on handling negotiations over the serialization of *Romance* (1903), in his observations on how literary influence is exerted and prestige acquired and lost, and his (not always successful) attempts to strike deals outside of the terms of the Pinker-Conrad contract. To their literary-historical importance, we might also add their value to social, political, cultural and intellectual historians. As Edward Said was one of the first to recognize: 'Conrad's letters ... provide us with an almost embarrassingly rich testimonial to the intensity and variety of his intellectual life'.[15] His letters to the Cardiff-born Pole Spiridion Kliszczewski bemoaning the outcome of the 1885 general election, to his friends the socialist politician and writer R. B. Cunninghame Graham and the schoolmaster 'Ted' Sanderson analyzing the Boer War (with vehement rhetoric to the former, in measured tones to the latter), and to his acquaintance Roger Casement advising him on his campaign to bring to light Belgian abuses in the Congo, all provide fascinating glimpses of an active and enquiring mind considering some of the major issues of the age, including ones into which Conrad had personal insight.[16]

Conrad's letters written during the First World War are among the most illuminating historically and biographically, first-hand accounts of a man of letters caught between shifting geopolitical forces, then supporting the war effort, and finally bearing the emotional burden of having a son (and friends' sons) on the Western Front. Conrad found himself in the summer of 1914 in potentially hostile territory as he had chosen that moment to take his family to visit Austrian Poland. Despite being at times in genuine danger of imprisonment, and faced with what must have seemed at times insuperable logistical challenges to return home (finally achieving this via Vienna and Genoa), Conrad was conscious of being a witness to epochal events. To Ada and John Galsworthy, for example, he wrote after his return, 'You must know that I started on our journey from Austria with an already gouty knee. It was a propitious moment which I dared not miss; the great rush of German and Austrian re-inforcing troops was over for a time and the Russians were falling back after their first advance' (*Letters*, V, 424). Whilst still in Zakopane in then-Austrian Poland's Tatra Mountains, he told Pinker he would 'have an awful job to get out of this country' before adding, 'I am getting a mental stimulant out of this affair – I can tell you! And if it were not for the unavoidable anxiety I would derive much benefit from the experience' (*Letters*, V, 411). Two years later, Conrad was enrolled into Britain's propaganda effort, for which he was invited by the Admiralty on a tour of Royal Naval operations. From Lowestoft – where he had first made landfall in Britain in 1878 – he described breathlessly his activities to his wife, Jessie:

> I have moved a lot, seen a lot and heard even more. Last night after being on my feet from 3.30 to nearly seven – in engine-rooms, up masts, down magazines, on bridges, down forepeaks on gun-platforms (practicing aiming – great fun) in sheds, store-rooms[,] workshops ... I went out in a vessel of a special kind to try a new 13-pounder gun. We stuffed cotton-waste in our ears (there

> was nothing else) and started her barking. The report is certainly very sharp but with one's ears well stopped all one gets is only a sort of friendly tap in the pit of one's stomach.
>
> (*Letters*, V, 662)

His records of his days on HMS *Ready*, a Q-ship (a heavily armed Royal Navy ship designed as a merchant vessel to lure German U-boats to the surface) are understandably less forthcoming, but a message to Pinker reveals a boyish excitement at being in a nautical adventure at the age of fifty-eight: 'All well. | Been practice-firing in sight of coast. | Weather improved. Health good. Hopes of bagging Fritz high' (*Letters*, V, 678). When his eldest son, Borys, was commanding a company on the Western Front, Conrad conveys the complex mixture of pride, anxiety, horror and grief that so many parents must have felt in those years, pithily summed up in February 1917: 'Our eldest boy has just been here on a 10 days' leave after 13 months at the front. A fearful joy. His contemporaries (he celebrated his nineteenth birthday here) are falling like cornstalks under the scythe' (*Letters*, VI, 27).

These examples show that the value of the letters extends far beyond their customary function to provide context for or commentary on the published work. What we might call the 'war letters' provide not only eyewitness accounts and an artist-intellectual's response to events, but also stories, charting a narrative arc from Conrad's surprise, apprehension and response to danger in Central Europe, to excited involvement in the war effort around Britain's coast and, finally, to disillusioned reflection in his study in Kent.

We can find many other examples of such extended first-person narratives in the letters: the ups-and-downs of Conrad's mental and physical health as he struggled with the emotional demands of writing and countless, frequently debilitating, attacks of gout; his reactions to his wife Jessie Conrad's fall in London's Oxford Street in 1904 and the subsequent twenty years of pain and surgery, with at times the looming threat of amputation; the tragic progress of his relationship with Ford, as a genuine personal and intellectual friendship with Ford undergoes (to borrow Aristotle's terms) a catastrophic reversal followed by Conrad's recognition of his friend's flaws. Conrad's gout prompted anguished but also extraordinarily creative responses, as for example that shared with his friend and fellow novelist Hugh Walpole in 1920: 'Since Saturday morning the improvement, as far as pain is concerned, has been rapid; but otherwise the experience has dismalised me. Not dismayed. Observe the shade of meaning. The flatness of this piece of paper on which you read these words is like a mountain compared with the flatness of my spirits' (*Letters*, VII, 111). The breach with Ford prompted some of Conrad's most ferocious writing when he recounted events to Pinker:

> I told him in effect to go to the devil and warned him that if I heard any more of that nonsense I would take steps to make it perfectly clear that his interference (whatever it was) in my affairs is an unauthorised and impertinent assumption on his part, completely without my knowledge and highly distasteful to me. … His conduct is *impossible*. All this will end badly. He's a megalomaniac who imagines he is managing the universe and that everybody treats him with the blackest ingratitude. A fierce and exasperated vanity is hidden under his calm manner which misleads people. Writing to you *in confidence* I do not hesitate to say that there are cases, not quite as bad, under medical treatment. This is not a joke. I have suffered too much mental worry and moral discomfort to joke upon the matter.
>
> (*Letters*, IV, 265–6)

There are short stories too among the long narratives, some of which reveal Conrad writing in an unfamiliar genre. His travel writing includes a caustic observation to Pinker on the inhabitants of his hotel in Ajaccio:

> There are also a few mature wandering women and a small proportion of (rather better class) frumps. An atmosphere of intense good form pervades the place. Low tones – polite smiles – kind inquiries – small groups. The only disreputable looking person is the unavoidable Clergyman of the C[hurch] of E[ngland] who looks as tho' he must have had a few adventures in his time.
>
> (*Letters*, VII, 256)

Perhaps most surprising are his letters to children, including one written during the scorching summer of 1923 to the eleven-year-old Lorna Watson, granddaughter of Sir Robert Jones, Jessie Conrad's surgeon, in which simplicity, directness and an apparent artlessness conceal an authorial knowingness that touches on the central, Conradian issue of truth in storytelling:

> At 2 P.M. on Thursday last I watched from my chair a wagtail crossing our so-called tennis-court. He could hardly put one foot before the other; he was positively dragging his tail after him. I suppose no such sight was ever seen since the creation of wagtails. I could not bear it. I closed my eyes; and when I opened them (3 hours afterwards) the wagtail was not to be seen anywhere. I wish I knew what became of him.
>
> What a tragic mystery. …
>
> Give my love to your Grandfather but don't tell him the story of the wagtail. He may not believe it – and that would hurt my feelings.
>
> (*Letters*, VIII, 133)

To the student of literature, the story from Conrad's correspondence of his 1890 Congo journey will appear particularly valuable; alongside the diary that Conrad kept while in Africa, they might be seen to provide an inside perspective on the people, scenes and events that, nine years later, became *Heart of Darkness*.[17] A letter sent from Freetown, Sierre Leone, to his cousin Karol Zagórski for instance, details the frenetic preparations that perhaps lie behind Marlow's 'I flew around like mad to get ready' (50.14):

> If you had only seen all the tin boxes and revolvers, the high boots and the tender farewells; just another handshake and just another pair of trousers! – and if you knew all the bottles of medicine and all the affectionate wishes I took away with me, you would understand in what a typhoon, cyclone, hurricane, earthquake – no! – in what a universal cataclysm, in what a fantastic atmosphere of mixed shopping, business, and affecting scenes, I passed two whole weeks.
>
> (*Letters*, I, 52)

Some of the atmosphere and narrative technique of the novella are also adumbrated in the same letter with Conrad's unease at hearing that '60 per cent. of our Company's employees return to Europe before they have completed even six months' service. Fever and dysentery! There are others who are sent home in a hurry at the end of a year, so that they shouldn't die in the Congo. God forbid! It would spoil the statistics, which are excellent, you see!' (*Letters*, I, 52). Five years before the publication of *Almayer's Folly*, we can here see the incipient novelist, deploying figures of speech, rhythmic prose, and techniques such as prolepsis; similarly, in 'The Congo Diary' we can witness the literary impressionist at work, recording in staccato prose the 'boom' of a bird as resembling 'the very distant baying of a hound' (*LE*, 125.19), or 'another dead body lying by the path in an attitude of meditative repose' (126.9–10).

These are resources of immense value, but there are risks in citing Conrad's correspondence, memoirs and diaries, especially in support of literary-critical judgments. If for example one were to make a case (as so many critics have) that Conrad's powers were in decline after the publication of *Under Western Eyes* (1911), it is not difficult to find support from the letters to suggest that Conrad struggled with a particular work or regarded it as inferior, such as his comment to Cunninghame Graham in January 1914: 'I am glad you find *Chance* tolerable. I don't' (*Letters*, V, 336). However, less than eight months earlier, Conrad had told Pinker that *Chance* was 'the biggest piece of work I've done since Lord Jim. As to what *it is* I'm very confident' (*Letters*, V, 229). Indeed, Conrad's evaluative judgements on his own work are consistent only in their inconsistency; the letters are dotted with deprecatory references to admired works such as 'An Outpost of Progress', *Heart of Darkness* and *Nostromo*. Conrad warned André Gide, for instance, that he would find the latter 'badly made and difficult to read – boring even' (*Letters*, V, 79). Critics who despise the 1913 short story 'The Inn of the Two Witches' – and in 1924 Conrad himself told Eric Pinker, who took over his father's literary agency after the latter's death, that he was 'not very much in love' with the story – might be surprised to see it included a month later in a letter to the same correspondent, in Conrad's putative list of selected stories for a Doubleday volume (*Letters*, VIII, 265, 310).

Conrad's comments on his work need to be seen in light of the rhetorical strategies he employs in the letters, strategies that varied according to the situation and the recipient. As Laurence Davies, the general editor of *The Collected Letters of Joseph Conrad*, has pointed out, they 'are distinguished by sharply delineated points of view in the manner of James or Ford': Conrad's 'extraordinary talent for camouflage' means that his 'epistolary personae' are 'not so much fictions as filtrates'.[18] Conrad's description to H. G. Wells of *The Mirror* as 'a wretched little volume of mine which is going to be shot out on the rubbish heap' (*Letters*, III, 356) might seem a damning verdict, but his use of the same term about *Nostromo* suggests rather that this was part of a code of epistolary behaviour between the two writers. The larger point, however, is that the protean rhetoric identified by Davies is evident throughout his correspondence, in which, as in his novels, we should beware of a simple identification of author with narrator. As Owen Knowles has put it, the letters are 'sometimes just as artifactual in their self-performance as his fictional reminiscences or autobiographical fictions'.[19]

Davies has also suggested that the publication of the letters extends what we have customarily viewed as Conrad's canon, and anyone who has read the corpus would find it hard to disagree. On all but the most trivial matters, the letters show the development and deployment of what Conrad often called 'treatment' – the application of techniques that we may label 'literary' or 'impressionist' or 'fictive' to subjects that range from war to painting to gout. Indeed, at the risk of falling into the trap of quoting Conrad selectively in order to clinch a critical argument, we might conclude with his observations on the relationship between life and art to his journalist friend Richard Curle. Conrad recalls a critic's remarks 'that there was no difference in method or character between my fiction and my professedly autobiographical matter' and comments: 'My own impression is that what he really meant was that my manner of telling, perfectly devoid of familiarity as between author and reader, aimed essentially at the intimacy of personal communication, without any thought for other effects' (*Letters*, VIII, 131). Conrad's literary artefacts seek to resemble letters ('personal communication'), while his letters resemble literary artefacts, just as autobiography and fiction keep intruding upon each other. Conrad's efforts to work memories into impressions and, through the power of imagination, to make the actual yield to the ideal are not confined to his most admired novels but are evident throughout his writing.

NOTES

1 On Conrad's financial position in this period, see J. H. Stape, *The Several Lives of Joseph Conrad* (London: Heinemann, 2007), p. 134.
2 Owen Knowles and Gene M. Moore, *Oxford Reader's Companion to Conrad* (Oxford: Oxford University Press, 2000), pp. 230–33.
3 Conrad considered 'The Art and the Life' as a possible title for what eventually became *A Personal Record* (*Letters*, IV, 139). *Notes on Life and Letters* was published in 1921.
4 Conrad uses the technique of personification quite explicitly in, for example, the section on winds, 'Rulers of East and West'.
5 *The Mirror of the Sea & A Personal Record*, ed. Zdzisław Najder (Oxford: Oxford University Press, 1989), p. 164.
6 For Nostromo's identification with Dominique Cervoni, see Norman Sherry, *Conrad's Western World* (Cambridge: Cambridge University Press, 1980), pp. 163–5.
7 See Zdzisław Najder, *Joseph Conrad: A Chronicle*, trans. Halina Carroll-Najder (Cambridge: Cambridge University Press, 1983) pp. 47–9, and Stape, *The Several Lives*, pp. 29–30.
8 Max Saunders, *Ford Madox Ford: A Dual Life* (Oxford: Oxford University Press, 1996), I, 242, 254.
9 Ford Madox Ford, *Return to Yesterday* (London: Victor Gollancz, 1931), p. 195.
10 For the *Review*'s significance in the career of Modernists such as D. H. Lawrence, see Saunders, *Ford Madox Ford*, I, 246–9.
11 Conrad's state of mind and the breakdown of his relationship with Ford in the spring of 1909 prevented him from writing further *Reminiscences* at the time, while his aspirations to add a second part or volume, which he retained until his death, never reached fulfillment. On this and on the making of the volume, see 'Introduction', *A Personal Record*, ed. Zdzisław Najder and J. H. Stape (Cambridge: Cambridge University Press, 2008), pp. xxi–xxii.
12 H. Porter Abbott, 'Writing and Conversion: Conrad's Modernist Autobiography', *Yale Journal of Criticism* 5, no. 3 (1992), 135–63.
13 Douglas Kerr, 'Going About: Conrad's Progress in *A Personal Record*', Conference paper, University of Cape Town, December 2011.
14 Pinker acted in effect as Conrad's banker after the failure of Conrad's bank in 1904. For Conrad's own warm estimation of the extent and value of these services, see his letter to Pinker of 19 April 1921 (*Letters*, VII, 271–2).
15 Edward Said, *Joseph Conrad and the Fiction of Autobiography* (Cambridge, MA: Harvard University Press, 1966), p. vii.
16 See *Letters*, I, 15–16; II, 206–07, 210–12; III, 95–7.

17 The critical text of 'The Congo Diary' is published in *Last Essays*, ed. Harold Ray Stevens and J. H. Stape (Cambridge: Cambridge University Press, 2010), pp. 123–37.
18 Laurence Davies, 'Listening for the Silences: Lacunæ and Restraints in Conrad's Letters', *Conradiana* 23 (1991) 5–9 (8–9).
19 Owen Knowles, 'Conrad's Correspondence: A Literary Dimension', *Conradiana* 23 (1991), 19–27 (25).

6

STEPHEN DONOVAN

Serialization

Were it not for his prolific contributions to newspapers and magazines, Joseph Conrad might well be unknown today. Periodicals enabled him to maintain himself by writing after he lost his inheritance on an ill-fortuned gold-mining venture at the start of his career in 1896. Commissions and invitations from editors inspired him to submit essays on topical subjects, reviews of new books and personal memoirs, and the instalment schedules and space requirements of periodical publishing played midwife to almost all of his major fictions as they evolved from short story to novella or full-length novel. In more than a dozen countries, serialization additionally brought Conrad's name to the attention of national audiences. Shapers of public opinion figured prominently in their number, a phenomenon reflected in the observation of a book-of-the-month-club judge that Conrad was 'more read by newspaper men than any other writer'.[1] Perhaps most importantly, serialization drew Conrad, albeit unwillingly, into a creative dialogue with the readers, editors and illustrators of his work – a career-long interaction that was to decisively shape both the themes and the style of his writing.

Conrad was serialized to an extraordinary extent. Even before he made his English magazine début with the short story 'The Idiots' in *The Savoy* in October 1896, his first novel, *Almayer's Folly* (1895), had appeared in Dutch translation in the Amsterdam daily *Het Nieuws van den Dag* (May–July 1896).[2] In turn, his death in August 1924 prompted the publication of his last and unfinished essay, 'Legends', in *The Daily Mail* (London), *The New York Times*, *The Manitoba Free Press* (Winnipeg) and, with an accompanying translation into Japanese, the Tokyo literary magazine *Eigo Seinen*. During the intervening quarter-century, his work had been published, republished, syndicated and extracted in no fewer than 250 periodicals around the world. Virtually everything he wrote was serialized, usually more than once, and it was magazine and newspaper serializations that pioneered the translation of his work into Dutch, French, German, Japanese, Polish and

Swedish between 1896 and 1904. Above all, it was in serial form that many of Conrad's works made their first public appearance.

The variety and complexity of this phenomenon has few parallels in modern letters. Major Victorian authors such as Dickens or Hardy, who relied upon serialization, typically associated themselves with, at most, a handful of titles, and even those Modernists, notably Ezra Pound and Virginia Woolf, who did write for periodicals only seldom strayed beyond *avant-garde* little magazines and well-established literary journals.[3] The relatively few instances when Conrad's contemporaries did permit their work to appear in trade journals or mass-circulation publications often marked either the start of their literary career, as with James Joyce's short story submissions to *The Irish Homestead* and interviews for Dublin's *Daily Express*, or its decline, as with what F. Scott Fitzgerald called his 'whoring' for *The Saturday Evening Post* and *Collier's Magazine*.[4]

By comparison, Conrad's own massive reliance on serials seems almost nonchalant. From early obscurity to the heights of international fame, he allowed his work to appear in an ever-widening circle of periodicals. In Britain, these included prestigious reviews (*Blackwood's Edinburgh Magazine*, *The Cornhill Magazine*, *The Fortnightly Review*, *New Review*, *Cosmopolis*), large-circulation fiction magazines (*Pall Mall Magazine*, *London Magazine*, *The Strand Magazine*, *Cassell's Magazine*, *Lloyd's Magazine*), social and political miscellanies (*The Illustrated London News*, *T. P.'s Weekly*, *Land & Water*, *The Outlook* (London)), literary journals (*The London Mercury*, *The Bookman*, *The Academy*), military magazines (*Reveille: Devoted to the Disabled Sailor & Soldier*, *The Granton Magazine*, *Fledgling: The Monthly Journal of the No.2 Flying Corps Cadet Wing*), pulps (*The Grand Magazine*) and a host of niche publications, including *The British Legion Journal*, *The Empire Magazine*, *Countries of the World*, *The Oxford and Cambridge Review* and *The Blue Peter: The Magazine of Sea Travel*. His writing also made numerous appearances in the pages of Fleet Street's leading titles: *The Times*, *The Star*, *The Daily Chronicle*, *The Daily News & Leader*, *The Tribune*, *The Speaker*, *The Standard* and, in particular, *The Daily Mail*, to which Conrad contributed more than a dozen essays and reviews between 1904 and 1924.[5]

In North America, where the passage of the International Copyright Act of 1891 had delivered a major check to literary piracy, Conrad's agent, the canny J. B. Pinker, managed to get his client's work into print, often for the second or third time, in an equally wide range of venues: major fiction magazines (*Metropolitan*, *Harper's Magazine*, *McClure's*, *Munsey's Magazine*, *Collier's Weekly*, *The Saturday Evening Post*), literary miscellanies (*The Living Age*, *Appleton's Booklover's Magazine*, *The Critic*), women's magazines (*The Pictorial Review*, *The Delineator*) and journals of current affairs (*Harper's Weekly*, *The North American Review*, *Current History*, *The Outlook* (New York), *Current Opinion*, *The Canadian Magazine*, *The Forum*). Other writings appeared in an even more diverse array of periodicals: 'The Brute' (1906), his most widely reprinted short story, in *The Ocean Wireless News* (1912), a colour monthly compiled and distributed aboard American passenger ships; *One Day More*, his first play, in the mouthpiece of political gadfly H. L. Mencken, *The Smart Set* (February 1914); *The Rescue* in the twenty-cent pulp magazine *Romance* (November 1919–April 1920); and 'Geography and Some Explorers' in the august and photo-illustrated *National Geographic Magazine* (March 1924). As importantly, Conrad's work was a feature in the metropolitan presses of New York, Boston, Los Angeles, Chicago, Kansas, Baltimore and Washington, DC, to name but a few, as well as in influential Modernist magazines on both sides of the Atlantic, among them *The English Review*, *The Dial* and the *transatlantic review*.

These are just some of the English-language periodicals to have serialized a complete Conrad work during his lifetime. To their number can be added the appearances of personal letters and extracts; the journal publications in other English-speaking territories and colonies such as Australia, New Zealand and Singapore; a host of posthumous reprintings; and an astonishing proliferation of foreign-language serializations that continued apace until mid-century. The Bogotá daily *El Tiempo* offered a translation of 'The Anarchist' in its fiction supplement for 13 December 1913; *La Nación*, a Buenos Aires newspaper with the largest circulation in Latin America, published a translation of 'The Lagoon' (1897) on 20 February 1921; the French Communist Party's official organ, *L'Humanité*, ran a feuilleton of 'Gaspar Ruiz' (1908) in July 1928; and the same novella appeared in Icelandic in the Reykjavik literary quarterly *Eimreiðin* (October 1936–September 1937). As late as 1946, that brash tabloid, the *New York Post*, could advertise a full serialization of Conrad's 'Youth' (1902) on the front page of its 9 August edition alongside reports of American-Soviet tensions. And new serializations, including works thought never to have been serialized in Conrad's lifetime, are continually coming to light: *Romance* (1903), his collaborative novel with Ford Madox Ford, in Minnesota's *St. Paul Globe* (27 March–3 July 1904); *Almayer's Folly* in *The Boston Post* (9–30 September 1923); and even 'Falk' (1902), a short story about cannibalism that Conrad once thought 'too strong for readers', in *La Revue de Paris* (1 December 1930–15 January 1931).

Largely inaccessible until the advent of digitization, this global archipelago of texts has been gathered into a single digital resource, *Conrad First:*

The Joseph Conrad Periodical Archive, that enables its users to reconstruct the intersecting strands of Conrad's dissemination in the public media of his day. In turn, a longstanding scholarly interest in the serial publication of Conrad's writings has been lent further impetus by the rise of the field known as Book History,[6] such that serialization is now widely recognized as an indispensable factor for how we understand the shape and dynamics of his literary career and those of Modernist authors more generally. As we shall see, the appearance of a Conrad text in an individual magazine or newspaper, although seemingly ephemeral and unvalued, in fact represents a unique kind of threshold between the world of the author and that of his audience, a threshold whose codes and conventions exerted profound influence upon the composition, publication and reception of his major works.

From the author's perspective, serialization has three principal attributes. The first is its periodicity; the literary work in serial is divided into instalments that appear at different times, often further divided among subsections of a single number, with the periodical assuming responsibility for defining the nature of their appearance and interconnectedness. The second is its extension; periodical publication is necessarily ephemeral and open-ended, being in essence a chronicle of recent events, feature items and topics of interest upon which it does not impose narrative form. The third is its authorizing function; individual articles or feuilleton chapters are subordinate to the larger identity of the newspaper or magazine in question. Unlike a regular staff writer, an occasional contributor in Conrad's day might reasonably expect a byline, but the sheer fact of publication in a serial implicitly cast the periodical as the sponsor or even co-author of an article.

All these factors can be observed at work in Conrad's very different relationships with his serial publishers, and collectively they are essential for an understanding of his idiosyncratic compositional method. Whether describing *Typhoon* (1902) as 'quite the thing that finds room in Xmas numbers', insisting to a magazine editor on the impossibility of 'faking a "sunny" ending to my story', or urging the American collector John Quinn not to read *Victory* (1915) in the 'double columns and crowded type' of *Munsey's Magazine*, Conrad's correspondence bears ample testimony to his accommodation to the demands of serial publishing. Moreover, the fact that the serial versions of longer works such as *Lord Jim* (1900), *Nostromo* (1904), *Under Western Eyes* (1911) and *Chance* (1914) began appearing *before* Conrad had completed them not only spurred him to produce copy but also made it impossible for him to ignore that he was writing for a specific community of readers.

The Mirror of the Sea (1906), a collection of nautical essays and embellished memoirs, presents a good example of how writing in the first instance for periodicals shaped the development of a major work. A perennial favourite with contemporary audiences and a cornerstone of Conrad's reputation as a maritime writer, this highly composite volume draws on articles published in seven different British and American newspapers and magazines: *Pall Mall Magazine*, *Harper's Weekly*, *Blackwood's Edinburgh Magazine*, *The Reader*, *The World's Work and Play*, *The Tribune*, *The Standard* and *The Daily Mail*. Of these, the last warrants particular attention. By the time its literary editor contacted Conrad in early 1904 about the possibility of writing a series of personal articles with a maritime flavour, this upstart halfpenny daily, whose audience included Conrad's own household, had established itself as an arbiter of public taste and opinion by expounding nationalist and populist doctrines while hawking a startling array of branded '*Daily Mail*' commodities ranging from brown bread and hats to sweet peas and fiction anthologies. Cash-strapped as always, Conrad seized the opportunity even though it meant interrupting his revision of *Nostromo* for book publication.

The resulting three articles were published as '"Missing!"' (8 March 1904), 'Overdue' (16 November 1904) and 'Stranded' (2 December 1904) and later incorporated as sections XVI–XXI of *The Mirror of the Sea*. Written in what their author characterized as an 'Easy narrative style' (*Letters*, III, 114) and sharing a structure that reflects both their occasional origin and the changing conventions of newspaper writing, they implicitly address a suburban readership – condescendingly evoked by Conrad as 'Mr Jones or Mr Robinson of Maida Vale or Finsbury' (*Letters*, III, 504) – whose knowledge of the sea extended no further than the pages of a newspaper. In each instance, Conrad interweaves personal anecdote with philosophical speculation and curious details of professional seafaring. Memories of killer ships and rogue ice-floes in '"Missing!"' are punctuated by references to peculiar cloud formations and reflections on the 'intimacy' between sailor and ship (58); an account of marine reinsurance in 'Overdue' prompts the tale of a steamer adrift in polar seas and a meditation upon its 'unearthly existence' (64); and a recollection of running aground in 'Stranded' includes a description of the mental shock delivered by a vessel touching bottom and a listing of the methods used to refloat it 'scientifically' (70).

Writing for the world's largest daily newspaper influenced Conrad in other ways, too. Mindful of *The Daily Mail*'s fondness for eye-catching maritime topics such as submarines and ship-building, and its publication of sensational serial fiction by popular sea-writers, such as Morley Roberts (1857–1942), he dispensed with his customary emphasis upon the unbridgeable gap separating landlubbers from professional sailors. Instead, each of his articles engages newspaper readers directly by encouraging them to speculate – about how a doomed liner went down ('"Missing!"'), about the thoughts of passengers aboard a 'dead ship' ('Overdue') (64) and about the anguish felt by the master of a beached vessel ('Stranded'). Likewise, in contrasting individual doubt with heroic solidarity, as illustrated by the case of the pessimistic underwriter who buys reinsurance only to find 'the men on board of a finer temper than he has been willing to take for granted' (62), Conrad repeatedly validates the same ideological qualities of British pride, loyalty and deference that *The Daily Mail* sought to foster in its million-strong readership.

Even the typography of newsprint played a part in the genesis of *The Mirror of the Sea* to judge from a letter, written shortly after Conrad submitted '"Missing!"', in which he describes himself as having 'invented five headlines for an article of 1000 words to please the Dly Mail' (*Letters*, III, 121). That newspaper headlines were pressing upon his consciousness at this time is evident from a range of other writings: his complaint in 'Autocracy and War' (1905) that 'the large page, the columns of words, the leaded headings exalt the mind into a state of feverish credulity' (*NLL*, 76.29–30); his depiction of Comrade Ossipon in *The Secret Agent* (1907) as tormented by the phrasing of the news headline '"Suicide of Lady Passenger from a cross-Channel Boat"' (228.29–30); and his approving recollection in *A Personal Record* (1912) of how a shipwreck had received 'no large headlines – no headlines at all' (*NLL*, 177.16). Like his addition of an exclamation mark, Conrad's reference to supplementing '"Missing!"' with 'five headlines' – more precisely, one sub-heading ('The Passing of a Ship at Sea') and four crossheads – 'The Funeral Oration', 'A Subtle Difference', '"Look, Sir!"' and 'The Turn of the Wheel') – reveals his adaptation to the house-style of a newspaper that was notorious for using sensational headlines such as 'Death Struggle At Sea'.[7] No less significantly, the fact that the title of Conrad's article appears in inverted commas confirms that its subject is as much the reading of newspapers, and specifically the headlines 'Shipping Intelligence' and 'Ships on the Overdue Market', as it is the sea itself.

Conrad's début in *The Daily Mail* was auspicious on several counts. As well as initiating a twenty-year association with the Amalgamated Press stable of journals, which in time brought him the patronage and friendship of its mercurial owner, Alfred Harmsworth, later first Viscount Northcliffe (1865–1922), it heralded his integration into the *Daily Mail*'s cultural universe, even seeing the offer of a regular book review column in 1910. (In the event, short-lived, as Conrad found such work and writing to a tight deadline uncongenial.) Although Conrad later quipped that its fulsome review of *Nostromo* was a 'consecration' of his genius (*Letters*, III, 181), the word was apt enough as a description of the newspaper's importance in helping to establish an immigrant Pole as Britain's pre-eminent commentator on maritime affairs, not least for the numerous American and Australasian journals that routinely reprinted its news and features. When the SS *Waratah* disappeared without trace off the coast of South Africa in July 1909, *The Daily Mail* turned to Conrad for a public statement, as it did during the thrilling transatlantic pursuit of the murderer Dr. Crippen in 1910. It opened its editorial pages in 1912 to his memoir of the London Sailors' Home and, again, in 1918, to his celebration of maritime courage in wartime. Conrad's identification with *The Daily Mail* received its most public confirmation the following year when his essay 'Confidence', a commissioned tribute to the Merchant Navy's role as a bulwark of empire, was accorded pride of place in its special Golden Peace Number, printed in gold ink and without advertisements, to commemorate the signing of the Treaty of Versailles.

The influence of serialization on the composition of Conrad's writings only rarely ended with the dispatch of his typescript to the editorial offices of the periodical in question. Between their appearances as serial and as book (or part thereof) his texts typically underwent a number of changes. Most of these fall into one of two categories. The first is interventions by editors and printers (including excisions, suppressions, emendations, house-styling, headlining and chapter division), which Conrad somewhat idiosyncratically incorporated, restored or rejected when redrafting his texts for book publication. The second is revisions (additions as well as cuts) of his own, which in at least some cases clearly resulted from his experience of the serialization process. The complexity of this evolution from serial to book – a development that may now be traced in detail thanks to the publication of critical editions of Conrad's works in the Cambridge Edition – has understandably made his writings an intriguing object of study for textual scholars. Yet it also has important implications for all readers and students of Conrad.

Nostromo, Conrad's panoramic treatment of South American revolution, offers an illustrative example. The novel appeared between 29 January and 7 October 1904 in *T. P.'s Weekly*, a left-leaning miscellany of literature and current affairs, before being issued as a book by Harper & Brothers on 14 October. Begun while the novel was still unfinished, serialization proved traumatic, even by Conrad's standards; and the pressure of a looming deadline forced him on at least one occasion to turn to Ford to take dictation. In this light, it would be reasonable to assume that his extensive revising and expanding of the serial version was a simple case of improving a flawed text produced under conditions of enforced haste. (The date of the book publication indicates that he must have revised the serial text even as it was appearing in *T. P's Weekly* and before he had written the ending.) However, close comparison of the serial and Harper's texts reveals that Conrad, even while indisputably improving his work at numerous points, also removed material necessary for narrative coherence (for example, an explanation of Charles Gould's complicity with the Ribierist regime) and extended the novel with swathes of second-rate or what he himself called 'magazineish' dialogue.[8] It is not possible, in other words, to say that the serial version of *Nostromo* is uniformly inferior – aesthetically or formally – to the book version that superseded it. Indeed, the fact that some of the least successful additions are to Part III (notably, Nostromo's courtship of Giselle Viola), while many of the least successful deletions occur in the novel's first third, suggests that in trying to ameliorate what he saw as serialization's distorting influence, Conrad weakened parts of his novel.

The existence of two substantially different versions similarly complicates an understanding of *The Secret Agent* (1908), which first appeared in print, in the United States, between 6 October 1905 and 15 January 1906 in the somewhat incongruous setting of *Ridgway's: A Militant Weekly for God and Country*, a muckraking Saturday magazine. Although he had initially offered to help cut the typescript text, Conrad was deeply dismayed by the serialization and confided to his agent: 'Ridgways are sending me their rag. It's awful .... I see they are "editing" the stuff pretty severely' (*Letters*, III, 369). His disgust was understandable. *Ridgway's* numerous suppressions included key details of Adolf Verloc's relationship to his wife (variously referred to as 'Winnie' and 'Minnie') – a crucial factor in the novel's climax – notably the information that Winnie had only accepted her charmless husband after an earlier sweetheart, a butcher's boy, proved unwilling to offer a home to Stevie, her mentally disabled brother.[9] Downplaying these domestic themes, *Ridgway's* effectively reduced *The Secret Agent* to what an appended sub-heading announced as 'A Novel with the Anarchists of London, with Complications of Diplomatic Intrigue and Anarchistic Treachery'. Conrad's correspondence shows that, just as with *Nostromo* in *T. P.'s Weekly*, he had the serial version before him when he began revising the novel in late 1906. Almost a third longer, this expanded version featured a new ending in which, perhaps uncoincidentally, a stereotyped newspaper report titled 'Suicide of Lady Passenger from a cross-Channel Boat' is shown mysteriously oppressing Comrade Ossipon by 'the rhythm of journalistic phrases' (*SA*, 231.19–20). In foregrounding the mental life of its protagonists and the centrality of Winnie to the plot, it is an altogether more ambitious and recognizably Modernist work of fiction than that in the serial.

The existence of alternative versions of Conrad's major works in serial form is now attracting considerable attention from scholars interested in recovering the material histories of Modernist writing. For example, in *Ridgway's*, a magazine published simultaneously in separate local editions in fourteen cities across the United States, *The Secret Agent* appeared in eleven discrete parts, accompanied by a plethora of crude line-drawing illustrations and surrounded by topical news items and display advertisements for household commodities ranging from condiments to washing machines. Embedded as they are within these complex social, economic and literary contexts, Conrad's serial publications clearly offer a rich pedagogical resource with which to explore the early-twentieth-century publishing of literary work in demotic venues. At the same time, it must not be forgotten that mangling at the hands of periodical editors and printers has also indirectly resulted in the circulation of highly edited texts and, in essence, unauthorized ones – notably, the book edition of *Victory* – that at several points traduce, misrepresent or outrightly replace the author's own work. For instance, Conrad bitterly, and bootlessly, complained to his agent about the division (necessitated by serialization) of 'An Outpost of Progress' into two parts; and he likewise grumbled about the division of *The Shadow-Line* by the *English Review,* likening it to 'doling it out in drops, as if it were poison' (*Letters*, VI, 25). There, at least, the novella appeared in its entirety, whereas in New York's *Metropolitan*, it suffered even more severely; only half the text, in fact, made it into print, while its other 20,000 words were blue-pencilled out by editors. *Heart of Darkness* suffered as well, being published in three instalments of *Blackwood's Edinburgh Magazine*; these divisions affecting the novella's texture were in place until they were finally deleted in the Cambridge Edition (2010). *Victory*'s chapter and part divisions, as it turns out, are in large part, especially in the novel's later sections, the work of its serial editors, Conrad himself having divided the novel into five, not four, parts. Moreover, the text that has circulated for a century was specifically tailored to an American audience by editors chary of its sensibilities; Ricardo's 'damn' and 'damned' were systematically edited out and references to the 'devil' changed to the 'deuce'; anti-Teutonic references were softened or deleted for an audience with a large population of German descent at a time when America was vividly engaged in a debate about the European war; and some of the novel's erotic content was flattened. Additionally, whole paragraphs were deleted, sentences were reshaped and rewritten, emphases were added, and the rhythms of Conrad's prose were altered.[10] Beyond its immediate archival and textual challenges, serialization thus raises urgent questions about the nature of collective 'authorship', authority and literary composition.

Serialization assumes an additional and arguably even greater significance when considered in relation to the reception and dissemination of Conrad's work. What might be called the 'consumption side' of periodical publishing is predicated on a series of factors that are largely unique to serials. Foremost among these is the specificity of their demographic profile. That Conrad was published in so many different venues (well over a hundred periodicals in Britain and the United States alone) strikingly illustrates the historic proliferation of newspapers and magazines during his career as an author. This expansion, which was driven by a combination of technological innovation, capital investment and rising literacy, prompted the periodicals industry to adopt two parallel strategies: mass appeal and audience specialization. Conrad's writing straddled both developments in spectacular fashion, as can be seen from the serialization history of 'An Outpost of Progress'. First published in summer 1897 in *Cosmopolis*, a pan-European liberal monthly of art and politics aimed at a niche polyglot readership, this short story was reprinted in March 1906 by New Journalism pioneer George Newnes (1851–1910) in his mass-circulation pulp *Grand Magazine*. In the interim, Conrad's fictional indictment of Belgian colonialism had appeared as a feuilleton in a Swedish-language daily issued in Helsinki (*Aftonposten*, 10–28 January 1899), as a single instalment of a German short-story miscellany (*Vita's Novellenschatz*, January 1901) and as a photo-illustrated feature in a Parisian current affairs magazine (*Les Nouvelles Illustrées*, 22–9 January 1903). In its various book editions, too, 'An Outpost of Progress' was subject to a range of other forces that shaped its appeal to particular audiences – publishing format, pricing, editorial policy, promotional campaigns, translation style and illustration, to name but a few; yet these pale almost into insignificance alongside the exceptional social heterogeneity represented by its serial publication venues.

Periodical readers also encountered Conrad in radically different ways to book readers. Their reading experience was inescapably defined by various forms of interruption, including division between and within individual issues, page layout, headlining, synopsis, editorial interpolation and, above all, the juxtaposition of unrelated text and images in what Marshall McLuhan memorably called 'the jazzy, ragtime discontinuity of press items'.[11] These experiential or phenomenological aspects of periodical reading were underpinned, in turn, by a new economic model of serial publishing. By using advertisements as a way to reduce cover price below the cost of production, modern newspapers and magazines fundamentally changed the relationship between periodical readers and texts. The former, strictly speaking, no longer purchased a serial but rather sold their attention to its advertisers in exchange for content selected according to strict aesthetic and ideological criteria.[12] In Conrad's many references to advertising, magazine-writing conventions, the expectations of periodical readers and even his own status as a recognizable literary commodity, we see his conscious negotiation of this new relationship as well as his accommodation to the process today known as 'name branding'. Thus, he recommended 'Freya of the Seven Isles' in February 1911 to a correspondent who had solicited one of his stories on behalf of a new Parisian monthly: 'It's quite good magazine stuff, quite Conradesque (in the easier style).... Perfectly safe. Eastern sea setting, but not too much setting' (*Letters*, IV, 413).

Perhaps the most striking aspect of serialization, however, is that it allows us to infer with some precision the way in which Conrad's work was read. Unlike the reception of his books, for which we have only aggregated sales figures and contemporary reviews, serial publications supply that exceedingly rare thing in literary study: hard data about the reading experiences of actual audiences. Such experiences are doubly important because they coincided with the début appearance of Conrad's work, when it garnered arguably the greatest amount of attention from readers of all classes and, with few exceptions, its single largest audience in his lifetime. Because how Conrad's reception was read has long been a central concern for scholars – witness the endless debate over whether *Heart of Darkness* reinforced or subverted contemporary views on race and imperialism – the periodicals that published his writing are uniquely valuable as records of the production of textual meaning. 'Amy Foster', Conrad's bleak tale of an Eastern European emigrant shipwrecked in England, would have held a very different significance for readers of *The Illustrated London News* (14–28 December 1901), where it was illustrated by naturalist painter Gunning King (1859–1940), than for readers of the American-Polish Chamber of Commerce's *Poland* (June–August 1924), where it was accompanied by studio photographs of real emigrants and boxed advertisements for package tours to Poland. Similarly dramatic shifts in meaning doubtless also occurred between the serializations of Conrad and Ford's Caribbean adventure *Romance* in New Brunswick's *St. John Daily Sun* (10 March–1 June 1906) and in the Dutch colonial newspaper *Amigoe di Curaçao* (6 March 1936–6 February 1937) and between the first appearance of *The Rescue* in Hilaire Belloc's conservative weekly *Land & Water* (30 January–31 July 1919) and its reissue as a 'photoplay serialization' by Elizabeth Meehan in Singapore's *Malayan Saturday Post* (30 March–20 May 1929).

The mediating influence of the editor is easily detected in this dialectic between periodical text and readership, especially during wartime, when underlying ideological bias often gives way to outright propaganda. After the Japanese Imperial Navy's historic engagement with Russian forces in February 1904 at Port Arthur (present-day Lüshun, China), the Tokyo magazine *Eigo Seinen* suspended its serialization of 'To-morrow' and immediately began serializing 'Youth' instead, justifying its decision on the grounds that the former (with its roustabout character who has sometimes been at sea) was unflattering to mariners; presumably, the latter story, with its sense of adventure and courage, was deemed more appropriate for a climate of national resurgence.[13] Similarly, when the New York monthly *Current History* extracted Conrad's 'Tradition' in May 1918, it juxtaposed his account of a ship being torpedoed with an article titled 'Typical U-boat Methods'. There can be no doubt here about the mood that the magazine's editors were seeking to elicit in Conrad's American readers: anger.

Long downplayed as a matter of financial expediency – a mere strategy for extracting double and even triple payment for writing destined to be published in book form – Conrad's lifelong involvement with periodicals is now acknowledged as a determining factor in the genesis of his major works and his reception by contemporary audiences. As the full extent of his sprawling presence in the international press comes into view, it is no longer possible to ignore serialization's role in shaping both the trajectory of his literary career and the peculiarly hybrid nature of his appeal to popular and *avant-garde* readerships. Barely a year after T. S. Eliot quoted *Heart of Darkness* in the epigraph to his landmark Modernist poem 'The Hollow Men' (1925), a ten-cent educational magazine could ask its audience of American high school students, 'Was Conrad a "popular" writer? Were any of his books "best sellers"? To what type of person do you think his writings would appeal?'[14] If nothing else, the history of Conrad's work in serial promises to overturn some commonly held assumptions about the answers to these questions.

By 1897, Conrad was the author of two critically acclaimed novels and three short stories in major magazines. Recognizing that he needed to secure a leading publisher's patronage, he began writing his next novel with the ambition of placing it in the *New Review*, whose editor, W. E. Henley (1849–1903), was a formidable backer of literary aspirants. Henley's selection of *The Nigger of the 'Narcissus'* for serialization in autumn that year was, Conrad later recalled, 'the first event in my writing life which really counted' (*Letters*, III, 115). The appearance of Conrad's novella in this particular periodical, with its crucial mixture of ultraconservativism in politics and avantgardism in culture, confirmed his accession to the ranks of Britain's literary elite.[15] While not lucrative in itself, serialization in the *New Review* conferred cultural capital that could be redeemed economically in several ways. In the short term, it brought Conrad's writing to the notice of prize committees, pension funds and influential publishers, such as William Blackwood (1836–1912), whose *Blackwood's Edinburgh Magazine* would soon serialize *Heart of Darkness*, 'Youth' and *Lord Jim*; in the long term, it established him as an object of interest for new literary magazines that aimed at reaching a mass audience, such as *Pall Mall Magazine* (est. 1893) and

Metropolitan (est. 1895). On this view, the serialization of *The Nigger of the 'Narcissus'* in the small-circulation *New Review* stands in stark contrast to the appearance (September–December 1923) of Conrad's last novel, *The Rover*, in the biggest selling monthly magazine in the world, *The Pictorial Review*.

Yet this easy narrative has been challenged by the recent discovery that *The Nigger of the 'Narcissus'* was syndicated in autumn 1897 in at least nine daily newspapers across the United States. That Conrad's writing should have been published in mass-circulation periodicals from the very start of his career is nothing less than extraordinary. Spanning the entire country – New York, Texas, Colorado, Iowa, California – this (apparently unauthorized) syndication brought the novel to an audience that was far removed, literally and figuratively, from that of the *New Review*. More numerous by an order of magnitude, these readers encountered Conrad's novella in highly truncated weekly instalments alongside local news items, display advertisements, features for women and a set of black-and-white cartoons by the artist George Young Kauffman (1868–1940), who had recently illustrated Stephen Crane's *The Red Badge of Courage* in *The Boston Post*.

Revealing Conrad's status as a marketable global commodity a mere two years after his literary début, the syndication of *The Nigger of the 'Narcissus'* illustrates the diversity of methodological and theoretical questions posed by serialization generally. How did American newspaper readers, many of them women, respond to this dense psychological drama of shipboard racial and class tensions? And why was Conrad deemed suitable for a weekly feuilleton in the first place? His American publishers famously changed the novel's title to *The Children of the Sea*, a decision that has variously been interpreted as the suppression of an offensive epithet and as a concession to readers prejudiced against stories featuring black protagonists. However, the novel was also presented to newspaper readers under its original title.[16] What does this discrepancy tell us about the different political sensibilities of newspaper readers versus book buyers or, for that matter, about the geographical disposition of book sales versus newspaper syndication?

We are not the first to weigh such matters. Conrad's peers were divided over the value of serializing fiction by major authors but in no doubt about its power to shape readers' experience. Thus a reviewer for the *Houston Daily Post* could assert that the literary merit of *Heart of Darkness* was guaranteed by its serialization in *Littell's Living Age* and *Blackwood's Edinburgh Magazine*, both 'journals ... of the highest order', even as *Lord Jim*'s appearance in the latter moved *The New York Tribune* to complain: 'As it runs through the columns of "Maga" the effect of serial publication upon it is appalling ... to an author like Mr. Conrad subtlety, atmosphere, mood, are everything, and how can they play their parts when the narrative to which they belong is broken into lengths and published month by month?'[17] For the most part, however, contemporary observers were inclined to see that serial publication offered an economic lifeline to struggling artists and a rare opportunity for cultural self-improvement to the great reading public. When New York's *Evening Telegram* began a daily feuilleton of *Lord Jim* in May 1903 – a serialization discovered only recently – the newspaper's editors explicitly cast the enterprise as an effort to remedy its author's failure to secure 'that larger acceptance that has been given to many a smaller man'.[18] In the same year, the popular British weekly *Black & White* went still further by suggesting that the advent of writers specializing in magazine fiction threatened to deprive literary writers such as Conrad of 'a great stimulus to good work – the serialisation of their novels ere they appear in book form'.[19] Whether a shaping force on the creative imagination, a time-capsule of reading events or a global network of textual remediation, the history of Conrad's work in serial promises to occupy the attention of students of Modernism for a good while yet.

NOTES

1 Christopher Morley, *Pipefuls* (Garden City, NY: Doubleday, Page, 1920), p. 40.

2 See Robert Steltenpool, 'The First Serialization and Translation of Conrad: *Almayer's Folly* in *Het Nieuws van den Dag* (Amsterdam), May–July 1896' (conradfirst.net/conrad/scholarship/authors/steltenpool).

3 See Robert Scholes and Clifford Wulfman, *Modernism in the Magazines: An Introduction* (New Haven, CT: Yale University Press, 2010), and Linda Brosnan, *Reading Virginia Woolf's Essays and Journalism* (Edinburgh: Edinburgh University Press, 1999).

4 Ernest Hemingway, *A Moveable Feast* (New York: Charles Scribner's Sons, 1964), p. 153.

5 For a discussion, see Stephen Donovan, 'Conrad and the Harmsworth Empire: *The Daily Mail, London Magazine, The Times, The Evening News*, and *Hutchinson's Magazine*', *Conradiana* 41, nos. 2–3 (2009), 153–77.

6 See, for example, the special issue 'Conrad and Serialization', ed. Stephen Donovan, Linda Dryden and Robert Hampson, *Conradiana* 41, nos. 1–3 (2009).

7 *The Daily Mail*, 2 December 1904, p. 7.

8 Cedric Watts, '*Nostromo* in *T. P.'s Weekly*,' *Yearbook of Conrad Studies* 3 (2007), 97–113.

9 [S. W. Reid], 'The Texts: An Essay', *The Secret Agent*, ed. Bruce Harkness and S. W. Reid (Cambridge: Cambridge University Press, 1990), pp. 249–59.

10 On these alterations, see the Cambridge Edition of *Victory, An Island Tale*, ed. J. H. Stape and Alexandre Fachard (Cambridge: Cambridge University Press, forthcoming 2015).

11 Marshall McLuhan, *The Mechanical Bride: Folklore of Industrial Man* (London: Routledge & Kegan Paul, 1967), p. 3.
12 For a full account of this epochal development, see Richard Ohmann, *Selling Culture: Magazines, Markets, and Class at the Turn of the Century* (London: Verso, 1996).
13 Personal communication: Yasuko Shidara.
14 *World Review*, 1 February 1926, p. 271.
15 For a detailed discussion of this topic, see Peter D. McDonald, *British Literary Culture and Publishing Practice, 1880–1914* (Cambridge: Cambridge University Press, 1997), pp. 22–67.
16 Curiously, *The Times* of Washington, DC, altered it to *The Negro of the 'Narcissus'*.
17 *Houston Daily Post*, 20 July 1902, p. 15; *New York Tribune*, 19 November 1899, p. 12. Accessed via the Library of Congress's *Chronicling America* (chroniclingamerica.loc.gov).
18 *The Evening Telegram* (New York), 2 May 1903, p. 6.
19 *Black & White*, 23 May 1903, p. 686.

7

J. H. STAPE

Texts

With rare exception, critical work on Conrad has been built upon surprisingly unstable foundations. Indeed, as will be seen here at least glimpsingly, stylistic and narrative investigations that have depended upon unreliable texts can arrive at conclusions that are unwarranted or that can be overturned by research into a text's history of production and dissemination. A recent example will suffice to show the perils of basing critical conclusions upon a received text that, as it turns out, is signally defective; subtle and discerning commentary on how the part and chapter divisions of *Victory* develop the narrative and affect pace are insecurely based, with several of the novel's divisions turning out to be the work, not of the author, but of the American editors tasked with adapting the novel for serialization.[1] The case is hardly an isolated one, and critics, their attention mainly engaged elsewhere, do not, for better or worse, generally interrogate the reliability of the texts they cite. A greater wariness about reliability that has set in during the past couple of decades in the wake of theoretical and technological advances in the field has yet to become or foment a universal scepticism.

As long ago as the late 1960s, it was realized that a scholarly edition of the Conrad canon was needed, preliminary research having revealed that the historical texts varyingly and – in some cases quite seriously – misrepresent the author's own work. During the decade following, closer investigation and scholarly discussion led to the birth of the Cambridge Edition of the Works of Joseph Conrad, with the intention of eventually replacing the texts in general circulation with reliable ones based on modern scholarly principles and practices. Actual work for that Edition – locating and describing the original documents, collecting the relevant book texts and serializations, and transcribing the primary and printed texts – got underway in the 1980s, precisely at a time when literary studies were generally in ferment, even upheaval, with the triumph of 'theory' seemingly assured, and when advances in digital technology gave a glimpse of new, more reliable comparisons required for a full-scale recension of long prose texts.

Enter Jerome McGann's 1983 *A Critique of Modern Textual Criticism*, an attempt to upset the apple cart in its vigorous questioning of what had until then been received wisdom in scholarly editing – the Greg-Bowers-Tanselle school that had held more or less undisputed sway.[2] The publication of Sir Walter Greg's foundational 'The Rationale of Copy-Text' (1951) laid down the central tenet of this school; that is, a base text – the 'copy-text' – was for well-reasoned arguments chosen and then emended by reference to the surviving evidence (usually original documents) in order to eliminate errors made by the author during drafting or engendered during the production process. McGann, who closely interrogated the adequacy of the copy-text tradition, proposed, by way of contrast, a 'social' view of texts that democratically celebrated the participation of the various agents involved in their production. Based upon the premise that instability is in the very nature of things literary, his argument was extended to a concept of versions of more-or-less equal validity, with the author becoming but one participant – the collaborator-in-chief, as it were – amongst several stakeholders in a given work's production. The view also fed into, and in part derived from, the then still novel idea of the death of the author, notably promulgated by the French theorist Roland Barthes, and it was, in a way, a continuation and elaboration of funeral rites celebrated festively in Paris, Prague and elsewhere. Whatever the ultimate value and applicability of McGann's views to long prose narratives – he himself was a specialist on poetry – the debate breathed new life into textual studies. It also helped to encourage a view whereby the provenance of a text being dealt with in the classroom or in one's study (or on one's tablet) should no longer be anonymous, lacking a clear 'parentage', or, indeed, any parentage at all.

Conrad studies have benefitted from this increased wariness about the source(s) and authority of a given text and from recent work on serials and versions. A scholarly generation or two ago, popular editions, widely cited in critical exegeses and intended for classroom use, could get away with making no statement at all about the text used as the basis for the reprint cited, whereas it is now commonplace to find editorial notes on this matter – even if not always wholly informed ones – in reading or popular texts designed for the university and general market. Both Penguin's 'Black Classics' series and Oxford 'World's Classics', for example, reflect the greater awareness that what the reader is offered needs to be identified. Even more, Conrad textual scholarship has by now firmly overturned the once widely held article of faith, based not upon actual investigation but upon a casual statement in a letter by Conrad that reflected a desire rather than a reality, that the Heinemann Collected Edition (1920–21) of his work represented his final word and would best represent his texts for posterity.[3] As it turns out, that venture proved to be only a frustrated testamentary act; although he supplied Author's Notes to the volumes of the series, Conrad ceased to be involved in the texts after the first few volumes were in print, whether overwhelmed by the new work he then had in hand or simply unexcited by the prospect of revising writing that, in some cases, was decades old. That collected edition underwent thorough editing by in-house agents so that unidiomatic or ungrammatical words and phrases were replaced with 'proper' ones and standard punctuation was imposed. As a result, the rhythms of Conrad's prose were damaged, and this meddling, however well intentioned, served to gentrify the writer, removing unsightly warts and making him appear more idiomatic and fluent in English than he in fact was, both in his early and even in his late career when the occasional infelicity could still occur.

The damage was initially confined, however, to that edition, concocted for the collectors' market and limited to 750 copies, its type being distributed after printing. It had no progeny until the Norton Critical Edition revived it for the American university classroom during the heyday of the New Criticism and when Conrad's reputation was at a high-water mark; boasting 'authoritative' texts, the Norton enterprise put into wide circulation the defective Heinemann Edition texts of *Heart of Darkness* (1963), *Lord Jim* (1968) and *The Nigger of the 'Narcissus'* (1970). The Norton editions not only revived corrupt editions that had quietly died an early, and well deserved, death, but also gave credence to a viewpoint based upon mere say so rather than scholarly investigation.

The rot, however, had set in much earlier than the Heinemann Collected Edition; Conrad himself saw into print, by force of circumstances – occasionally highly fraught ones – versions of his work that were variously imperfect. Errors began at his own desk. He could drop a word that was later guessed at by a typist; his attractive but somewhat florid and Continental hand on occasion offered insuperable challenges to his typists; in the haste to get his ideas down on a page he omitted essential punctuation; a word in dictation could be misheard or, because of his strong accent in English, misunderstood or it could not even be English at all ('inabordable' in *The Nigger of the 'Narcissus'*, 'invasation' and 'vertige' in the manuscript of *Victory*); he almost never referred back to earlier versions of a text when reading the typed transcriptions of his manuscripts or when proofreading; and at times a given manuscript or typescript was unavailable to him during production as he had already sold it before a book or story had seen its way into proofs. Typists could – and did – wreak havoc on sense, compositors played god with phrases that seemed wrong and editors systematically tidied according to both their own lights and house protocols. Magazine editors carved out chapter divisions according to the expectations (or presumed expectations) of their audiences, and long sentences and sinuously meandering paragraphs were systematically divided up into smaller units to conform with house-style practices.

The texts produced by these energies, variously applied, were undoubtedly 'social' ones; but they were not always those that Conrad himself had authorized other than, at the very most, in a passive or casual way. Desirous to see his work into print and earning his daily bread from it, he could wink at an imperfection or close his eyes altogether, as he did with the American serial market, which only rarely provided him with proofs.[4] Claiming to have an 'intense dislike for all these American humbugs in the publishing line' (*Letters*, IV, 306), he was mainly indifferent, or at least claimed to be, as to how his texts were treated in the rough-and-tumble (and normally quite lucrative) American marketplace that had been secured for writers of British and other nationalities by the Chace Act of 1890, which made provisions for copyright not previously obtaining in the United States.

Examples give flesh to these assertions and clarify the extent of the vexing, complex and sometimes insoluble editorial problems faced in the attempt to restore a text traduced by the non-authorial agents that helped see it into print. As it turns out, the 'Conrad' widely read and admired is not always, in fact, Conrad – even a century after his works began to appear in book and serial form.

As a writer, Conrad was not always his own best friend. Until 1917, he generally wrote out his work in longhand, either having his wife – not, as was long believed, a professional typist[5] – type it up for his revision or for sending directly to his literary agent, J. B. Pinker, to be typed by professional typing agencies. After *The Shadow-Line* (1917), which was partly dictated to agency typists, he produced the remainder of his work by dictation, working closely with Lilian M. Hallowes, a professional 'typewriter'.[6] From time to time he had resorted to dictation earlier in his career (*Nostromo*, for instance, was in part composed in this way), but at this stage it was not a matter of choice, his hand being afflicted by gout, a painful condition that prohibited regular and planned writing. As a result of this chosen method, Conrad's later work tends towards prolixity, and a marked stylistic looseness not free from grammatical or syntactical oddities.

His manuscripts are normally drafts, sometimes rather preliminary ones lacking normal punctuation, which, in the haste of composition, Conrad was not interested in supplying, the issue generally left to the typescript stage, when he added full stops, supplied inverted commas for dialogue and (sometimes) gave commas to interlocutory statements. At times, he almost seemed to invite his typists' active collaboration in delivering to them texts that were, at times, quite roughly hewn. Already by the time of *Lord Jim*, however, he had clearly tired of such intervention, writing atop pages for retyping: 'Type exactly as written', evidence that his handwriting and slapdash punctuation had previously proved problematic and had engendered 'correction'.

Conrad was conscientious about his work and took an interest in its graphic presentation, complaining, and even fussing on occasion, about type fonts, layout and binding, but even his best efforts did not always guarantee that his work got into print as he hoped it would. For example, the American compositors of the first edition of *Victory* misread his handwriting so as to alter the physical description of Martin Ricardo: 'He was a muscular, short man with eyes that gleamed and blinked, a harsh voice, and a round, toneless, pock-marked face ornamented by a thin, dishevelled moustache'.[7] The word Conrad added in proof was, in fact, not 'toneless' but 'colourless'. He had no opportunity to see the American revise proofs, upon which Methuen's English first edition is based; he read both sets of proofs under pressure and to tight deadlines, and if he looked at this passage at all, he overlooked this compositorial error. Both book texts contain, then, a description concocted not by the author himself but by a compositor unable to read his handwriting.

It can, of course, be argued that Conrad might have 'approved' the change, but the grounds for this assumption are weak, speculative and, ultimately, merely a kind of wishful thinking that would see the author in supreme control over every element in his texts, the responsibility for what got into print under his name absolute and unwavering. This is, in fact, far from the case, few authors enjoying such control once a work made its way off their desks and into the hands of others. Whether this is to be lamented or deprecated has now, however, become a matter of discussion. Another clear example of Conrad's having no control over what got into print is the case of the American serial version of *Victory*, published by *Munsey's Magazine* in its February 1915 number; Ricardo emits 'a grunt of astonishing ferocity as if proposing to himself to eat the livers of the local people'; the phrase 'the livers of' was interpolated by the American serial editor, and the English serial editor tidied out the phrase 'to himself'. This is a social text, indeed, but since the serials were not the basis of the book text, this description appears only in *Munsey's Magazine* in the United States and the London *Star* (derived from it), which audiences read in 1915 but which has until relatively recently been accessible only in archival collections.[8] In the scheme of things, this alteration, made at the serial proof stage, is small beer; the text of the novel as a whole is seriously flawed. American editors hacked the text about, changed Conrad's paragraphing freely and systematically and made hundreds of verbal changes that descended to the book texts so that a severely mangled version of the novel got into widespread distribution and has represented, or, rather, misrepresented, this work of Conrad's mid-period for a century.

The case of *Victory* is atypical in the extent of non-authorial intervention (traditionally styled 'corruption' in a textual discourse that also invokes the word 'purity'), but it signals problems that lurk for the critic who builds a case for a particular reading out of what can be a misreading, a casual mistyping or the deliberate interventionist proclivities of an editor or compositor. Whither, for instance, characterization, and even a subtler matter such as tone, in all this? In *Lord Jim*, for instance, the received text, until the Cambridge Edition of 2012 (155.28–29) corrected it, had the butterfly-collecting Stein assert 'Only one specimen like this they have in *your* London'. The manuscript shows that the emphatic 'your' (at best, somewhat odd in context) is merely an elongated capital 'T' from the next line, carried over by the typist as an underlining and in due course appearing in the print texts, duly and dutifully proofread by Conrad, as italics.

What case can be made for his 'approval' of this uninvited collaboration? Theoretically, at least, one might consider that the typist hit upon a happy formulation inadvertently; her work, as opposed to the writer's, serves to highlight the ethnic differences between Marlow the Englishman and Stein the German, ones even more preoccupying in 1900, when, in the years leading up to the First World War, England and Germany began to enter a period of even frostier relations than those of the novel's time period, the Bismarckian 1880s. The '*your*' then can be read as dramatically separating Stein and Marlow and bringing attention to a cultural divide: the triumph of rigorous German science over British amateurism. If not simply oddly inflected, the phrase arguably engages Stein, the sage of Semarang, in playing off ethnic rivalries. But this is not the author's emphasis, or at least was not so originally. It can be argued that it became so with his proofreading, although that would be to assume, on the part of a busy man already engaged in his next project, an attention to minute detail that is more the textual critic's province than the practising author's. The tone, in short, matters, and the emphasis is simply a casual typist's error, perpetuated in every reprinting of the novel throughout the whole of the twentieth century – and, even if in a minor way, disfiguring this scene and touching upon characterization. Interpretation can and does hang upon such thin threads. The error certainly leaves open the possibility that the readers of Conrad's time saw this in a light different than the author himself intended, and the critic who might cite this sentence with its *faux* emphasis would be led astray. A similar instance where the typist's work trumps the author occurs in *Victory* at an important juncture; the received text has Heyst regard the arrival of Mr Jones and his party as a 'visitation', a word the typist made out of Conrad's impossible 'invasation' in the manuscript, a rare and scientific word in French for 'attack' and in English best rendered as 'invasion'. The change in meaning is nothing less than dramatic.

Much larger issues than these illustrate the problematic nature of the received texts. Only with the Cambridge Edition are large-scale restorations finally available in the narrative texture of 'An Outpost of Progress', *Heart of Darkness* and *The Shadow-Line*. Conrad vigorously, and even with some spirit, objected – unavailingly – to the division of 'An Outpost' into two parts, made to suit *Cosmopolis*, which, like any magazine, needed to accommodate other articles in a given issue. Occasioned by the circumstances of the story's initial publication context, this division was maintained when the story was collected in *Tales of Unrest* (1898). The scholarly editor must decide between alternatives: Did Conrad forget his earlier strictures about the story's division? Or did he belatedly sanction the serial editor's work? Put another way, should the context of serial publication – no longer at issue – determine how modern readers read and receive this text?

The same question confronts the editor of *Heart of Darkness*, originally delivered to readers in three instalments of *Blackwood's Edinburgh Magazine*, and *The Shadow-Line*, which stretched over seven instalments of the *English Review*. In the latter instance, Conrad again objected to how his text was being carved into pieces, vigorously complaining to his agent that the magazine's editor, had been 'doling it out in drops, as if it were poison' (*Letters*, VI, 25). The pressure to retain the instalment breaks in the book form came from the publisher, J. M. Dent, who was keen to make a small book look larger by chapter divisions that would begin on a new page. Neither of these situations are now compelling reasons to perpetuate divisions to which the author himself objected, even if he did eventually concede to them, by force of circumstance.

A first-person narrative, reminiscent in tone and mood, *The Shadow-Line*, like *Heart of Darkness*, gains in intensity and thematic coherence by its presentation as a unified, continuous text, and the illusion of oral delivery (the 'confessional' aspect of its sub-title) is considerably strengthened by suppressing the arbitrary editorial divisions that are disruptive, on the one hand, and, on the other, even damage Conrad's explicitly Modernist project, informed by impressionism and famously enunciated in the Preface to *The Nigger of the 'Narcissus'*: 'to make you hear, to make you feel … above all, to make you *see*'. Conrad's contemporary editors both helped and hindered him in his self-imposed task.

As is the case for any major author, the critical editing of Conrad's texts demands bringing to bear judgement, and, although it is not a word much bruited in rarefied textual circles that aim a scientific objectivity, taste. It requires an in-depth knowledge of the writer's life and compositional habits as well as of period printing practices. In Conrad's case, an awareness of the influence of Polish and French can prove invaluable, some linguistic oddities explained by reference to his other languages. Editing is not merely a mechanical task, and the scholarly editor of Modernist texts must, like those of much earlier ones (as in the case of the Classics, for example), make decisions based upon evidence that is sometimes inconclusive and, on occasion, contradictory. Some decisions are water-tight; correcting a word that has simply been mis-transcribed or mangled by an amanuensis offers such an instance, and restoring the author's own work from the interventions made by an editor's red pencil another.

It might be well to point out that the word 'editing' itself is, and remains, notoriously porous as regards the several activities it describes. Writing an introduction to a cosmetically corrected reprint goes by the name of 'editing', although such projects have more recently involved the selection and justification of a copy-text (sometimes on not thoroughly examined grounds). By contrast, critical editing engages in the painstaking analysis of a given text in all its surviving authoritative forms, from original documents through to editions corrected by the author in his lifetime. The identification of relevant forms, their collection and accurate transcription, and their comparison and analysis are the lifeblood of this kind of editing, with the editor responsible for recording decisions in an apparatus that lays out variants and emendations, describing the editorial principles involved and arguing for the selection of a particular copy-text that is emended as warranted by the surviving evidence. In Conrad's case, scholarly editing is a complex and involved task because of the multiple versions that he saw into print, much of his work appearing in both the English and American serial markets as well as in book editions on both sides of the Atlantic.

There are also typically several preprint documents to examine, transcribe and collate. In the case of *Victory*, for instance, no fewer than thirteen versions of the text require collation: the manuscript at the Harry Ransom Center at the University of Texas at Austin; the Philadelphia Free Library typescript (two texts: the one that emerged as the result of the typist's copying of the manuscript and that revised by Conrad); the New York Public Library Berg Collection typescript (four texts – that produced by the typist, that revised by Conrad, and those altered by the American serial editor and the American book editor); the American and English serial texts in *Munsey's Magazine* (based on the Berg typescript) and the London *Star* (set up from *Munsey's Magazine*); the unrevised and revised states of the first American edition book proofs at Princeton's Firestone Library; and the first American and English editions. (The order is deliberate here: the novel was first published by Doubleday, Page, & Company in the United States, and Methuen's English edition was set up from a set of American revised proofs.)

Some scholars hold on to the authority of the first edition as an act of faith, as it were; this position absolves them from the nitty-gritty work of examining various widely scattered originals, whether in preprint or print forms. In Conrad's case, and in light of the complex circumstances of publication and printing, the authority of the first edition texts needs to be investigated and evaluated. The last in line in production, the book texts underwent cumulative interventions that, in some cases, seriously traduce both the author's meaning and stylistic effects. *Victory* illustrates this dramatically, with the first edition only intermittently authoritative, at times outrightly corrupt and, on a whole, seriously misrepresentative of Conrad's own work. A single paragraph serves to demonstrate the extent of intervention, both deliberate and inadvertent, by his amanuenses:

> 'Why do you want to stick here?' he cried. 'It can't pay you people to fool around like this. Didn't you worry just now about moving your governor? Well, the police would move him for you; and from Singapore you can go on to the east coast of Africa.'
>
> (First English edition, Methuen & Company, 1915, p. 154)

Shorn of the typist's 'corrections' and errors and the editorial interventions and cuts documented in the surviving typescripts, the authorial text, in fact, reads as follows:

> 'Why,' he cried, 'do *you* want to stick here? Have you got a fit too? It can't pay you people to fool around like this. Don't you worry just now about moving your – your governor. Well. The Police would move him for you. And you can get on to the East Coast of Africa from Singapore.'
>
> (TS1 235 revised; Free Library of Philadelphia)

The original typist – in this case, Jessie Conrad – failed to carry over the italics for 'you' in the first question, dropped the second 'your' in the third sentence – eliminating an effect of hesitation (or, given the ambiguous psychological relationship between Mr Jones and Ricardo, a subtle periphrasis) – and neglected to carry over the manuscript's capital 'Coast'. The serial editor altered tense and capitalization, made a clause where none existed and also repositioned a phrase. Schomberg's statements are bolder, more emphatic and even more aggressive as Conrad cast them; cumulatively, restorations of this kind to a critical text offer a subtly different version of this quintessential Teuton, who, in the received version, tends to speak in a somewhat hysterical fashion generally because of the exclamation marks given to his speech by *Munsey's* editors. No less telling an example of

Conrad's not getting what he wanted is the case of the following statement by Lena to Heyst, given first in the author's own form and then in its editorial ('social') one:

> 'You know it seems to me somehow that if you were to stop thinking of me I wouldn't be in the world at all.' (MS 502)
>
> 'Do you know, it seems to me, somehow, that if you were to stop thinking of me I shouldn't be in the world at all!' (Methuen, 1915, p. 188)

Myths, however, die hard deaths, and the editor of a reading edition of the novel, who also mistakenly asserts that no marked proofs survive, can claim, on the basis of the handful of mainly minor changes that Conrad made for the novel's first English edition, that that version 'preserv[es] the text that Conrad wished his readers to see'.[9] To the contrary, one must conclude on the basis of an analysis of the primary documents and printing history that the text of the novel Conrad wanted his readers to read, despite his efforts, never made its way into print at all – or rather did so only in part and mainly unsatisfactorily.

A frequent charge made against texts emerging from the close study of preprint documents and emended so as to reinstate authorial preferences over those of a variety of amanuenses – typists, editors, compositors, in-house proofreaders – is that these are not the texts that Conrad himself or his contemporary audience read. Those, of course, are available in the first editions and later reprints based on them. That these texts, even when discovered to be corrupt, should forever determine the 'Conrad' read by later readers, seems an odd proposition, but it is an unquestioned article of faith among some, based on an assumption that the author (theoretically, at least) had control over them and that that closes the case. An unwillingness to engage with, or even a fear of, textual eclecticism partly motivates this belief; national pride and even little Englandism seem to linger in the background ('English texts for English authors', to parody *Victory*'s Schomberg, who advertises his *table-d'hôte* as 'catering, "white man for white men"'); and several other premises, some naïve and others unexamined, stand unabashedly in the foreground. The overwhelming evidence demonstrates, to the contrary, that the texts of Conrad's fiction and non-fiction that appeared during his lifetime are, first, inherently 'eclectic', derived from several distinct stages of composition and revision, and, secondly, as we have seen, influenced by complex circumstances only varyingly under the author's control, with several agents responsible for aspects of them.

On the most obvious level, for instance, the texts that Conrad dictated saw control over their punctuation at least partly ceded to his typists, with consequences for rhythm and emphasis and, ultimately then, characterization. True, he went on to revise these texts after the sheets were removed from the typewriter, and his concern for his work was both professional and painstaking, but it was hardly absolute, and the work is, by necessity, 'social'. The typed section of *The Shadow-Line* indicates that the 'typewriter' (as typists were then called) hired to help complete the novella encountered problems in understanding Conrad's rather pronounced accent. She heard 'Won't' as 'Once', 'through' as 'to', 'came at' as 'cannot', and confused 'weary' and 'wary'.[10] Perhaps the most notable of these misunderstandings is the transcription of 'Forwards' as 'Four words' (in a sentence later deleted) and 'moral isolation' as 'mobilisation'.[11] Conrad often enough corrected his typists' errors and dealt with their misprisions, but, *mutatis mutandis*, others escaped his notice. For example, the received text of *Heart of Darkness* contained some thirty misreadings of Conrad's handwriting by his first typist (again, his wife), and only after more than a century have these finally been caught and corrected.[12] Not every error has signal consequences for interpretation, being variant wordings, but others most certainly do.

Engaging with the texts at this close level undoubtedly demythologizes the author as traditionally constructed, and the editorial theories and technologies now available allow, as is the temper of the age, for an indeterminacy that would largely have been unappealing a scholarly generation or two ago. One can, indeed, celebrate the wider availability of printed texts once, and not long ago, accessible mainly in archives and major libraries, sites of 'privilege' visited in person at considerable expense.[13] Electronic editions have encouraged active collaboration on the part of the patient and curious, laying out the genesis of a given text through variant hypertexts and encouraging a sense of a work as an evolving dynamic process rather than an achieved static entity passed on through time in a form that has remained (varyingly) stable.

No Conrad work has fully entered the digital domain, as have those of a number of canonical authors. Although copyright in Conrad's published writings has lapsed, that in unpublished work remains in perpetuity with the Conrad Estate. Assuming its cooperation, the true challenge might lie elsewhere; the physical forms containing Conrad's works are housed in several repositories, with, at times, the preprint materials for a single text being variously held, one archive preserving the manuscript, another (or more than one) holding typescript materials and still another preserving proofs. The collaboration of several institutions would thus be required even to lay the groundwork for such a venture, assuming the funding necessary for it and for converting the original documents into digital form. Unless, then, proprietary rights over the physical documents (a matter different than copyright) were ceded by the several stakeholders involved, the future of a digital Conrad remains uncertain, perhaps even bleak. In the best of worlds, however, one could celebrate, on a democratic model, the availability of all versions, preprint and print, to all comers for readers to make of them what they will.

The recent interest in versions has been stimulated by technological and theoretical advances in the digital humanities. Criticism has yet to assimilate this new material, and in Conrad studies this remains at an early stage, with a likely future development being a considerably more nuanced and sophisticated appreciation of the historical contexts in which his works appeared and were marketed to various audiences. This will also ultimately stimulate an even greater awareness of the complexity and diversity of his achievement. At the same time, the general reader's needs are still likely to be served by a single text, whether available digitally or in print. Making available the various versions in which Conrad's writings appeared is a useful preliminary stage that will allow, and no doubt encourage, detailed investigations by specialists, but the gap between the scholar, who will appreciate and perhaps even revel in the dynamic and shifting text(s) revealed by the availability of multiple versions, and the general reader, who will probably wish to approach a given work in a static and unitary form, might remain unbridged. The needs of that reader not interested in textual variants, hypertext possibilities or the innate instabilities of any Conrad text would, then, arguably be best served by a reliably produced edition that takes into account the plethora of material available but that, in the end, continues to privilege one text over several competing possible ones, with the scholarly editor presenting that unitary text in full awareness that it is but one of several that at various times circulated in print.

It may well be that future publishing conditions will allow for the wider recirculation, whether in digital or print forms – with contemporary production values – of the serial texts of *Nostromo*, *The Secret Agent* and *Chance*, for instance, reviving versions of these works produced at distinct historical and cultural moments. That would be a welcome development and assist in a real understanding of both the variety of Conrad's audience and the role these texts played in the shaping of his reputation and the complexity of the Conradian textual situation generally; however, it is unlikely to render redundant the need for research into the original documents, the contexualization that accompanies it or advanced textual scholarship and its traditional end-product in a critical edition, a project that, by its nature, is alert to the several, sometimes competing, forms in which a work originally and subsequently appeared. The historical analysis of a text's production is, and will almost certainly remain, a major scholarly endeavour requiring, as minimum conditions, not only the 'blear-eyed wisdom' gained only by frequent converse with the work itself and the canon as a whole, but also a wide knowledge of the social, political and cultural history of the period and the contexts of writing. This is to say nothing of a necessary bent for patient, close work, the *sine qua non* of textual scholarship. In short, the need for critical editions under the care of specialists, even in forms quite different than those currently available and still widely produced at present, will almost certainly remain, whatever theories of the moment might inform them and guide their production.

NOTES

1 See Fausto Ciompi, *Conrad: nichilismo e alterità* (Pisa: Edizioni ETS, 2012), pp. 191–5. Conrad only settled on the part and chapter divisions in the second typescript. The novel's four-part division is an editor's work, Conrad himself having divided the novel into five parts. For details, see *Victory, An Island Tale*, ed. J. H. Stape and Alexandre Fachard (Cambridge: Cambridge University Press, forthcoming 2015).

2 For a useful overview of contemporary trends and issues in scholarly editing, see *The Cambridge Companion to Textual Scholarship* (2013), ed. Neil Fraistat and Julia Flanders.

3 For a history of the Heinemann Edition, see Alexandre Fachard, 'The Production and Publication of the Heinemann Collected Edition of Joseph Conrad's Works', *The Conradian* 38, no. 1 (2013), 72–85.

4 For a discussion of the serialization of Conrad's work in the United States, see S. W. Reid, 'American Markets, Serials, and Conrad's Career', *The Conradian* 28, no. 1 (2003), 57–99.

5 On this issue, see J. H. Stape, *The Several Lives of Joseph Conrad* (London: Heinemann, 2007), p. 78.

6 For biographical accounts of these central figures in Conrad's writing career, see, David Miller, 'Amanuensis: A Biographical Sketch of Lilian M. Hallowes, "Mr Conrad's Secretary"', *The Conradian* 31, no. 1 (2006), 86–103, and J. H. Stape, '"The Pinker of Agents": A Family History of James Brand Pinker', *The Conradian* 34, no. 1 (2009), 111–43.

7 *Victory* (New York: Doubleday, Page, 1915), p. 112; *Victory* (London: Methuen, 1915), p. 101.

8 The website *Conrad First: The Joseph Conrad Periodical Archive* (conradfirst.net) has made digital versions of both texts readily available to the researcher, permitting access not only to the texts but also to their full original publication contexts. For further discussion, see 'Serialization' in the present volume.

9 'Note on the Text', *Victory*, ed. Mara Kalnins (Oxford: Oxford University Press 2004), p. xli. Some of the word forms that appear for the first time in this edition are clearly editorial – the correction of 'lie' to 'lay' and 'further' to 'farther' – and offer another warning that close investigation and the sifting of evidence, not *a priori* assumptions, must provide the basis for textual work.

10 *The Shadow-Line*, ed. J. H. Stape and Allan H. Simmons (Cambridge: Cambridge University Press, 2013), pp. 74.18, 75.12, 75.13.

11 Ibid., pp. 79.1, 101.20.

12 See the critical edition of the novella in *Youth, Heart of Darkness, The End of the Tether*, ed. Owen Knowles (Cambridge: Cambridge University Press, 2010).

13 The digitized texts available through Project Gutenberg do not always provide provenance and are of varying accuracy. The Internet Archive (archive.org) and the Open Library (openlibrary.org) make available page-views of several of Conrad's first English and American editions. The Bodleian Library provides access to Heinemann's (now discredited) Collected Edition. The Modernist Versions Project (mvp.uvic.ca) is currently engaged in a project that will provide access to various editions of *Nostromo*.

8

MICHAEL GREANEY

Conrad's Style

Conrad couldn't seem to decide whether or not he was a stylist. 'Style is a matter of great concern to me' (*Letters*, II, 460), he wrote to a friend in December 1902, a sentiment he would echo some two decades later in an interview with his French translator Henri-Durand Davray that stresses his '*souci du style et de l'expression*' ('concern for style and expression').[1] When quizzed by American interviewers about his style, however, he blithely dismissed it as 'something I never bother about',[2] a trifling distraction from the serious business of storytelling. It probably should not surprise us to find Conrad playing the roles of fastidious Gallic stylist and Anglo-Saxon plain-speaker with equal gusto. Such contradictory attitudes towards style are one small measure of the complex authorial persona that he developed during a life in which he changed his name, profession, homeland and language in a process of self-reinvention that was extraordinary even by the standards of a Modernist era of masks, personae and literary shape-shifting.

For some writers, the art of self-stylization is a pleasurable corollary of the literary vocation; for Conrad, who sought to fashion a coherent cultural identity from the formative traumas of political exile, cultural displacement and linguistic transplantation, it was an existential necessity. And for him the process was underway well before his début as a novelist. Perplexed by his Eastern European accent and foppish appearance, Conrad's fellow ships' officers, with whom he was not terribly popular, nicknamed him 'the Russian count'. His flamboyant dress – bowler hat, stylish tailoring, fancy trousers, gold-tipped cane and so forth – reveals an unexpected streak of dandyism in an author with a reputation for dourness.[3] But even the name 'Joseph Conrad' is a gesture of stylization that quietly assimilates elements of the author's Polish identity as Józef Teodor Konrad Korzeniowski into a new selfhood that is recognizably, but by no means exclusively, British. The process is continued and complicated by his use of narratorial personae, most famously of Charlie Marlow, who serves as Conrad's Anglo-Saxon *alter ego* in a number of works – although as we shall have reason to note, Marlow is, in some respects, hardly a conventional Englishman.

Nor was Conrad's English strictly conventional. '*Et puis l'Anglais m'est toujours une langue etrangère*' (*Letters*, III, 401)[4] he wrote to his marriage relation and fellow writer Marguerite Poradowska, in 1907. There is more than a whiff of false modesty in this claim – Conrad was, after all, writing in his capacity as the author of several major works of modern English fiction – but it is nevertheless true that he never quite achieved the kind of inconspicuous competence that would make his written English absolutely indistinguishable from that of native speakers. Tell-tale slips – odd choices of vocabulary or eccentricities of word order – occasionally reveal layers of French and Polish that are imperfectly buried beneath the surface of his prose.[5] In *Heart of Darkness*, when the Manager of the Central Station vents his exasperation with Kurtz's idealistic imperial rhetoric, he does so by growling '"Conceive you – that ass"' (76.6–7). 'Conceive you' is an intelligible but jarringly unidiomatic English transliteration of the French *Concevez-vous*. Would the dialogue have worked better if the Manager had said 'Can you believe it?' or 'Can you imagine it?' Or should we take the Gallicism as an indication that we are eavesdropping on a conversation conducted in French – that is, as a subtle reminder of the linguistic context of Marlow's journey in the Belgian Congo? We cannot rule out the latter possibility and, for this reason, cannot dismiss 'Conceive you' as nothing more than a regrettable linguistic blunder. Here and elsewhere, Conrad's tendency to hover *between* languages produces effects without which his writing would be all the poorer; his 'mistakes' generate new semantic possibilities precisely because they deviate from linguistic norms.

Working in a complex inter-linguistic space, Conrad achieved something far more impressive than mere competence in English; he acquired, with astonishing rapidity, a powerful and sometimes overpowering command of his adopted tongue, which in his hands became a curiously defamiliarized medium, capable of all sorts of rich and strange literary effects, and every bit as stylistically distinctive as the language of great Modernist contemporaries such as James Joyce and Virginia Woolf. One test of the distinctiveness of any literary style is that it is deemed parody-worthy, a test Conrad passed when he was imitated for fun by Max Beerbohm in 'The Feast by J*S*PH C*NR*D' (1912). Like many of Conrad's early fictions, Beerbohm's send-up has a dual focus: In the foreground is a glazed European expatriate, caught in a trance of inertia, while in the background is a luxuriant tropical environment seething with violence, beauty and unrecognized danger. In its response to that environment, the mock-Conradian prose of 'The Feast' faithfully imitates the portentous adjectival music of 'The Lagoon'.

The opening of Conrad's story contemplates a landscape 'unclouded and dazzling' (*TU*, 155.9–10), 'motionless and silent' (155.10), 'enormous and heavy' (155.14), 'perfect and final' (155.17–18); the landscape envisioned by the 'The Feast', meanwhile, is 'murmurous and unquiet', 'tenebrous and shifty', 'private and eternal'.[6] Parody of this kind affectionately hugs the original's linguistic contours and pays an indirect tribute to the imaginative power of the writer whom it spoofs. Further evidence of the sheer imaginative force of Conrad's style is provided by Graham Greene, who banned himself from reading Conrad for decades in a bid to shake off the overpowering influence of 'That Blasted Pole'.[7]

What were the components of this style? Conrad lists some of them in a self-deprecating letter of 1896 to his friend Edward Garnett that describes the imagery of 'The Lagoon' (1897): 'the usual forests river – stars – wind sunrise, and so on – and lots of secondhand Conradese' (*Letters*, I, 301). What might we add to this catalogue of stock Conradian imagery? Rattan screens, torch-lit campongs, bamboo fences and shady verandas; thrilling and chastening empty vistas of land and sea; unspeakable horrors tinged with a lugubriously playful sense of the absurd; secrets urgently trafficked between men in scenes of hushed nocturnal storytelling. There is, moreover, a distinctive Conradian syntax. He is fond of weighing contradictory extremes of experience against one another: 'the curse of life and the consolation of death' (*AF*, 85.23); 'The day of joy and of anxiety, of hope and terror' (*AF*, 111.9–10); 'the presented vision of regret or pity, of terror or mirth' (Preface, *NN*, x); 'The Claim of Life and the Toll of Death' (*Re*, Pt VI). Conrad's is an unapologetically high style that soars above the trivialities of everyday life to speak with sonorous Olympian detachment about the unavoidable truths of human existence. Needless to say, such a style is not without a strong capacity for bathos. In his evocations of intense, obsessive psychological states, Conrad occasionally lets himself be carried away by a breathy, rhapsodizing style that is too easily mesmerized by its own magniloquence. One such moment is the account of Tom Lingard's love for his brig in *The Rescue*: 'To him she was always precious – like old love; always desirable – like a strange woman; always tender – like a mother; always faithful – like the favourite daughter of a man's heart' (10). With these elaborate but uninspired variations on the ship-as-woman cliché, we do indeed seem to be in the presence of 'secondhand Conradese'.

There are obvious limits to what any simple catalogue of tropes, images and verbal tics can tell us about Conrad's style. Tempting though it might be to proceed by further itemizing his most conspicuous linguistic idiosyncrasies, we really need to attend to the *interactions* between Conrad's different voices and discourses in the context of his ambitious and elaborate narrative methods, if we are to get a genuine sense of how his prose works and why it is worth reading. His style, we will find, is typically divided between its commitment to the virtues of monosyllabic understatement and its appetite for expansive loquacity; it is tugged between a fascination with the immediacy of the human voice and its inescapable involvement in the impersonality of writing. It is also a demanding style whose idiosyncrasies have at times tested the patience of even his most sympathetic readers. Prominent among these demands is its implied insistence that if we are to become fluent in 'Conradese' then we must acquire proficiency in something that his heroes are not always very good at: waiting.

'"Kaspar! *Makan!*"' Readers of Conrad's first novel, *Almayer's Folly* (1895), have to negotiate a couple of unfamiliar words – a Dutch proper name and a Malay expression that roughly translates as 'dinnertime!' or 'let's eat!' – before the narrative settles down into something resembling ordinary English prose: 'The well known shrill voice startled Almayer from his dream of splendid future into the unpleasant realities of the present hour. An unpleasant voice too. He had heard it for many years, and with every year he liked it less. No matter; there would be an end to all this soon' (5.4–7). It would once have seemed appropriate to describe the world of *Almayer's Folly* as 'exotic', but we have learned to be wary of such labels. Postcolonial theory has taught us that there are no exotic places, only ways of seeing spaces as such, and the Western dream of South-East Asia as an exotic place – enigmatic and luxuriant, harbouring fabulous wealth and terrible danger – is one that Conrad's Malay fiction both perpetuates and calls into question. This ambiguity is there from the outset. An 'exotic' voice opens *Almayer's Folly*, but it speaks on behalf of the everyday rather than the oneiric or fantastical; it speaks an unfamiliar language but addresses itself to a decidedly non-exotic, humdrum necessity – food – that is sharply counterpointed to the nebulous fantasies of self-aggrandizement entertained by the novel's title character. It is also worth noting the *gender* of the first voice to speak in Conrad's first novel. Rightly or otherwise, Conrad has acquired the reputation of being a male-dominated novelist whose narratives are rooted in the masculine cultural activities of sailing, spying, gun-running, adventuring and trading, and whose fiction is pervaded by what one critic calls the 'dream of a homocentric universe'.[8] We cannot deny that there is at least some truth in this allegation, but we should also remember that the first voice in Conrad's first novel is a *female* voice that punctures a masculine dream of a self-centred universe.

Succinctly dramatized in the opening lines of *Almayer's Folly* is what we may assume to be an entirely representative non-meeting of minds between the protagonist and his wife. Almayer's inner life, as Jeremy Hawthorn has shown, is explored via free indirect style, that subtle compromise between third- and first-person narrative in which characters are narrated from within, brought to life by an anonymous narrator who participates in the conversations that fictional people have with themselves.[9] For example, the words 'there would be an end to all this soon' belong to Almayer – they are his unvoiced, desperately hopeful thoughts – but they also belong to the external narrator, for whom they mean something entirely different. Things *will* indeed be over soon enough for Almayer, but not in a way that remotely satisfies his vision of the future.

Already perceptible here is Conrad's ironic handling of chronological time, his sense of how easily life makes a nonsense of our efforts to articulate experience into meaningful and orderly temporal sequences. Almayer, in this scene, seems absent-mindedly unstuck from time – for how long, we wonder, has he been dreaming wordlessly on his veranda? – but he is soon plunged back into turbulent flow. The past, present and future of his marriage are sketched in these opening sentences – the dragging weight of those unhappy years, the painfulness of the here-and-now (the rhyme of 'present' with 'unpleasant' is suitably jolting), and the ardent, listless dream of a better future. We should note here that Conrad's prose stumbles, ever so slightly, in the phrase 'dream of splendid future', which should presumably be 'dream of a splendid future' – or perhaps 'dreams of splendid futures'. It does seem strangely apt that the prose should falter when it comes to expressing a clear sense of the future, the very subject on which Almayer is so notably cloudy and misguided.

'He hesitated for years' (24.11): these words account for Kaspar Almayer's protracted career of indecision. They also say, or imply, something about the significance of narrative hesitation in Conrad's style. *Almayer's Folly* is a novel that invites us to join Almayer in waiting, and to measure our capacity for patience against his. Not all of Conrad's readers have been happy with the tarrying, lingering qualities of Conradian narrative; Virginia Woolf, who greatly admired Conrad, reports with some regret that his style can be 'a little somnolent sometimes in repose'.[10] Conrad himself sheds interesting light on this aspect of his style when he ruefully describes himself as: 'the slowest writer on earth' (*Letters*, VIII, 63). He was talking about the excruciatingly ponderous business of literary composition when he said this, but he might equally have been reflecting on the artful sluggishness of his prose, the lingering style that doubles back on itself when conventional narrative would be keen to forge ahead. Progress, inhibited by all sorts of obstacles, can be a decidedly slow business in Conradian narrative. Getting anywhere takes time and patience, and anywhere might turn out to be nowhere. 'Youth' (1898) concerns a steamer that faces one delay after another and never reaches its destination. Some of the most significant journeys in *Heart of Darkness* are conducted on all fours. In *The Shadow-Line* (1917), the ship is becalmed in a windless Gulf of Siam for weeks. The central image of *The Rescue* – a novel begun in 1898, periodically abandoned and revived over many years and finally published in 1920 – is of a yacht stranded on a mudbank. Conrad was the master not of suspense but of suspendedness, captivated by the spectacle of what happens when things fail to happen and fascinated by how people conduct themselves in the limbo of delay and deferral.

Uncoiling with languorous indirectness, Conradian narrative often involves its heroes in the quintessentially modern, Beckettian predicament of waiting for nothing – for meaning that never fully reveals itself or relief that will never arrive. In an essay on the value of waiting, the philosopher Harold Schweizer defines impatient people as those who have no idea what to do with an 'unwanted gift' of time.[11] It is a gift that Conrad's heroes have a habit of squandering. '"To-morrow we shall see the steamer"' (*TU*, 93.25) is the mantra with which Kayerts and Carlier, the tragicomically inept Belgian trading agents in 'An Outpost of Progress' (1897), comfort themselves as they play out empty months waiting for external salvation from the absurdly inconsequential business with which they fill their lives. Captain Hagberd also lives a life of futile waiting in 'To-morrow' (1903), another tragicomic short story about the perils of locating meaning in a future that may never arrive.

Confident that the future will handsomely reward them for the time that they invest in waiting for it, Conrad's waiting subjects – Almayer, Kayerts, Carlier, Hagberd – are too eager sacrificing the present to the future to notice that there might be value in the *act* of waiting as well as in the object of waiting. In this sense, they misread the very texts in which they are represented. Waiting, in Conradian narrative, produces meanings even as it defers them. There is an important clue to the significance of Conradian narrative hesitations and suspensions in the surname of Almayer's mentor and father-in-law, Tom Lingard, the recurring though frequently offstage hero of the trilogy-in-reverse, *Almayer's Folly*, *An Outcast of the Islands* and *The Rescue*. Indeed, the split-second that we might need to hear 'lingered' in 'Lingard', and thus to sense that an aesthetic of deferral might be important to Conrad, is one small example of the kinds of meaning that Conrad's prose makes visible in moments of narrative or semantic delay.

Somnolence, repose and delay are stylistic traits that all contribute to what can seem like a peculiar unforthcomingness in Conrad's style, an unwillingness – or inability – to comply with the naive appetite for answers and revelations that all readers, however sophisticated, cannot but help bring to narrative. As the titles of some of his major works indicate – *The Secret Agent* (1908), 'The Secret Sharer' (1910) – Conrad is fond of writing about secretive people; what is more, he often does so in a style that can seem ostentatiously secretive, belabouring as it does the challenges of incomprehensibility, unrepresentability and unsayability that bedevil the modern storyteller. When his friend and reviewer Hugh Clifford remarks that Conrad is 'no apostle of the obvious' (*CR*, I, 307), he is putting it mildly. The narrative of *Heart of Darkness*, in particular, is notoriously thick with talk of what it cannot say. In this novella, the Conradian thesaurus of negations is seemingly endless: incomprehensible, inconclusive, innumerable, insoluble, indefinable, inscrutable, impenetrable, implacable, interminable, inconceivable, inestimable, impalpable, unspeakable, inadmissible, improbable, inexplicable, inaccessible, unapproachable, intolerable, incredible, inappreciable, incalculable, indistinct. Can any writer ever have been quite so verbosely lost for words? 'His style is like river mist', H. G. Wells commented in his review of *An Outcast of the Islands*: 'for a space things are seen clearly, and then comes a great grey-bank of printed matter, page on page, creeping round the reader, swallowing him up' (*CR*, I, 110).

The Cambridge critic F. R. Leavis was even less forgiving of Conrad's stylistic obscurity. *The Great Tradition* (1948), which makes an influential case for Conrad's eminent position in the literary canon, insists that the author's tendency to 'make a virtue out of not knowing what he means' is nothing short of disastrous for the style of *Heart of Darkness*. [12] Two responses are commonly given to these allegations of linguistic haziness. The first is that such strictures, impatient as they are for sharp outlines and definitive clarity, misunderstand Conrad's impressionistic way with words. Rather than aiming for a spurious clarity of vision, his prose wants to capture reality as it is subjectively perceived, with all its blurred edges and fuzzy outlines.[13] The second is that the Conradian language of negation and uncertainty is in keeping with modern philosophical scepticism about the ability of words to impart truth and meaning in any transparent or direct manner.[14] Acutely aware of the slipperiness of all verbal communication, Conrad's writing warns us that language is often at its most powerful when at its most duplicitous. Language is something that Conrad frequently denounces – think of the sinister eloquence of Kurtz in *Heart of Darkness*, the torrent of political verbiage in *Nostromo* (1903), or the fraudulent advertising campaigns of de Barral in *Chance* (1914) – but there is no question of his renouncing it. Suspicious of language but wholly committed to the practice of writing, he has no choice but to trust that words will own up to the truth of their own untrustworthiness. A style of uncertainty, hesitation and negation is one way of registering the force of that paradox.

For Conrad, our linguistic and cognitive relationship with the external world is never less than vexed. Plagued by misperception, false starts and faulty assumptions, subjective impressions must continually be revised and corrected to achieve a rounded view of external realities. The act of seeing rarely coincides with the moment of understanding, and the time lag between the two is often filled with dubious guesswork as we grope towards a secure knowledge of what we think we have observed. 'Delayed decoding' is Ian Watt's term for the 'double take' that Conrad's fiction so frequently performs in the face of vivid, confusing sensory input.[15] In *Heart of Darkness*, Marlow has a worrying habit of seeing innocuousness where he should be sensing danger: a flurry of little sticks proves to be a shower of arrows, whilst carved ornaments turn out to be human heads mounted on posts. In *Typhoon* (1903), Mr Jukes experiences an altogether more tactile version of delayed decoding as he flails and staggers on the deck of the *Nan-Shan*:

> as soon as he had commenced his wretched struggles he discovered he had become somehow mixed up with a face, an oilskin coat, somebody's boots. He clawed ferociously at all these things in turn, lost them, found them again, lost them once more, and finally was himself caught in the firm clasp of a pair of stout arms. He returned the embrace closely around a thick solid body. He had found his captain.
>
> (42)

Jukes plays a desperate game of hide-and-seek with reality in this scene, frantically fumbling for purchase on an external world that eludes his clutches as it disintegrates into a collection of disconnected things – a face, a coat, a pair of boots. He fails to get a secure grasp on things but is saved from chaotic uncertainty when things get a grasp on him, in the person of his commanding officer, Captain McWhirr. Intelligible reality asserts itself in the guise of professional authority and status, a truth that outranks – literally, in this case – the partial, confusing welter of sensory impressions in which Jukes flounders. But not everything in this passage is fully decoded. When Jukes and his captain embrace, they experience the kind of intimacy between men that extreme physical danger can license, a dangerous intimacy that frequently plays around the edges of Conrad's novels and stories. Currents of homosocial desire ripple between his characters, but the secret sharing of masculine intimacy is never fully acknowledged as an 'official' theme of Conradian narrative; rather, it remains ambiguously encoded in his texts long after other perceptual conundrums have been neatly decoded.

The darkness in which Jukes and McWhirr (re-)discover each other is, as always in Conrad, highly ambiguous. On the one hand, it is associated with uncertainty and diminished perception; on the other, it provides the opportunity for a hands-on encounter with reality. And this is by no means the only moment in Conrad where the 'downgrading' of the visual lets other regions of sensory experience come into their own. The darkness that so often engulfs his characters also makes possible a rediscovery of the traditional oral and aural practices that permeate, and often dominate, Conrad's fiction. Texts such as 'The Lagoon' and *Heart of Darkness*, where the narrative is framed as an oral report delivered at nightfall, position the storyteller as a nocturnal creature whose gift flourishes in the absence of the light on which reading and writing are dependent. Storytelling in Conrad is an activity that colonizes the night for truth, meaning and value; but, as we shall see, the oral culture that he wants to idealize is not lacking its own dark and disturbing qualities.

In its fascination with traditional oral culture, Conrad's fiction taps into a generative resource that Modernist literature, with its labyrinthine bookishness, often denies itself – word-of-mouth traditions that circulate between communities of tellers and listeners. Conrad's great contemporary T. S. Eliot once fantasized for himself an audience that could 'neither read nor write',[16] an unlettered audience receptive to the sheer music of his poetry. Conrad's fiction seems to harbour its own version of this fantasy, opening up as it does a space for stories and storytellers in a culture dominated by what he once called 'cold, silent, colourless print'.[17] His narratives often present themselves as having originated in an irrepressibly vibrant culture of gossip, anecdote and yarn-spinning whose traditional wisdom and companionable pleasures have been lost in the modern transition from oral to print culture. A sidelong glance at a newspaper vendor in 'Karain: A Memory' (1897) is enough to take in modern print culture in one devastating glance: 'a ragged old man with a face of despair yelled horribly in the mud the name of a paper' (*TU*, 48.40–41.1). Conrad perceived the mass circulation newspaper as a debased narrative form, a commodity pitched to everyone and no one by an anti-storyteller whose voice despairingly proclaims its own subservience to modern print culture.

The malaise of a culture cut off from the imaginative resources of traditional storytelling is also personified by Kaspar Almayer, who among his other woes, suffers from the predicament of being 'traditionless' (35.14). He has no story to tell, and even if he did he would have no audience to hear it, isolated as he is from the rich oral culture of gossip, rumour and myth that flourishes on the banks of the Pantai. Almayer's abject traditionlessness is exemplarily modern, and it points up the urgency of Conrad's attempt to reconnect novelistic discourse with oral culture, a project of 're-traditionalization' that finds its most characteristic expression in the narratives that he entrusts to Marlow.

Charlie Marlow, the storyteller in 'Youth', *Heart of Darkness*, *Lord Jim* and *Chance*, is the most significant of Conrad's raconteurs, a major technical resource but also an invaluable proxy self for his creator. For Conrad's biographer Zdzisław Najder, Marlow is nothing less than 'the embodiment of all that Conrad would wish to be if he were to become completely anglicized'.[18] But what kind of Englishman is Marlow? A ship's captain, he is an avuncular man of action who combines savvy practical awareness with a brooding, philosophical cast of mind; he has a genius for friendship, and a constant willingness to lend a sympathetic ear, and generous practical assistance, to men and women whom he finds in desperate circumstances. Puzzled by this unlikely combination of personal qualities and by Marlow's capacity for eccentric long-windedness, Henry James used to refer to him as 'that preposterous master mariner'.[19] Perhaps James was being more generous than he knew. Pre-posterous, in the sense of back-to-front, isn't a bad description of the way Marlow operates as a storyteller. His stories have beginnings, middles and ends, but not necessarily in that order. He has a habit of talking *around* his subjects at prodigious length in ways that sorely test his listeners' patience. If we measure a storyteller's impact by his ability to hold an audience, then we would have to concede that Marlow does not always meet with unqualified success. He often manages to lose or to alienate his audience in one way or another. Some melt away, or fall asleep; others are stung into protest by his calculatedly waspish asides. '"Try to be civil, Marlow"' (*YHET*, 77.39), says one irate listener in *Heart of Darkness*. Yet Marlow *is* trying to be 'civil' in this context. Unpicking the myths of progress in which Western imperialism likes to clothe itself, Marlow realizes that loyalty to civilization can entail a calculated flouting of some of its more trivial proprieties.

Marlow can be abrasive, and is more than willing to taunt and antagonize members of his audience; however, he is normally as generous as he can be towards the objects of his narrative. In this, he is the polar opposite of those storytellers in Conrad – notably the German hotelier Wilhlem Schomberg in 'Falk', *Lord Jim* and *Victory* – who aim to ingratiate themselves with their listeners by loudly denigrating others. Gossip, especially when motivated by destructive *Schadenfreude* or cruel prurience, circulates in Conradian narrative like a debased counterfeit of the authentic currency of traditional storytelling. His narratives are often sympathetically concerned with *victims* of narrative, those who have been roughly or unfairly treated by powerful voices, bullied by the language of others. Exemplary in this regard is 'Amy Foster' (1901), Conrad's reverse Robinson Crusoe narrative, a tale in which the people and landscapes of the so-called Home Counties become an unhomely *terra incognita* for the Carpathian peasant Yanko Gorrall when he is washed up on the shores of Kent. Yanko is on the receiving end of violence, abuse and fearful incomprehension from almost everyone he meets: pelted with stones, lashed by a whip, assaulted with an umbrella. He is also on the sharp end of the linguistic violence of gossip. The story is told, retrospectively, by Dr Kennedy, a raconteur of Marlow-like humanity; but on the fringes of 'Amy Foster' is a sizeable chorus of minor characters, all of whom chip in with their – usually unsympathetic – verdicts on the stranger in their midst. Those who have sighted Yanko variously describe him as '"a hairy sort of gypsy fellow"' (*TOT*, 118), a '"funny tramp"' (119), a '"troublesome lunatic"' (121), and '"a bit of a Hindoo"' (126). The advent of this needy stranger exposes some difficult truths about the cultural needs of the community whose hospitality he so desperately solicits: a need for a coherent sense of its own identity, its own story, its own limits – and a need to police those limits through acts of violent linguistic exclusion designed to keep the gypsies, tramps, lunatics and Hindoos firmly on the outside. If all storytellers were like Marlow or Kennedy, then Conrad would have been able to pursue his project of re-traditionalization with unalloyed nostalgia, but 'Amy Foster' shows that he was under no illusions about the power of the spoken word to divide and exclude.

'Amy Foster' is a characteristically Conradian meditation on the relationship between the power of language and the pathos of inarticulacy. Loquacious storytellers may provide one obvious model for Conrad's narrative methods, but those who struggle with words offer a no less powerful source of inspiration. Yanko Goorall, Jim, Stevie – none of these characters enjoys anything approaching linguistic fluency, but their stumbling efforts at self-expression invest their words with a pre-stylized authenticity that literary discourse cannot help but envy. In *The Secret Agent*, when Stevie utters the words '"Bad world for poor people"' (132.19), for example, he articulates, with a kind of stammering eloquence, what is perhaps the only authentic political sentiment in a novel of bad faith and rhetorical grandstanding.

Conrad's fiction often asks that we listen most intently and sympathetically to the words of those who are not at home in, or with, language. Consider, in this regard, the sublimely unimaginative Captain MacWhirr in *Typhoon*. Quotations from his comically phlegmatic letters home – '"The heat here is very great"', '"we fell in with some icebergs"' (5) – appear as patches of lifeless prose amidst the surging energy of Conrad's descriptive writing. But Conrad's narrator does not cite McWhirr's letters simply to hold them up as objects of mild ridicule; the text takes a lesson in understatement from the *Nan-Shan*'s laconic skipper even as it finds humour in his humourlessly unimaginative relationship with words. MacWhirr probably could not write a stylish or stylized sentence if he wanted to, but the novella seems to envy him his ability to live in a world of guileless plain-speaking and undemonstrative matter-of-factness, and the final sentence of Part 5 pays him a suitably understated tribute. Guiding the *Nan-Shan* through the Formosa Channel to Fu-chau, MacWhirr risks losing his vessel to a hurricane of ferocious power. Will the *Nan-Shan* be destroyed? Conrad delivers us from suspense with five simple words: 'He was spared that annoyance' (90). Here, the novella's style affectionately mimics the linguistic style of its taciturn hero.

If Conrad's fiction responds admiringly to plainness and inarticulacy, it often deals harshly with the stylish and the over-stylized. His most flamboyant stylist, the Frenchified journalist Martin Decoud in *Nostromo*, struggles to define himself in the absence of the kind of sophisticated metropolitan readership that he probably feels he deserves. It is hard not to feel that the novel punishes this self-regarding stylist by sending him into exile in a region where his gifts will not find an appreciative audience. Elegance and polish, fine writing and studied irony – anything that smacks of linguistic effortlessness is likely to meet with Conrad's disapproval. Undisguised *effortfulness* – what Fredric Jameson calls Conrad's 'will to style'[20] – characterizes his writing, a straining towards verbal and narrative inventiveness that has sometimes bemused more conventionally urbane and elegant stylists. Typical in this regard is Henry James, who, in his memorably supercilious review of *Chance*, declares Conrad to be 'absolutely alone as a votary of the way of doing a thing that shall make it undergo most doing'.[21] If we assume, in Jamesian fashion, that a good style is one that disguises the labour that went into producing its effects, then we will have to conclude that Conrad is not a very effective stylist. But if we understand that a necessary part of his will-to-style is a certain willingness, conscious or otherwise, to sabotage style in the name of truth and authenticity, then we will able to respond more generously than James to Conrad's prose.

If we can resist judging Conrad in Jamesian terms, we will also be in a better position to appreciate the quirks and hiccups of his defamiliarized English. From time to time, as we have seen, he will write a sentence that does not quite work. There will be a certain awkwardness or eccentricity in the phrasing. The sentence will not be quite right – but, awkwardly for us, nor will it be quite wrong. Even native speakers will struggle to decide on what counts as a 'mistake' in Conrad, because his polyglot English exposes the 'native speaker' – the privileged 'expert' who will generously applaud Conrad's many virtuosities and regretfully note his occasional mistakes – as an apocryphal figure. No one is born speaking the English language, and it takes a writer like Conrad, one of whose greatest achievements was to make English a powerful, awkward '*langue etrangère*' for all of his readers, to remind us of this.

NOTES

1 Cited in Martin Ray, comp., *Joseph Conrad: Memories and Impressions: An Annotated Bibliography* (Amsterdam: Rodopi, 2007), p. 33.
2 Cited in Martin Ray, ed., *Joseph Conrad: Interviews and Recollections* (London: Macmillan, 1990), p. 184.
3 Zdzisław Najder, *Joseph Conrad: A Life*, trans. Halina Najder (Rochester, NY: Camden House, 2007), pp. 129–30.
4 'And then English is always a foreign language to me.'
5 For more on the influence of Polish and French on Conrad's English, see Mary Morzinski and Véronique Pauly, 'Language' in *Joseph Conrad in Context*, ed. Allan H. Simmons (Cambridge: Cambridge University Press, 2009), pp. 18–25, and for a wide-ranging discussion of multilingualism as both the theme and condition of Conrad's writing, see M. S. Ray, 'The Gift of Tongues: The Languages of Joseph Conrad', *Conradiana* 15 (1983), 83–109.
6 Max Beerbohm, 'The Feast' in *A Christmas Garland* (London: William Heinemann, 1922), p. 113.
7 Cited in Norman Sherry, *The Life of Graham Greene: 1904–1939* (London: Cape, 1989) I, 311. For Conrad's influence on Greene, see the interview with Ronald Harwood in *Conversations with Graham Greene*, ed. Henry J. Donaghy (Jackson: University Press of Mississippi, 1992), pp. 90–6.
8 Nina Pelikan Straus, 'The Exclusion of the Intended from Secret Sharing in Conrad's *Heart of Darkness*', *Novel* 20, no. 2 (1987), 123–37 (126).
9 See Jeremy Hawthorn, *Joseph Conrad: Narrative Technique and Ideological Commitment* (London: Arnold, 1979), pp. 2–4.
10 Virginia Woolf, 'Joseph Conrad', *The Essays of Virginia Woolf: 1925–1928*, ed. Andrew McNeillie (London: Hogarth Press, 1986), I, 227.
11 Harold Schweizer, 'On Waiting', *University of Toronto Quarterly* 74 (2005), 777–92 (782).
12 F. R. Leavis, *The Great Tradition: George Eliot, Henry James, Joseph Conrad* (1948; rpt. London: Chatto & Windus, 1962), p. 179.
13 For Conrad and impressionism, see Eloise Knapp Hay, 'Joseph Conrad and Impressionism', *Journal of Aesthetics and Art Criticism* 34, no. 2 (1975), 137–44; Ian Watt, *Conrad in the Nineteenth Century* (London: Chatto & Windus, 1981), pp. 169–98; and John G. Peters, *Conrad and Impressionism* (Cambridge: Cambridge University Press, 2009).
14 For Conrad's linguistic self-consciousness, see Michael Greaney, *Conrad, Language, and Narrative* (Cambridge University Press, 2002); and Jeremy Hawthorn, *Joseph Conrad: Language and Fictional Self-Consciousness* (London: Arnold, 1979).
15 Watt, *Conrad in the Nineteenth Century*, pp. 175–9.
16 T. S. Eliot, *The Use of Poetry and the Use of Criticism* (London: Faber & Faber, 1933), p. 152.
17 'Autocracy and War', *NLL*, p. 71.16.
18 Najder, *Joseph Conrad: A Life*, p. 267.

19 See Ford Madox Ford, *Joseph Conrad: A Personal Remembrance* (London: Duckworth, 1924), pp. 160–1.

20 Fredric Jameson, *The Political Unconscious: Narrative as a Socially Symbolic Act* (London: Methuen, 1981), p. 200.

21 Henry James, 'The Younger Generation' in *Selected Literary Criticism*, ed. Morris Shapira (Cambridge: Cambridge University Press, 1981), p. 331.

9

PETER LANCELOT MALLIOS

Conrad's Reception

One writes only half the book; the other half is with the reader.
Conrad to R. B. Cunninghame Graham, 5 August 1897
(*Letters*, I, 370)

What does the body of work and thought we refer to as 'Conrad' mean to other people? How has 'Conrad' been read at different times and places and among different communities of readers? What elements in his writings prompt and connect, and divide and differentiate, these responses?

These are questions of reception. In a certain sense, they are the oldest and most foundational questions the writer has to offer. For Joseph Conrad has always been known as a writer of unusual international range and implication, his works subject to their vantage points. His writings not only offer unusually wide latitudes of response, but also require those latitudes to do full justice to understanding those writings and the world they represent on such a wide canvas. Counterpoint has thus been an essential motor of Conrad's reception throughout the twentieth century and into the twenty-first. His various British, French, Irish, Polish, variously European, widely colonial and postcolonial, American, Asian, male and female, radical and conservative, seafaring and white collar, aristocratic and popular, critical and creative readers and rewriters have all driven his reception in complex response to one another, each contributing special vantage points in important ways unavailable to the others. More so than for most literary authors, to talk about reception is to talk about the only way to know Conrad and the world to which he lays claim; half of his books really does lie with other readers, upon whom one is unusually dependent.

Reception, moreover, is built into the foundations of his art of fiction. When the frame narrator of *Heart of Darkness* famously describes Marlow's mode of storytelling as one in which 'the meaning of an episode was not inside like a kernel but outside, enveloping the tale which brought it out only as glow brings out a haze' (45.36–38), this is in part a commentary on

Conrad's own experimental fiction, whose meaning so significantly depends upon the outside and enveloping presence and power of the reader. Similarly, reception is a central concern raised by many other signature aspects of Conrad's writing, including dramatized relations between narrators and audiences and impressionistic and otherwise indeterminate registers of language foregrounding the need for the reader's interpretive collaboration to make meaning. In the Preface to *The Nigger of the 'Narcissus'*, Conrad describes his 'task' as an artist as 'by the power of the written word to make you hear, to make you feel – it is, before all, to make you *see*' (p. x). Even as these words come to emphasize sight, the true underlying emphasis falls upon 'you'. It is the bridge with the reader, or rather, the management of the fundamental unruliness and autonomy of readers in their acts of reception, that is the fundamental concern driving the technical and sensory imperatives of Conrad's art, not the other way around.

To some extent, the pursuit of difference (that is, differences of perspective, place, culture and modes of understanding and expression) and its management, even its erasure and containment, lie at the core of how Conrad's writings have been received since they were first published. Yet this emphasis on difference, and the importance of differences of interpretation generated from different places and times that it implies, does not preclude several strong continuities interlinking different moments of Conrad's reception.

Perhaps most striking among these is a paradox of intermittent prophecy. On the one hand, every generation of Conrad's readers has had occasion to remark his works' hauntingly prescient anticipation of so many baseline aspects of twentieth and twenty-first century psychological and political experience. Writing in the context of the First World War, the British publisher J. M. Dent observed to Conrad in 1916: 'We are witnessing the birth throes of a new world, and you of all men, it seems to me, should be the prophet of its psychology' (*Letters*, V, 681 *n.* 5). Since that time, Conrad's anticipations of failed internationalist idealism after the First World War, the Russian revolution and autocracy, fascist atrocity and psychology, imperialist crisis and decolonization, economic globalization, transnational human movements of migrants, refugees and diasporic populations, terrorism, crises of democracy and mass media ecology and more have all been observed – as if Conrad stands to greet each post-1900 generation at the threshold of some of its own most vital concerns and challenges. This is so, one should add, even though Conrad relentlessly parodies the idea of 'prophecy' in texts like *The Secret Agent* and even as many commentators have objected to the specific representational claims he advances about the modern and postmodern world, whose general fault-lines he nevertheless seems to perceive with unusual breadth and clarity.

Yet at the same time, Conrad has also proved unusually vulnerable to receding from view and being forgotten for significant stretches of time during the course of the 'long' twentieth century. If he is in rare literary company when it comes to anticipating concerns of political, human and expressive consequence, he has also been subject to much more volatile fluctuations in reputation and attention than his modern literary peers. His interest seems to have proceeded through recurrent and uneven cycles of rise and fall, rather than following any consistent standard of recognition, simple linear pattern of rise or decline or the more abrupt model of 'sea change'. During his lifetime, Conrad's earlier critical but not popular recognition was followed in the 1910s and early 1920s – *after* most of his major works were written – by soaring heights of both popular success and general critical acknowledgement, affirming his status as England's finest living novelist and a permanent figure in the English literary pantheon. By the time of his death in 1924, however, debate on these latter points was so severe that a critic could credibly write:

> We begin to see … that he was not the great stylist we had fancied, that he has had no influence on either the popular imagination or even his fellow-artists, and that … he does not lie in any English tradition at all, nor has he in the least influenced English thought or English writers as lesser artists have done.
>
> (*CR*, IV, 540–42)

Similarly, the critical reception of Conrad since his death has been anything but stable in its intensity. Although one should be wary of oversimplification, as Conrad has too many audiences, many of which we are still discovering and recovering, to fit neatly any standardized pattern, there is important truth in the proposition that after a relative disappearance from critical consideration in the later 1920s and 1930s, there have been strong renewals of interest in Conrad arising out of the Second World War and its ensuing contexts of the Cold War; out of the later 1960s and 1970s, harnessing critical energies from both decolonization and post-structuralism; and out of the dawn of the twenty-first century, as it has come to seem that the 'end of history' is no more settled or satisfying, nor certainly any less globally interdependent in its troubled irresolution, than it is at the end of *Nostromo*. These surges, moreover, dependably succumb to periods of dissipated interest in Conrad, in which Conrad seems more alone and outside established 'traditions' than ever before, and these cycles of renewal are further accompanied by remarkable upheavals of assessment, rises and falls, concerning as well which texts constitute the 'major' Conrad.

One reason why Conrad has consistently cycled back into view is that, at the turn of the twentieth century, he perceived acutely, if not necessarily prophetically, certain historical conditions and possibilities of expression and critical and moral reflection that have continued deeply to frame and implicate the world since. There are also more general qualities of interest (qualities of loneliness, of fatality and tragedy, of the necessity of illusion, of the deceptive nature of language and inescapability of 'ideas') whose history and potentialities of appeal are not so easily reducible to twentieth-century concerns or even those of modernity more generally. But if there is an answer to the specific paradox of prophetic volatility that seems to characterize Conrad's reception over time, if there is a means of accounting for both his fluctuating patterns of interest and the extraordinary differences of voice and concern that become articulated in relation to him through those swings of interest, the answer may lie somewhere in between history and the abstract, in Conrad's status not simply as an artist of particular historical developments but, in light of them, as an artist of modern historical unrest and its crises of transition.

In November 1914, the American critic Van Wyck Brooks described Joseph Conrad as the defining writer in an 'epoch of alien turmoil' in whom 'the spirit of revolt, of 'unrest' is prefigured'.[1] Since that time, Conrad has tended to become 'received' in moments of upheaval, with the very controversial nature of his reception and understanding in those moments – debate, tension and dialogue generally constituting the mechanism of Conrad's assertion – being connected to those conditions of upheaval. In moments in which social limits are being called into question, Conrad, as a bard of borderlands and a strange, perhaps even exotic, combination of impulses of radicalism and conservatism, finds the horizons of his own fiction's meaning changing – and his fiction itself becoming acutely, if ever provisionally and unstably, at public issue.

These are propositions one can explore by considering what the late Terry Collits has called four different 'moments' in Conrad's critical reception.[2] These moments are tied to particular places and communities of Conrad's readers, themselves subject to reconsideration through the on-going recovery of others. Many other moments and vantages could be chosen, but these four, which have in various ways predominated in English-language criticism of Conrad during the past century, are illustrative of significant terms and patterns that have recurred in his reception while also highlighting key differences – and relationships to difference – that have emerged over time. Reception is a vital centre of the study of Conrad today, and it is through engagement with past modes that one is able to apprehend new modes and opportunities of discerning the writer's reception in the past and on into the future.

The Original Moment: Britain, Ireland, the United States

The first critical moment is Conrad's popular and critical reception during his lifetime in Britain, Ireland and the United States. These were dominant sites of Conrad's publication and review, although there were also important European, British colonial and other world markets and communities of reception for his writings.

The importance that ideas of 'unrest' and 'horizon' play in Conrad's reception during this period is usefully suggested by the map of the writer's works, widely reprinted by his publishers and in contemporary newspapers and periodicals, that first appeared as the front endpapers of the first American edition of *Victory* (1915).[3] Commissioned by his publisher, F. N. Doubleday, as part of an aggressive marketing campaign, the map plots the settings of Conrad's works and their sea-voyages against the backdrop of the world. These bearings are presented through a tangle of bold red circled numbers, labels and dotted lines that touch and interpenetrate every Asian, Australian, Latin American, African, Russian and maritime space the map offers – all the world, with the conspicuous exception of the United States, the one blank country simultaneously at the map's centre and in excess of which all of Conrad's grounds for provocation extend.

Explicitly designed for American audiences, the map thus presents Conrad as a writer of interest precisely in the comprehensive access he offers to the world as it exists beyond American domain, knowledge and experience. This appeal, moreover, is deeply rooted in contemporary conditions of national and global unrest. American readers would quickly embrace *Victory* – the tale of a man of profoundly isolationist temperament who perilously, although perhaps heroically, becomes involved with the world – in part because they understood it as a haunting echo of their anxieties about entering the First World War. More generally, Conrad's fiction served Americans during this crisis period and its aftermath as a means of accessing and understanding, as well as engaging and debating with, a larger world whose vast latitudes of political and social convulsion could no longer be distinguished from their own.

Doubleday's map thus suggests something of the wide field of concerns, international and domestic (for the map raises questions not only about the place of the United States in the world but also about its comparative and circumscribed implications for it), which helped propel Conrad's remarkable rise as a popular and critical celebrity in the United States during and after the war.[4] But the map also falsifies as peculiar to one nation qualities of estranged and expanded borders that are, in fact, characteristic of Conrad's works and reception more generally. For Conrad's fiction is presumptively set in distant and 'alien' places, at least as concerns most of the dominant audiences the writer assumed and even as audiences from those places have long and actively responded – often with their own senses of estrangement – to Conrad as well.

In Britain, one finds a sense of Conrad's writing of what lies beyond the horizon present from the earliest reviews of *Almayer's Folly* (1895): 'To the wearied reader', one reviewer writes, 'there is nothing so fascinating as the discovery of a new world' (*CR*, I, 23). A central line of British reception follows this lead, emphasizing Conrad's 'unusual fund of first-hand knowledge of the out-of-the-way places of the earth' and his 'special power of conjuring up for the reader an alien environment' (*CR*, I, 217, 388) – whether it may be the Malay Archipelago, sea-life in the merchant marine, the Congo under Belgian misrule, an imaginary country in Latin America, political enclaves in Russia and Geneva, or, especially as observed by Irish reviewers, the invisible coordinate of Poland that for some arguably underwrites all of Conrad's fiction, making that fiction unusually expressive of 'oppressed peoples' generally (*CR*, IV, 71–2).

Observing these various frontiers of expanded insight and imaginative accountability, Edward Garnett, Conrad's friend and arguably his best reader of this period, wrote: 'The artist has spoken: a new world finds voice, and we understand. The blank solid wall of the familiar, the strange world of new and old that fronts the puzzled sensations of those peoples far away, has melted away before the artist, and he has seen in everything the *significant* fact' (*CR*, I, 255). Concentrating specifically on English thought, Garnett crucially adds in two later essays that Conrad's 'especial interest' lies in his 'liberating force to our English insularity. The scope of his valuation is not bounded by the special illusions our English society cherishes'; 'it is good for us English to have Mr. Conrad in our midst visualizing aspects of life we are constitutionally unable to perceive' (*CR*, II, 471, 369).

The politics, of course, of all these appeals to English spheres of experience are complicated. Those reviewers who extolled Conrad for imaginatively 'annexing Borneo' or becoming the 'Kipling of the Malay Archipelago' (*CR*, I, 13, 47) were not experiencing a shift in British imperial thought so much as extending and reinforcing basic premises. Moreover, the many reviewers who objected to Conrad, ever the subject of controversy in his courting of 'other' viewpoints, did not necessarily object to the stereotypes in which he too trafficked. What makes Garnett's formulations especially helpful, however, is their ultimate concentration less on capturing all the truths of the world's distant places and peoples than on demonstrating how contact, however variously well or little Conrad might have known them, resulted in estrangement of the British point of view.

Many reviewers followed Garnett in observing that it is not simply distant spaces *beyond* the horizon but rather the hybrid spaces at the *borderlands* of the horizon that provided Conrad with his true subject matter. These spaces 'at the edge of the [known] world' (*CR*, II, 22), 'on the borderland of the possessions of the Dutch in Asia' (I, 88), in various 'little-known borderland[s] between civilization and barbarism' (I, 219), featuring 'boundary rider[s]' (II, 46) and 'communities with their curious blending of races – Malay, Arab, Chinese, European' (I,146), and presenting 'strange links [between] civilizations' (I, 297) – these are the spaces of contact through which British thought becomes troubled, challenged and estranged, comparatively and contingently exposed as less stable; less probative, singular and distinctive; less natural, moral and legitimate; and less comprehensive in understanding than one had thought.

The borderlands of Conrad's fiction thus provide as much a battleground of British self-and-world understanding as in the United States, albeit open to different concerns and vantages of unrest. Moreover, Conrad's art as well is continually received in terms that reflect these concerns of limit and borderland. For contemporary commentators, the significance of his artistic creations was not simply that they had 'broken new ground', that the writing is so original and unprecedented in form and mode that it 'leaps at once to a place of his own' (*CR*, I, 148, 5); it is also that as Conrad writes in what might seem radically alien ways, he estranges English fiction by establishing how many of its conventions – of plot, linear form, character, sentimentality, didactic message, space and subject, romance machinery – the art of fiction can do without. For these commentators, he further made a borderland of English literary fiction, not only by importing influences from French, Russian, Polish and other literary traditions, but also by combining and hybridizing, within his practice of English fiction, oppositional aesthetic categories – of aestheticism and naturalism, realism and romance, visual art and the oral tale, non-fiction and fiction, popular genre and high art, short story and novel – whose separations the field of English writing had relied upon as a matter of its own fundamental sense of organization and self-understanding.

The Humanist Moment: The 1940s and After

A second critical moment arose during the Second World War and in its aftermath with Conrad's institutionalization in universities as a 'great' literary figure in English literature and the modern novel. Drawing energy from economic critiques predating the War and concerns of British imperial decline and Cold War culture following it, Conrad criticism during this period nevertheless tended to position itself at some remove from politics, with the 'prophetic' Conrad less a part of than a superior and anterior vantage from which to gain an understanding of the whole – and its fundamental human stakes and elements. Although significantly diverse and contentious, this moment of reception is generally 'humanist' in the sense both that its practitioners looked to the writer as an instrument of humane and humanizing culture and that they understood 'Conrad' to cast valuable light on the fundamental question of what it means to be human.

In Britain, the seminal figure of Conrad's humanist inception was the upstart Cambridge professor F. R. Leavis (1895–1978), co-founder of the influential journal *Scrutiny*, begun in the early 1930s as a forum to re-imagine and justify the study of 'English' literature in higher education and for society generally. In *The Great Tradition* (1948), Leavis draws on essays originally published in *Scrutiny* in 1941 to lionize Conrad, along with Jane Austen, George Eliot, Henry James and D. H. Lawrence, as the central figures of the English literary tradition of the novel. Although the 'foreign' Conrad might seem a peculiar choice to centre so self-consciously 'English' a sense of tradition, Conrad in fact, precisely because of his 'uprooted' and 'deracinated' qualities and sensitivities, becomes the perfect interlocutor of the vision of English literature and its social purposiveness that *Scrutiny* had been trying to articulate for nearly a decade. It is a vision that, with the coming of the Second World War and the opportunities of institutional reform it would eventually entail, Leavis sought to use to transform education to meet contemporary and continuing problems of British domestic and international unrest.

Although its specific strategies evolved over time, *Scrutiny*'s central project throughout its existence was to challenge and check the destructive forces of modern industrialization, mass commercialization and scientific efficiency on humane culture and society. This project was to achieve its ends not by adopting a Marxist alternative, whose industrial premises Leavis understood to replicate the underlying problem, but rather by imagining a longstanding organic tradition of English culture, epitomized in its literature and extending from before and semi-autonomously across the nation's historical phases of industrialization, through which capitalist excess could be contained and held to humane critical account.

Conrad was a remarkable fit for this project of critical and moral awareness, which in important ways transposed Matthew Arnold's nineteenth-century vision of 'Culture' to twentieth-century terms. For in Conrad's signature sensitivity, beginning with his departure from Austrian Poland to horizons of thought and culture that become displaced from and embattled in their sense of grounding, his works mirrored the basic condition of corrosion and deracinating atomization posed – in Leavis's view – by modern industrialization to traditions of English culture. Moreover, in Conrad's emphasis on fidelity, solidarity and disciplined commitment to time-sanctioned traditions, social formations and communities as a locus of value against the shocks of history, his works licensed the intense imagining of a trans-historically continuous 'organic' English culture whose critical and humanely redemptive power was at the heart of Leavis's vision. Indeed, in Conrad's specific distaste for industrial modernity; in his resistance to capitalist celebration combined with a refusal to embrace Marxist counter-measures; in his odd combination of radical political critique and ultimate conservatism; and in his very fascination with looking backwards and exploring the compulsive appeal of anterior and romantic myth for its energizing critical value (and liabilities and perils) in the present, Conrad offered Leavis a highly congenial frame, less for asserting a particular political point of view than for claiming an external vantage – in literature – from which critically to understand and humanely to account for the conduct of politics generally. His works were not simply 'great' instances of the English novel; they implicitly instanced an entire programme of understanding the form's social purposiveness.

At least two significant developments extend from Leavis's formulation of Conrad. First, it effectively takes the central antagonism of Conrad's reviews and commentaries of the earlier period – that is, the debates concerning whether Conrad, estranging as he is, ultimately confirms or undermines a dominant and normative British point of view – and integrates both sides into a harmonized new order in which idealized English culture itself is defined precisely by its capacities to elicit critical estrangement and resistance – to produce 'misfits', as a colleague of Leavis wrote[5] – with respect to dominant economic and social forces. It is *order*, and, indeed, a strangely uniform and generalized conception of moral order, not to mention 'misfits', that Leavis ultimately emphasizes, whereas in the earlier period conflict predominated. But it is a distinctive characteristic of Conrad's reception across time that his works seem simultaneously to prompt strong assertions of both order and resistance, each often articulated in the same period or even instance, perhaps because his fictions understand these two temptations as vitally connected.

A second development is Leavis's instigation of academic debate about *which* Conrad texts are truly 'great'. Ever provocative, he famously characterized *Heart of Darkness* and *Lord Jim* as deeply compromised and overrated texts. The 'adjectival insistence on inexpressible and incomprehensible mystery' in the former showed Conrad 'making a virtue of not knowing what he means';[6] in both texts, Conrad almost wilfully failed to offer the clear expression of human psychology and its relation to the social world that is essential for English fiction's redemptive power.

Nostromo and *The Secret Agent*, on the other hand, although widely undervalued during this period, are two masterpieces not only of the Conrad canon but also of English literature because of their epic dramatization not of the obscurities of individualized psychologies but of social totalities as they frame human experiences of engagement with history. *Under Western Eyes* and *Chance* are also major novels, but not more so than *Victory*, which, despite its melodramatic materials, is the one text 'that answers most clearly to the stock notion' of Conrad's 'genius'.[7] For the novel witnesses Conrad's most careful, intimate and perspicuous contemplation of what it means for a human being to be uprooted and isolated from any grounding and integrative organic community or tradition. All of these judgements, a direct assault on earlier assessments of Conrad as fundamentally an 'exotic' or 'sea' writer, deeply extend from Leavis's larger humanist purposes driving him to Conrad. And they set off, or at least rekindled with vitalizing energy, a debate concerning which Conrad texts matter most that has continued to drive – and remain unsettled in – his reception ever since.

In the United States, organicist efforts to understand Conrad have significant parallels with Leavis, notably among Southern critics coming out of the Vanderbilt Agrarian Circle; Robert Penn Warren's 1951 introduction to *Nostromo* is the masterpiece of this line.[8] However, for the most part, the American renaissance of interest in Conrad during this period strikes a different note, perhaps most distinctive in two works emphatically psychological in emphasis: Thomas Moser's *Joseph Conrad: Achievement and Decline* (1957) and Albert J. Guerard's *Conrad the Novelist* (1958), the latter building on his shorter book *Joseph Conrad* of 1947. Advancing one of the two most perennially revisited claims[9] in all of Conrad's reception – that is, that the works fall into two phases, one of achievement (through 1911), then of decline – Moser makes his case through a Freudian analysis of sex and women as 'uncongenial' subjects to the writer's mind and imagination, marring his fiction when they assume a prominent role. Guerard's book issues as forceful a claim to Conrad's significance to the modern novel as Leavis's does to the English one. But Guerard writes as a fellow novelist and without Leavis's sense of programme; his fundamental concern is with the art and technique of the fiction as they may be understood, through Freudian, Jungian and other psychological and anthropological vocabularies, to express what Lionel Trilling, extending Guerard's argument in 1973, would come to call the full 'authenticity' of Conrad's presentation of human psychological experience in all its obscurities and dark unruliness.[10]

These psychological emphases, in part informed by depoliticizing pressures on expression during the Cold War, are, in certain respects, the opposite of Leavis's emphases on social psychology, its cultural foundations and material and historical discontents. As a consequence, Moser and Guerard value Conrad's individual works differently than does Leavis, with *Lord Jim* as Conrad's summit for Moser and Guerard acutely valuing *Heart of Darkness* precisely for its insistent self-awareness even in moments of self-conscious opacity. Both have limited use for *Victory*.

But Leavis and Moser/Guerard are not so far apart as might at first seem. Leavis, whose discussions of Conrad are often quite formally technical and psychological, places Conrad as firmly at a distance from politics as do Moser and Guerard, whose psychological and technical emphases do not preclude sharp occasional appeals to politics.[11] Leavis's Conrad is an external vantage to conceiving politics, not a situated or partisan agent in politics. Moser and Guerard similarly present Conrad as medium of a strangely uniform, 'generally human', register of universal experience. Their Conrad speaks to and of us in fundamentally similar ways, and this – again strangely – despite the fact that Moser's premise is Conrad's fundamental misogyny, and Guerard's invocations of 'Africa' frequently threaten to collapse from strained abstraction.

These three commentators, and the different critical trends in Conrad's reception in this period, share certain abstract and generalizing humanist premises that, beginning in the 1960s, with a New Historicist and empiricist turn in Conrad scholarship, begin to see challenges, particularly in Eloise Knapp Hay's *The Political Novels of Joseph Conrad* (1963) and Avrom Fleishman's *Conrad's Politics* (1967), which conceive Conrad in terms of specific political traditions. Conrad's critical reception permanently changes through the work of Zdzisław Najder's making available the specific Polish cultural, moral and historical vocabularies and experiences underlying Conrad's writings and the work of Ian Watt, whose *Conrad in the Nineteenth Century* (1979) places Conrad – without displacing Conrad as a central or stable source of moral authority in himself – in a wide context of European intellectual history and historical experience.

The Postcolonial Moment: From the 1960s to the Present

A third critical moment in Conrad criticism arose out of the social ferment of the 1960s through intersecting developments of anti-colonial struggle and decolonization and the rise of post-structuralist theory. This is the moment when *difference* becomes the self-conscious engine of Conrad's reception, when a far greater range of world voices are heard than ever before in counterpointed relation to one another and in terms that insist upon their own authority, rather than Conrad's or generalized articulations of his meaning. In this moment, the imperial pretence of speaking neutrally of or through Conrad in the representative name of the world is radically questioned. Conrad's audiences here fight not simply over the writer's works but also in resistance to them; they query not only the estranging expanse of Conrad's horizons but also their limits and limitations. They insist on Conrad's being situated in the world and as a product of its discourses; and they treat as a terrain of troubled irresolution both the world Conrad represents and the textual means he uses. This is an especially rich moment in Conrad's reception, and to call it 'postcolonial' is neither to exhaust its range nor to suggest that anti-colonial/oppositional politics and post-structuralist theory always neatly come together in its execution,[12] but rather that the question of the relation between the two domains of anti-colonial political priorities and post-structuralist thought is persistently raised throughout it.

Postcolonial critique of Conrad arguably dates back at least as early as W. E. B. DuBois' 'The Souls of White Folks' (1920), Langston Hughes' 'Luani of the Jungles' (1927) and Jean Rhys' *Voyage in the Dark* (1934), all different kinds of engagements with Conrad's imperial facilitations of world colour-lines. However, Chinua Achebe's lecture, 'An Image of Africa: Racism in Conrad's *Heart of Darkness*' (1975), is the watershed event that makes the politics of Conrad's fiction not only a central but also almost unavoidable aspect of his discussion, present to readers even when the terms of discussion might seem distant. Conrad's fiction is no longer transcendentally outside or above or disinterestedly offering estranging or foundational guidance on the politics of nation, world and imperial relations. They are, rather, objects implicated in various kinds of political and imperialistic endeavour, their artistry also an agent in such concerns.

Achebe's well-known critique of *Heart of Darkness* as a racist text fatally undermined in its imperial critique by its essentialization of Africans, spurs an influential critical project of 'writing back' to Conrad. This project of countering and questioning the dehumanizing limits of Conrad's representations has an important parallel in the modern Latin American reception of Conrad, where, a year after Achebe's lecture and in a line of critique that continues through Colombian novelist Juan Gabriel Vásquez's *Historia secreta de Costaguana* (2007), Jean Franco drew attention to *Nostromo*'s inability to imagine any capacities for meaningful political agency and stable self-determination among the novel's non-European South American characters.[13] In the following decade, Nina Pelikan Straus similarly challenged the exclusion of women in *Heart of Darkness*, a line of consideration that other critics have followed up in exploring links in Conrad between female gendering and primitivization and colonial authorization.[14] However, just as Achebe cites Leavis to challenge Conrad's 'adjectival insistence' as an act of artistic bad faith, the Nigerian critic and novelist opened up a different door, one followed in different but important ways by critics including Frances Singh, Benita Parry, Edward Said, and Ugandan critic and novelist Peter Nazareth, implicitly transposing Guerard's (and Garnett's) borderland sense of at least provisional receptiveness to the unknown; the key claim here is the recognition, alongside the political situatedness and limits of Conrad's representations, of a self-conscious quality of *unknowing* whose "heterogeneous" register is a kind of threshold invitation to and incipient knowledge of Other voices.[15] Edward Said, whose body of work perpetually revisits Conrad from beginning to end, is perhaps the most influential writer articulating 'two' visions of Conrad, whom Said recognizes as ever a threshold figure of both global literary articulation and the recognition of the power of 'ideas' to wield Orientalist force.[16]

Post-structuralist thought finds a natural home in such questions of fraught meaning, although sometimes directly connected to anti-colonial and related political concerns, sometimes more tenuously so if at all. Deconstruction, for example, readily lends itself to Conrad's self-cancelling fiction, quite self-consciously predicated upon problems of indeterminate meaning and oppositional binaries reversed in their hierarchy and revealed in their interdependence. But such methods and allied concerns of narrative theory have been marshalled with great sophistication and interdisciplinary combination to the scrutiny of East/West, black/white, masculine/feminine and other imperial binaries – and also domains of religion, modern philosophy and temper, literary formalism, and genre, more distant and sometimes even positively resistant to politics *per se*.[17] Similarly, one of the most influential attempts to read Conrad in terms of the opaque and ulterior depths of his meaning is Fredric Jameson's chapter in *The Political Unconscious* (1982), a 'symptomatic' Marxist reading that has richly enabled subsequent postcolonial readings[18] and in many respects is at odds with the explicit representational and (critical/secular) humanist priorities foregrounded by writers like Achebe and Said. Finally, historicist and cultural studies that have grounded Conrad in literary, anthropological, scientific, popular cultural and other discourses and practices of his time, pursuing all the world and 'Conrad' alike as a species of text, reap their rich rewards from unexpected horizons of implication and application.[19] It is the question of how postcoloniality and post-structuralism can inform or impede one another, not a certainty or underlying homology of relation, that is a centring force driving Conrad's reception during this period.

The Present Moment: The Twenty-First Century

Beyond the 'end of history' and 'Third Way' of post-agonistic politics proffered by some in the 1990s, over the threshold of the twenty-first century, worldwide economic, political and military unrest seems again to have become the norm, and again Conrad has seemed urgently with us. Although terror, mass media and related concerns of propaganda and democratic liability were important triggering issues early in the century, the twin energies of a profoundly transnational reorientation of point of view and the rise of digital archival and research tools for recovering Conrad's history of planetary significance and contact with more variety and granularity than ever before seem to be the driving forces.

Reception itself – in the largest sense that includes not only the 'critical' reception partially sketched earlier, but also the histories of global literary rewriting and material book history, serialization and syndication discussed elsewhere in this volume – has become a driving inquiry through which our re-understanding of Conrad's many meanings in the past occasions the ability to think and generate global conversations about the future.

Since 1999, five studies of different postcolonial trajectories of global literature have meaningfully concerned Conrad's work and also advanced models of comparative and contrapuntal literary history beyond paradigms of 'writing back', 'influence' or even any filial relation.[20] There have also been published a meticulously edited four-volume set of Conrad's *Contemporary Reviews*, predicated on the challenge of opening up transnational views of Conrad's original readerships; individual volumes in the *Conrad: Eastern and Western Perspectives* series considering Conrad from vantages of France, Germany, Poland, Scandinavia, 'the Orient' and South Africa; intensive reception studies at different moments in Germany, Latin America and the United States and among Conrad's contemporary women audiences;[21] and generative work prompting more thinking along these lines concerning the idea of 'heterotopia'.[22] The present moment stands to offer many more 'moments' of Conrad's reception in the past and offers suggestive possibilities for his reception in the future.

NOTES

1 Van Wyck Brooks, 'A Study of Joseph Conrad', *New Republic*, 16 December 1914, pp. 26–7.

2 Terry Collits, *Postcolonial Conrad: Paradoxes of Empire* (New York: Routledge, 2005), pp. 11–20.

3 This map is reproduced in Peter Mallios, *Our Conrad: Constituting American Modernity* (Stanford, CA: Stanford University Press, 2010), pp. 20–21.

4 For a literary and cultural history of Conrad's modern American reception, see Mallios, *Our Conrad.*
5 Denys Thompson, 'Advertising God', *Scrutiny* 1 (December 1932), 245–6.
6 F. R. Leavis, *The Great Tradition: George Eliot, Henry James, Joseph Conrad* (New York: George W. Stewart, 1948), pp. 177, 180.
7 Ibid., p. 209.
8 On Conrad's reception among the Vanderbilt Circle and in the American South generally, see Mallios, *Our Conrad*, pp. 265–374.
9 The other is Chinua Achebe's argument, discussed later.
10 Lionel Trilling, *Sincerity and Authenticity* (Cambridge, MA: Harvard University Press, 1972), pp. 106–11.
11 Moser, indeed, quite forthrightly declares of Conrad: 'we see him as a political prophet, foretelling with appalling accuracy the political immorality of the twentieth century; see *Joseph Conrad: Achievement and Decline* (Cambridge, MA: Harvard University Press, 1957), p. 11. Guerard makes pointed references to Conrad's critical anticipations of complicity with fascist evil before and during the Second World War, and American Cold War propaganda and nuclear hysteria; see *Conrad the Novelist* (Cambridge, MA: Harvard University Press, 1958), pp. 35, 37–8.
12 For a discussion of postcolonial criticism and its impact on Conrad studies, see the chapter by Andrew Francis in the present volume.
13 See Jean Franco, 'The Limits of the Liberal Imagination: *One Hundred Years of Solitude* and *Nostromo*', *Punto de Contacto/Point of Contact* 1, no. 1 (1976), 4–14.
14 See Nina Pelikan Straus, 'The Exclusion of the Intended from the Secret Sharing in Conrad's *Heart of Darkness*', *Novel* 20, no. 2 (1987), 123–37; Marianna Torgovnick, *Gone Primitive: Savage Intellects, Modern Lives* (Chicago, University of Chicago Press, 1990), pp. 141–58; Padmini Mongia, 'Empire, Narrative, and the Feminine in *Lord Jim* and *Heart of Darkness*' in *Contexts for Conrad*, ed. Keith Carabine, Owen Knowles and Wiesław Krajka (Boulder: University of Colorado Press, 1993), pp. 135–50. See also Debra Romanick Baldwin's chapter on feminist criticism in the present volume.
15 Wilson Harris, 'The Frontier on which *Heart of Darkness* Stands' (1981); reprinted in *Heart of Darkness: An Authoritative Text, Backgrounds and Sources, Criticism*, 3rd edn. (New York: Norton, 1988), ed. Robert Kimbrough, pp. 262–8. See also Frances Singh, 'The Colonialistic Bias of *Heart of Darkness*' (1978), reprinted in Kimbrough, pp. 41–54; Benita Parry, *Conrad and Imperialism: Ideological Boundaries and Visionary Frontiers* (London: Macmillan 1983); and Peter Nazareth, 'Out of Darkness: Conrad and Other Third World Writers', *Conradiana* 14 (1982), 173–87, and 'Conrad's Descendants', *Conradiana* 22 (1990), 101–9.
16 See Edward Said, *Culture and Imperialism* (New York: Random House, 1993), pp. 19–30 and *Reflections on Exile and Other Essays* (Cambridge, MA: Harvard University Press, 2002), pp. xi–xxxv, 70–82, 276, 81. See also the interview 'Traveling with Conrad' in *Conrad in the Twenty-First Century: Contemporary Approaches and Perspectives*, ed. Carola Kaplan, Peter Lancelot Mallios and Andrea White (New York: Routledge, 2005), pp. 283–303.

17 Three suggestive examples of the former are Jacques Darras, *Joseph Conrad and the West: Signs of Empire* (London: Macmillan, 1982); Christopher GoGwilt, *The Invention of the West: Joseph Conrad and the Double-Mapping of Europe and Empire* (Stanford, CA: Stanford University Press, 1995); and Marianne De Koven, *Rich and Strange: Gender, History, Modernism* (Princeton, NJ: Princeton University Press, 1991). Two influential examples of the latter are William W. Bonney, *Thorns and Arabesques: Contexts for Conrad's Fiction* (Baltimore, MD: Johns Hopkins University Press, 1980) and Daphna Erdinast-Vulcan, *Joseph Conrad and the Modern Temper* (Oxford: Clarendon Press, 1991). Geoffrey Galt Harpham's *One of Us: The Mastery of Joseph Conrad* (Chicago, IL: University of Chicago Press, 1994) is especially inventive in enlisting linguistic excess to reframe the foundational concerns of 'Poland', 'sea' and 'writing' as they inform Conrad's writings.

18 These include Collits, *Postcolonial Conrad*; Stephen Ross, *Conrad and Empire* (Columbia, Missouri: University of Missouri Press, 1994); and Tamás Juhász, *Conradian Contracts: Exchange and Identity in the Immigrant Imagination* (Lanham, MD: Lexington Books, 2011).

19 Three generative studies are Allan Hunter, *Joseph Conrad and the Ethics of Darwinism: The Challenges of Science* (London: Croom Helm 1983); Andrea White, *Joseph Conrad and the Adventure Tradition* (1993); and Stephen Donovan, *Joseph Conrad and Popular Culture* (New York: Palgrave-Macmillan, 2005).

20 In addition to Collits, these are Asako Nakai, *The English Book and Its Marginalia: Colonial Postcolonial Literatures after 'Heart of Darkness'* (Amsterdam: Rodopi 2000); Byron Caminero-Santangelo, *African Fiction and Joseph Conrad: Reading Postcolonial Intertextuality* (Albany: State University of New York Press, 2004); Natalie Melas, *All the Difference in the World: Postcoloniality and the Ends of Comparison* (Stanford, CA: Stanford University Press, 2007); and Christopher GoGwilt, *The Passage of Literature: Genealogies of Modernism in Conrad, Rhys, Pramoedya* (New York: Oxford University Press, 2010).

21 See, respectively, Anthony Fothergill, *Secret Sharers: Joseph Conrad's Cultural Reception in Germany* (Oxford: Peter Lang, 2006); Jennifer French, *Nature, Neo-Colonialism, and the Spanish-American Regional Writers* (Hanover, NH: University Press of New England, 2005); Mallios, *Our Conrad*; and Susan Jones, *Conrad and Women* (Oxford: Oxford University Press, 2009).

22 Especially influential are Cesare Casarino, *Modernity at Sea: Melville, Marx, Conrad in Crisis* (Minneapolis: University of Minnesota Press, 2002), and, among many works concerning 'mapping' by Robert Hampson, 'Conrad's Heterotopic Fiction: Composite Maps, Superimposed Sites, Impossible Spaces', *Conrad in the Twenty-First Century*, pp. 121–36.

10

DEBRA ROMANICK BALDWIN

Conrad and Gender

> A man who has had his way is seldom happy, for generally he finds that the way does not lead very far on this earth of desires which can never be fully satisfied.
>
> *Chance* (p. 396)

Introduction

The increasing popularity of gender studies in Conrad scholarship is the result of not only the burgeoning of various critical approaches themselves, but also the relevance and complexity of Conrad's human vision. As we now know more fully than did Conrad's contemporaries, this vision of humanity was informed by several cultural contexts, each offering different valences of masculinity and femininity and different parameters of sexual identity and experience. These contexts include the nineteenth-century classical gymnasium curriculum that shaped his education; highly literate parents and a family steeped in the Polish literary tradition; twenty years' cosmopolitan experience in the French and British Merchant Marine; travels through the Mediterranean and East Asia; and thirty years' subsequent settlement in England, with time spent in the urban whirl of London before moving to a largely domestic existence in the countryside of Kent with his wife and two sons and their occasional visitors.

Despite the cultural breadth of Conrad's experience and the complexity of his narratives, his approach to gender was long assumed to be relatively one-dimensional: that he was a masculine writer of sea stories in a man's world, indifferent to the experience of women. Subsequent criticism has both developed and challenged this assumption. Critics who maintain that Conrad's fiction reflects a masculine perspective either focus on how it ignores or distorts feminine experience for ideological ends, or how it challenges the very concepts of masculinity, embracing homosocial and homosexual aspects of masculine experience. In *Conrad and Masculinity*, Andrew Michael Roberts explores 'ways in which Conrad's fiction reproduces and re-enacts oppressive aspects of masculinity of his time' as well as ways in which his fiction offers 'a potential transformation, ironizing or destabilizing its own ideological formations of masculinity', arguing that these two forces in Conrad's fiction need to be taken together, 'as interlocking aspects of the same discourse'.[1]

Other critics have challenged an over-emphasis on the masculinity of Conrad's fiction. In *Conrad and Women* (1999), Susan Jones discerns the complexity and astuteness of Conrad's portraits of women, investigating his engagement and sympathy with feminine readers and writers, including in his intimate correspondence with his wife, the writer Marguerite Poradowska. Ellen Burton Harrington argues that works such as 'The Idiots', *The Secret Agent*, and *Chance* offer Conrad's critique of 'the patriarchal system that leaves women in the care of men who fail to understand them or even consider them empathetically', while Gail Fraser also finds in *Chance* Conrad's attempt 'to show the reader the social and moral implication of [his female protagonist's] victimization without denigrating her point of view'.[2]

Still other critics call into question the categories altogether. Carola Kaplan, for example, articulating Conrad's 'revisionist thinking' on matters of gender and sexuality, asserts that 'by the time he comes to write *Under Western Eyes*, Conrad creates powerful and independent female characters who help to undermine traditional patriarchal constructions of gender and sexuality by effacing the boundaries between male and female and by blurring the distinctions between homosexual and heterosexual relationships' and by demonstrating that 'gender is 'performative'... fluid, unstable, contextual'.[3] She finds in Conrad an argument 'for openness and indeterminacy'.[4] And Lissa Schneider explores the 'fugitive' ways that Conrad challenges Victorian norms, treating gender as conceptual and performative.[5] Taken together, all of these approaches invite the deeper question of what we mean when we speak of 'gender'.

Gender and the Problem of Categories

The term 'gender', unlike the more amorphous term 'sexuality', implies categories that contrast or differentiate – not only distinguishing 'masculine' from 'feminine', as we have seen so far, but also expressing other distinctions between various sexual identities. Yet until the mid-twentieth century, 'gender' was a grammatical term referring not to biological sex, but to classes of organizing nouns in some languages based on structure or sound. In those languages in which 'masculine', 'feminine', and 'neuter' are used as grammatical categories, these grammatical genders at times correspond to biological sex (for example, γυνή means 'woman' in Greek and is also a feminine word in its structural ending), and at other times, are unrelated, or even opposed, to any metaphorical meaning derivable from biological characteristics.[6] Precisely this complexity and inconsistency proved an opportunity to broaden the term's use to the sexual realm; because the biological characteristics of people do not simply predict how they identify themselves sexually, nor do understandings of what might constitute 'masculine' and 'feminine' qualities simply correspond to the characteristics of biological sex, those studying the subject began to use the more flexible and unpredictable grammatical term to capture the complexity of sexual identity.

However, if biological categories are insufficient, gender categories also turn out to be problematic, as seen by their proliferation and constant redefinition, as more or different categories are sought to provide salient and satisfactory descriptions of how individuals identify themselves.[7] Moreover, appropriating an asexual grammatical term to express complex sexuality has had the effect of sexualizing language – that is, introducing a sexual connotation where it might not have been previously heard, nor present. For example, current usage assumes that 'man' and 'mankind' are gendered – that is, that they refer to sex, and it is difficult for current readers to 'hear' the generic male pronoun taken for granted by some older readers, a sensibility that would allow an older female reader to assume that this essay's epigram is directed, on a human level, at herself – a sensibility possibly not shared with a younger female contemporary. This change in perception allows current readers to be more carefully attuned to instances where women have been excluded in older works, but it can also cause these same readers to assume that women were excluded at times when they might not have been. In the same way, words evolve to gain or lose prejudicial connotation – as the term 'homosexual' is deemed pejorative by some preferring the term 'queer', itself previously pejorative but now deliberately appropriated as a term of pride. Precisely because the affective connotations of words are so central to the experience of reading, the shifting valences of language – including their relation to gender and sex – pose particular problems for reading literary works, as readers continually impose their own changing affective associations on the words they encounter.

With these difficulties in mind, then, we turn to the problem of gender in Conrad's fiction, which refers not only to his treatment of male and female characters, but also to the more fluid and difficult categories of masculine and feminine, and then to the deeper vision of inner lives and longings, the *eros* underlying them.[8]

Because gender proceeds as an oppositional concept, it is worth beginning with *Heart of Darkness*, the narrative of Conrad's which brims most conspicuously with contrasting categories – not only masculine and feminine, but civilized and uncivilized, African and European, ancient and modern and darkness and light. Yet, as many critics have shown, in perspectives ranging from new critical to post-structuralist, the narrative also destabilizes the binary categories it sets up. Although Marlow engages his jingoistic audience, including the frame narrator, who waxes eloquent on the 'dreams of men, the seed of commonwealths, the germs of empires' (*YHET*, 45.8–9) by justifying the 'conquest of the earth' redeemed by 'an unselfish belief in the idea' (47.21), he soon begins to offer irony after irony undermining the pretence of this civilizing mission,[9] acerbically reducing 'the cause of progress' to the death of two black hens, the metonymic slaughter of a continent. So, too, the darkness that he leads his listeners to locate first in Africa as 'one of the dark places of the earth', (45.17–18) pales next to 'the barren darkness' he discovers within the pale high priest of ivory, Mr Kurtz and, more importantly, within himself. Even the African 'cannibals' (78.14) of Marlow's narrative, themselves 'eight hundred miles away' from their homes, turn out to exhibit more self-restraint than the European 'pilgrims' and 'civilizers' he encounters, whose 'desire was to tear treasure out of the bowels of the land with no more moral purpose at the back of it than there is in burglars breaking into a safe' (73.33–35), leaving all of these terms – 'cannibals', 'pilgrims', 'civilizers' – drenched in sarcasm. The 'exquisite brilliance' of daylight which opens the narrative (44.6) is replaced with 'an overcast sky' (126.15) at the end, marking the accumulated metaphorical resonances in which the 'idea' of a civilizing light is disclosed as the darkness of violence and hypocrisy.

But does this pattern of ironical destabilization extend to the categories of masculine and feminine, as well? As many critics have noted, it is difficult to disentangle the narrative's various binary oppositions from one another – difficult, for example, to see Kurtz's 'Intended' at the end separate from her status as a holder of the very ideals which the preceding narrative has led us to see in their horror. The feminine imagery itself undergoes an ironic transformation over the course of Marlow's journey. First encountering the dense and difficult coast of Africa, Marlow comments that it was 'as if Nature herself had tried to ward off intruders' (55.24) – using a conventionally feminine personification to express an ordering purpose. Once beyond the coast, however, the wilderness remains an androgynous 'it' – or, at one point, arguably double-gendered, when Marlow bifurcates its stillness into 'an implacable force brooding over an inscrutable intention' (77.23). Whether 'inscrutable intention' here is meant to connote a contrasting feminine element (echoing the 'Intended') or whether both terms in their active form connote traditionally masculine categories,[10] ambiguous gender broods over inscrutable abstraction. Only near the end of his journey does Marlow again ally the natural setting with femininity, when he likens 'the soul' of 'the immense wilderness' to an African political woman who deals with Kurtz: she is 'savage and superb, wild eyed and magnificent' (107.24–25) and, in 'tragic' pose, is gunned down by an 'imbecile crowd' (115.15). The feminine as ordering principle has been replaced by the feminine as tragic victim.

Yet in another light, Marlow presents his gender categories as fixed, as seen in his infamous explanation for the lie he tells Kurtz's fiancée at the end, a lie which denies the horror of all that he has seen and his complicity in it: 'They – the women I mean – are out of it – should be out of it. We must help them to stay in that beautiful world of their own lest ours get worse' (93.23–25).[11] Whatever one thinks of the ethical or humane claims for Marlow's lie – and, despite decades of criticism, it remains a crux of the novella – certainly it emerges as the structuring principle for the narrative, which presents Marlow's struggle to express the truth of his experience to his exclusively male listeners against – in reaction to, perhaps even in atonement for – the lie he feels compelled to tell a woman. And however rich the feminine imagery he uses, however important the female characters might turn out to be for his story, female subjectivity itself is absent: *Heart of Darkness* remains Marlow's story.

But what sort of narrative authority do Marlow's words hold? Why is he nested in a narrative frame that compromises – renders subjective – his narrative authority, underscores his limited point of view and distances him from both reader and author? How do his subjective opinions relate to the broader human vision of Conrad's art? These questions point to the fact that the issue of gender is inseparable from the problem of voice.

Gender and the Problem of Voice

Not only *Heart of Darkness* but all of Conrad's narratives are characterized by narrative structures that compromise narrative authority and resist omniscient narration. Conrad layers his voices in narrative frames, capriciously shifts the pronouns of the narration (*The Nigger of the 'Narcissus'*, *The Secret Agent*), and plays with free indirect discourse, ambiguously blending the narrator's voice with the words or thoughts of a character. Nevertheless, his narrators remain male. And of these, Marlow is the one most often recurring, at least by name, appearing in four narratives spanning from 'Youth' and *Heart of Darkness* in 1898 to *Chance* in 1913. The Marlow of *Chance* is crustier in his prejudices than the Marlow of *Heart of Darkness*, but these prejudices also encounter more resistance, not only from a frame narrator who repeatedly challenges him, but also from the counterexample of Flora, who develops into a complex and active agent ultimately eluding Marlow's ability to characterize her. Susan Jones has offered a valuable analysis of how this deliberate authorial reticence constitutes Conrad's deliberate response to Henry James over 'what can be "known" to the author'; she argues that 'by distancing himself as author from the chief narrator of the novel, Conrad appears sceptical of the storyteller's assumption of an overarching authority over the text'.[12] There is also another explanation for this authorial reticence to assume a feminine voice: Time and again Conrad repeated his conviction that his art rested upon fidelity to his own experience and sensations.[13] Might adopting an explicitly female narrator have transgressed what he perceived to be the limits of his experience?

Still the absence of a female narrator does not preclude exploring feminine subjectivity. Indeed, the very narrative distance provided by a multiplicity of voices or gendered perspectives can even deepen the effect of conveying a character's internal experience. *The Secret Agent* (1908), whose Author's Note (1920) refers to the novel as 'Winnie's story', is an example. 'Winnie's story' is told by an elusive and masculine narrator who steps in and out of the narrative as furtively as a patron frequenting Mr Verloc's shop, and Winnie begins as distant from the reader as one of the women in *Heart of Darkness*. The one psychological fact given about her, early and often, is her conviction that 'life doesn't bear too much looking into' – aligning her resistance to examining her own inner life (and the inner lives around her) with the reader's distance from her. Yet the narrative conveyed by a distant and ironic voice manages also to disclose or approach her internal state in the oblique and cumulative fashion usually reserved for male protagonists, such as Martin Decoud, Lord Jim and Axel Heyst – characters the reader meets from the outside, so to speak, introduced from an external perspective of their outward appearance but whose interior points of view emerge through a series of flashbacks and increasing narrative subjectivity. In the case of Winnie, as she recalls protecting her brother from her abusive father we are told:

> She remembered brushing the boy's hair and tying his pinafores – herself in a pinafore still; the consolations administered to a small and badly scared creature by another creature nearly as small but not quite so badly scared; she had the vision of the blows intercepted (often with her own head), of a door held desperately shut against a man's rage (not for very long); of a poker flung once (not very far), which stilled that particular storm into the dumb and awful silence which follows a thunder-clap. And all these scenes of violence came and went accompanied by the unrefined noise of deep vociferations proceeding from a man wounded in his paternal pride, declaring himself obviously accursed since one of his kids was a "slobbering idjut and the other a wicked she-devil." It was of her that this had been said many years ago.
>
> (183.13–26)

The passage first appears to be an instance of indirect discourse, the voice of a narrator who observes her actions of remembering and seeing, retaining ironical distance ('not quite so', 'unrefined', 'wounded') while replicating the details of her memory with such specificity and affective power that one has the illusion that the narrative voice is adopting her thoughts and pain. Or is it *she* who has adopted the *narrator's* voice, objectifying herself in retrospect and detaching herself in the face of her father's rage – 'a man's rage' that includes the gendered curse that she is a 'she-devil'? Either reading avoids what would be the sheer pain of felt subjectivity, and both emphasize the neutering effect of dehumanizing violence: how a 'she' and a 'boy' can be turned into simply 'scared creatures'. The detached observation that they were both still in pinafores accentuates their androgynous diminution in the face of their father's terrifying tyranny.

Although it is tempting to see the final conversation between Winnie and Verloc – as they talk past one another into two separate pits of incommunicability – as voices polarized along strict gender lines, the narrative denies us such easy correspondence. Winnie's increasing identification with Stevie after she learns of his death, her murdering Verloc by stabbing him with a knife after he insinuates he wants sex with her while lying impotent on a couch, only hints at the narrative's tangle of shifting gender roles, a tangle as complex as any multi-layered frame of Conrad's other narratives. Here, its effect is to convey the complete and utterly transgressive breakdown of her identity. The narrative's shifting, anarchic use of gender also forces us to face an *individual*, to contemplate a specific action burdened by a history that has been buried by its own violence and to confront a passion whose depth and complexity is conveyed not by conventional categories and authoritative voices, but by their explosion.

Gender and the Problem of *Eros*

Brought to the level of the individual, the question of gender – of the category to which one might belong – turns into the more amorphous question of *eros*, of internal desire. The erotic is not a simple topic in Conrad, although for a long time, indeed, he was regarded as a writer indifferent to the topic. Richard Curle described his art in 1914 as 'realism uncoloured by erotic imagination'; and eighty years later, Joseph Epstein wrote that 'Conrad was not a writer whose own passions were greatly engaged by the erotic.'[14] Opinions have shifted, but the question remains of just what form the erotic takes.

Perhaps the most overt and conspicuous form of *eros* in Conrad's world is also the strangest by modern standards: the captains' love for their ships.

While ships are conventionally referred to with the feminine pronoun, Conrad elaborates the image into a full-fledged romance. It is seen in the purple prose of *The Shadow-Line*'s young captain, who with 'a thump in [his] breast' (44.29) beholds his ship for the first time and likens her to 'some rare women ... one of those creatures whose mere existence is enough to awaken an unselfish delight' (45.18–20), or, in 'A Smile of Fortune,' when the old captain of the *Hilda* laments with 'trembling voice' (*TLS*, 28.14) the loss of his ship's figure-head, and 'Nobody could have guessed from his tone that the woman was made of wood' (28.12–13) – to the suggestion that he replace it, he responds, 'I've been a widower now for eight and twenty years come next May and I would just as soon think of getting a new wife' (28.32–33). Both of these examples perform a comic function in the scheme of these stories, setting up or contrasting the more complicated human predicaments to follow, but elsewhere the same level of passion is earnestly described. The narrative voice of *A Mirror of the Sea* describes a sailing ship as:

> a complete creation endowed with character, individuality, qualities and defects, by men whose hands launch her upon the water, and that other men shall learn to know with an intimacy surpassing the intimacy of man with man, to love with a love nearly as great as that of man for woman, and often as blind in its infatuated disregard of defects.
>
> (58)

It would be easy to dismiss a passage such as this as a form of displaced sexuality – either as a consciously romantic construct more palatable to the audience than a more complicated portrait of the erotic impulses we might imagine aboard a ship, or else as a less conscious manifestation of erotic urges repressed. How are we to read 'the intimacy of man with man', and what is the nature of the intimacy it describes? Does separating 'intimacy' from the 'love of man for woman' reflect a simple contrast between friendship and sexual love, or a deeper admission of authorial distance from the romantic trope being used?

Despite these and other questions that such a passage invites, a reading that seeks to reduce or explain away the *eros* avowedly directed towards the ships risks devaluing both the sense of dependence a captain feels for a craft in the face of hostile and unpredictable conditions and the aesthetic experience in its own right, in all its pleasure. In *The Rescue*, Tom Lingard feels 'a sense of acute delight' as he manoeuvers his responsive craft along a dangerous channel, and the narrative adds: 'It was in such moments that he lived intensely, in a flush of strong feeling that made him long to press his little vessel to his breast' (54). The moment has larger implications for Conrad's world: if an ever-present danger facing his protagonists is detachment and paralysis, Lingard's passion for his brig is intelligible for the sheer connectedness and active engagement with concrete realities that it affords him.

Conrad's vision of gender in these passages is double-edged. On the one hand, Lingard's implied use of the diminutive ('his little vessel') and his active manoeuvring suggest a model of masculine control over a passively feminine vessel. Yet the 'feminine' element of the ship to which Conrad appeals is less its passivity than an expression of otherness ('the mysteries of feminine nature' (*MS*, 56)) in the masculine world of the sea. Moreover, the captains' relations to their ships are not simply a one-directional matter of control, for the ships themselves react with idiosyncratic responsiveness, and the result is a sort of mutual effort that Conrad describes as 'a feeling of intimate, equal fellowship, the ship and the man, backing each other against the implacable, if sometimes dissembled, hostility of the world of waters' (*MS*, 137). In this way, Conrad appeals to the conventionally gendered categories of romance while also asserting a vision of intimate equality – combining love and intimacy, as it were. The question remains what the implications of this vision might be for human relationships.

In *Sexuality and the Erotic in the Fiction of Joseph Conrad*, Jeremy Hawthorn exhorts us not to assume the sexual naïveté that earlier generations assumed of Conrad's works but instead to recognize in his writings a more sophisticated and delicately deliberate understanding of sexuality from which we might discover much. Hawthorn offers a range of examples showing both the unconventional variety and sheer power of human sexual relations in the world of Conrad's fiction.

The springboard for his argument is the story 'Il Conde' (1907), which, on the surface, appears to be the story of an innocent count visiting Capri, who gets robbed at night in a deserted pathway during an outdoor musical entertainment. Tormented by a threat from his assailant, who belongs to a criminal gang, the sickly count leaves the healthful climate of Capri for an unfavourable winter in Europe and, we presume, his health's demise. After half a century of 'Il Conde' criticism indifferent to its sexually charged allusions – beginning with the nude statue of Hermes that begins the story and whose posture the assailant duplicates before the robbery – essays by Douglas A. Hughes and Theo Steinmann in 1975 explored the idea that the story contains a covert homosexual plot: that the count, far from sexually innocent, is involved in making a sexual advance on the young man who robs him.[15] Asking why it took critics so long to acknowledge the story's homoerotic content, Hawthorn answers himself by suggesting that one answer lies in Conrad's heterosexually conventional reputation.

To say that the plot of 'Il Conde' concerns a homosexual liaison gone wrong does not in itself, however, offer a reading of the story. If we accept this covert plot, what then? Is it a playful concealment of context for what remains a traumatic robbery of a gentle ('kind') soul? Is it a coded but sympathetic depiction of rejection, of violent insult following sexual offering? Or is it a moral tale: engage in this type of behaviour and getting mugged is a possible consequence? In any of these readings, can one separate the sexual material from the ethical or human implications of erotic desire and human discovery?

Any 'covert' (or esoteric) reading of a text also raises the question of critical suggestibility: How easily can a prompt influence what we impose upon a text? Hawthorn writes that 'Once we start to examine the story in light of a suspicion that the Count is sexually interested in young men, then many other details may seem less innocent', admitting that 'the details in question involve at the most hints and suggestions rather than unambiguous information'.[16] But insinuation is a powerful force, both narrative and critical. Moreover, all critical questions shape our readings. Asked to find 'dichotomies' in a text, for example, students will find them, but perhaps at the expense of seeing its triads. And sexual content is even more suggestible. At the same time, however – and this remains Hawthorn's concern – by *not* responding actively and imaginatively to the unstated realm that a text invites us to complete, we might miss an important part of what the author had hoped we might discover. We are left with a critical crux: When are we desexualizing what *is* sexual, and when are we sexualizing what is *not*?[17]

While Hawthorn acknowledges that Conrad portrayed emotionally charged relations between men sharing work and respect, most of his analysis engages the darker side of Conradian *eros*. He offers persuasive readings of an artistic world full of cruelty, voyeurism, exhibitionism, sadism, masochism and what he describes as the 'mesmerized desire for the writhing, death-linked intimacies and intermingling of an exotic, erotic and feminized space'.[18] He also poses the question of why characters in Conrad's world are not able to find 'passionate, loving relationships of a sexual nature' that are 'able to offer a way out of the existential solitary confinement that his characters fear so much',[19] suggesting that *eros* is never merely a private desire. Defining the erotic as 'sexuality clothed in the vestments provided by a particular cultural configuration',[20] he argues that Conrad portrayed sexuality as he did (despite what was by all accounts a happy marriage with Jessie Conrad) because he saw that the cultural inequalities and inhumanities around him pervaded the private realm he chose to depict.

But are there, in fact, no passionate and loving relationships in Conrad's world? It is worth turning, for a moment, to 'The Tale' (1917), a narrative whose sexual passion is explicit and that offers a vision of *eros* which broadens the vision of passion and intimacy to what one might call the aletheic realm of storytelling and shared understanding. The story opens in an overtly sexual key; a man and a woman are intimately engaged on a couch in a room whose dimming light leaves their actions discreetly in the shadows, as does the narrative voice, which describes their love-making ambiguously: 'the whispering of a man's voice, passionately interrupted and passionately renewed, seemed to plead against the answering murmurs of infinite sadness', and pausing to continue, 'At last, no answering murmur came' (59). Although the lines preceding this description shape our reading – suggestively drawing our attention to a window 'framed rigidly in the gathering shades', followed by 'the irresistible tide' of night flowing into the room – nevertheless when the man gets up and moves to a chair, we are told that he sees the woman's hands 'a moment before abandoned to his kisses', implying that he had only been kissing her hands. Hawthorn helpfully identifies this narrative tactic as typical of a method Conrad also uses in 'Il Conde': raising suspicion only to deny it, thereby adding a disclaimer that allows him to slip in more erotic content than his sense of propriety or his readers' expectations might otherwise allow. The extent of the sexual activity, however, is perhaps less interesting than what it grows into. For when they are done, the woman asks him to 'tell her a tale', and he responds, reluctantly at first, with a third-person account of an episode in the life of a Commanding Officer, who turns out at the end to be himself.

The Commanding Officer's tale, which forms the story's central narrative, at first seems overtly opposed to the erotic and to the private realm altogether. For it is a story situated in extreme political conditions antithetical to the leisure of erotic imagination: patrolling a coast during submarine warfare after seeing a ship in one's company 'blow up all of a sudden and plop under almost before you know what has happened to her' (64). Under these mental conditions, he causes the sinking of a neutral ship whose captain he has convinced himself is guilty of selling supplies to an enemy submarine. Only later does he doubt himself and feel the full horror of his action.

Why situate an ethical tale about war within this highly charged and highly gendered erotic frame? A Marlovian answer might be to suggest that the domestic realm offers an illusory solace from the political. Here, however, the erotic frame narrative is not an *escape* from the political reality of the man's tale, but the condition for its *disclosure*: the horror is manifest. And the woman not only listens to, but also elicits it, for at first he resists. When he evasively says that he likes the word 'duty', she replies, 'It is horrible – sometimes' (61), a two-sided retort that shows she understands the competing claims of difficult situations. When he replies that the word 'contains infinities', she responds, 'What is this jargon?' (61), correctly surmising that his use of abstraction is detaching him from reality. But still she presses him on, most of all with her sympathetic understanding. When she 'appreciatively' interjects, 'I can imagine', he 'soberly' responds: 'What is there that you can't imagine?' (63). With such engagement, she elicits the story that he tells about himself, with difficulty, in the third person. And as such, the narrative offers a reversal of Marlow's lie in *Heart of Darkness*; instead of lying to a woman and then confessing his complicity in the horror to his male companions, the Commanding Officer, after having received 'an infinity of absolution' in the conventionally manly world of warfare in which he has done his 'duty', confesses the deeper horror of his actions to his erotic partner, a woman, who listens and understands – and who, as their verbal repartee reveals, is anything but 'out of it'.

Their banter emphasizes the erotic charge of intelligent conversation, recalling other couples in Conrad's world who are intellectually matched and engaged with one another, including the political sparring of Decoud and Antonia in *Nostromo* and the extended conversation in *Victory* between Heyst and Lena, who though unlearned is extraordinarily perceptive. At one point, when she expresses pity for happy people destroyed in the Deluge, Heyst responds, 'I should have thought it's they specially who ought to be congratulated', and Lena immediately replies: 'Oh, yes – I understand what you mean; but there were forty days before it was all over' (191), quickly comprehending his point that the mere fact of death is less important than a life happily lived, but astutely observing that not all deaths are equal. Their intense conversation ranges for two chapters over topics high (Biblical exegesis) and low (the inn-keeper Schomberg's gossip) in a discourse full of gaps that each fills more quickly for the other than readers can fill for themselves – a conversation that finally culminates in sex then and there on the cliff. Understanding why these two relationships ultimately end tragically, rather than 'happily ever after', would require not only analyzing psychological forces beyond the erotic, but also considering the more general question of Conrad's indeterminate narrative endings, his aversion to easy resolutions. Of course, a Romantic conclusion to 'The Tale' would have been grotesque – trivializing the ethical significance of what the Commanding Officer has just confronted, precluding the meditative space his (and perhaps the reader's) reflection requires. So he kisses the woman and leaves the room.

If the intimate dynamics of intense conversation are themselves erotic, then where does that leave gender categories and the highly charged conversation at the heart of 'The Tale' between the Commanding Officer and the Northman? Indeed, the stylistic echoes between that scene and the frame narrative have not been lost on critics. Yet the scene also inverts the narrative's initially stark gender categories more deeply than simply complicating the nature of erotic charge. For at the beginning, the narrative voice (strongly aligned with the man) had described the Commanding Officer standing 'masculine and mysterious in his immobility', slightly angered 'for that feminine mobility that slips out of an emotion as easily as out of a splendid gown' – a conventional characterization, playfully echoing Verdi's '*La donna è mobile*', juxtaposing masculine constancy against feminine fickleness. But by the end, he embodies a parody of masculine constancy, maintaining his immobile 'certitude' of the Northman's guilt according to the immoveable categories into which he divides the world: 'friend' and 'enemy'. The Northman, however, defies these categories. He imaginatively depicts the complex individual circumstances that would lead a man to accept the gold he can see for the boxed supplies he cannot. He invites imagining a complex reality that the Commanding Officer, in his political position, cannot bear – that is, until he makes the appeal himself, in his own tale. Most importantly, the Northman is, in the end, unknowable: a mystery, much deeper than the questions of 'which side' he is on, or to which category he belongs. And in that mystery, too, he holds erotic attraction.[21]

Indeed, insofar as gender in Conrad expresses difference, it expresses the gaps and fissures not only between self and other, but also within oneself, between the desire to understand and the very mystery of being itself. For the internal realm in Conrad's world is, in the end, as mysterious as the cosmos that encloses it, defying intellectual categories and certain knowledge. For this reason, his art resists happy endings and easy resolutions not just in the manner of all Modernists in full flight from Victorian cliché but also because he mistrusts the most powerful erotic illusion that another human being contains one's good. His art invites us to consider the possibility that we might not always know what we are looking for, and that getting what we are looking for might not always satisfy.

Despite the erotic complexity that ever complicates the issue of gender, many gender studies continue to be defined by binary gender categories of 'masculinity' and 'femininity', even if their aim is to challenge or rethink such categories. And the risk of limitation and exclusion continues. When Nina Pelikan Straus writes: 'A woman's experience of the text is quite different … the woman reader has no access to the sense of pleasure and plenitude which male critics display in their readings of *Heart of Darkness*', she risks effacing those female (feminine?) readers who enter into narrative intimacy with Marlow as a human being.[22] Similarly, Jeremy Hawthorn ends his book saying, truly enough, that he 'cannot speak for the female reader',[23] but surely readers as diverse as Pelikan Strauss and myself suggest that it might be problematic to speak of *the* female reader and that a deeper affinity might rather be found between her reading and Andrew Michael Roberts' neo-masculine approach, each moving – to use Roberts' phrase – 'against the grain' of Conrad's text. Or is a woman critic's reading 'feminine' in ways in which she is unaware? The implication of this unknowability for gender studies is ever to hesitate over the categories we use and the 'knowing readings' we assert, instead acknowledging both their limitations and ours, and how little really we know about our own deepest longings, as readers, as critics and as human beings.

NOTES

1 Andrew Michael Roberts, *Conrad and Masculinity* (New York: St Martin's Press, 2000), pp. 6, 39.
2 Ellen Burton Harrington, 'Suicide, Feminism, and 'the miserable dependence of girls' in 'The Idiots', *The Secret Agent*, and *Chance*', *The Conradian* 37, no. 2 (2012), 56, and Gail Fraser, 'Mediating Between the Sexes: Conrad's *Chance*', *Review of English Studies* 43 (1992), 88.
3 Carola M. Kaplan, 'Beyond Gender: Deconstructions of Masculinity and Femininity from 'Karain' to *Under Western Eyes*' in *Conrad in the Twenty-First Century*, ed. Carola M. Kaplan, Peter Lancelot Mallios and Andrea White (New York: Routledge, 2005), pp. 267, 268, 273.
4 Ibid., p. 278.
5 Lissa Schneider, *Conrad's Narratives of Difference: Not Exactly Tales for Boys* (New York: Routledge, 2003).
6 For example, 'masculinity' is a feminine word in several languages, including *męskość* in Polish.
7 The issue is further complicated because gender identification does not always predict gender attraction.
8 This essay avoids speculating about Conrad's personal life, whether or not he harboured sexual secrets beyond what appears from his letters to have been an affectionate marriage producing two children. Several critics have identified homosocial and homoerotic themes in Conrad's works, and some have attempted to extend these elements beyond the fiction into the life. Yet the leap from art to life is precarious, and, in the absence of evidence about a specific event or relationship (and such evidence has yet to surface), biographical conjecture remains speculative.
9 As Conrad wrote about the narrative as he began to write it: 'The criminality of inefficiency and pure selfishness when tackling the civilizing work in Africa is a justifiable idea' (to William Blackwood, 31 December 1898 (*Letters*, I, 139)).
10 Masculinizing of the imagery here might support readings that argue for the homoerotic elements of Marlow's experience; see Richard Ruppel's *Homosexuality in the Life and Work of Joseph Conrad: Love Between the Lines* (New York: Routledge Press, 2008). But the ambiguous gendering of the wilderness not only anticipates transgressive sexual readings of the novella, but also invites philosophical readings that seek to move beyond gender and conventional categories.

11 Johanna M. Smith characterizes this lie as one that 'must be told by a man to a woman, so as to deny her the masculine truth, to confine her to 'that beautiful world' [Marlow] has constructed as a counter to the masculine world'; see '"Too Beautiful Altogether": Patriarchal Ideology in *Heart of Darkness*' in *Heart of Darkness: A Case Study in Contemporary Criticism*, ed. Ross C. Murfin (New York: Bedford/St Martin's, 1989), p. 194. Rita Bode has argued that, in fact, the women in *Heart of Darkness* are far from simply victimized; they hold a latent power that Marlow, threatened by it, attempts to conceal. See her '"They … Should Be Out of It": The Women of *Heart of Darkness*', *Conradiana* 26 (1994), 20–34.

12 Susan Jones, *Conrad and Women* (Oxford: Oxford University Press, 1999), pp. 129, 130.

13 In the early Preface to *The Nigger of the 'Narcissus'* (1897), Conrad set forth his artistic credo by contrasting the artist's fidelity to his own internal experience with the thinker's attention to 'ideas' or the scientist's attention to 'facts' (p. vii), and sixteen years later, he wrote, 'the artist[']s salvation is in fidelity, in remorseless fidelity to the *truth of his own sensations*. … All these things I have said in the plainest words in print and they are also implied in every line of my writings' (to Warrington Dawson, 20 June 1913 (*Letters*, v, 238)).

14 Richard Curle, *Joseph Conrad: A Study* (London: Kegan Paul, 1914), p. 12, and Joseph Epstein, 'Life Sentences: The Art of Joseph Conrad', *New Criterion* 12, no. 10 (1994), 24.

15 Douglas A. Hughes, 'Conrad's 'Il Conde': "A deucedly queer story"', *Conradiana* 7, no. 1 (1975), 17–25, and Theo Steinmann, '"Il Conde"'s Uncensored Story', *Conradiana* 7, no. 1 (1975), 83–6. Their analyses dovetail with later research detailing the historical Polish count whom Conrad had met, on whom he based the character, and who (according to a letter by his grandson to Zdzisław Najder) was at the time active in Capri's homosexual scene.

16 Jeremy Hawthorn, *Sexuality and the Erotic in the Fiction of Joseph Conrad* (London: Continuum, 2007), p. 28.

17 David Miller has spoken of the danger of sexualizing authors, as well – of equating their imaginative with their literal lives: 'Should not an author be imaginatively bisexual? Think Iris Murdoch, George Eliot, V. S. Pritchett' (p. 14). 'The Coastal Shelf: Conrad, Sex, and Marriage', Joint International Conference on Joseph Conrad of the Société Conradienne Française and The Joseph Conrad Society (UK), Université de Versailles–St-Quentin, 17 September 2010.

18 Hawthorn, p. 76.

19 Ibid., p. 156.

20 Ibid., p. 155.

21 The *eros* of mystery need not turn Conradian erotics into a matter of pure abstraction; surely erotic passion remains a mysterious hybrid that cannot neglect the physical. Yet the erotic charges that Conrad presents is also more confused, mingled with the moral, aesthetic and even ontological dimensions of human experience.

22 Nina Pelikan Straus, 'The Exclusion of Women from Secret Sharing in *Heart of Darkness*'; rpt. in *Conrad's 'Heart of Darkness': A Casebook*, ed. Gene M. Moore (Oxford: Oxford University Press, 2004), p. 208.

23 Hawthorn, p. 157.

11

ANDREW FRANCIS

Postcolonial Conrad

Following the decline of European empires in the wake of the Second World War, postcolonial studies developed in the late 1970s as an iconoclastic way of looking at colonial discourse as well as other manifestations of colonialism. Often vigorously assertive in style and attitude and arguing its corrective ideas about the nature of colonialism from social and political viewpoints, it has been one of several important influences on critical writing about Conrad since the 1980s and on literary criticism more widely.[1] As a result, we are offered a view of Conrad's works and his imperial world with different eyes. As importantly, we also see that Conrad wrote about the colonial world of his time in ways that foreshadowed the postcolonial interrogation of empire. Terry Collits writes that Conrad's novels 'mull over cracks in the edifice of imperial ideology instead of celebrating its magnificence', noting that others, including postcolonial critics, have worked with the aid of Conrad's foundational insights.[2]

Postcolonial discourse analysis, which was often allied early on to the theoretical field of deconstruction, seeks to reveal how imperial Western thinking infuses literary texts through spoken and unspoken assumptions about the colonized world, and how those texts bear out and share in colonization's violence and repression. In Collits's words, it is about 'the politics of representation'.[3] In its quest to expose these realities and injustices, postcolonialism has provided the literary critic with new and sharpened insights in social and political approaches to literature, insights that are now part of the currency of literary criticism. It has drawn attention to the history of those usually silenced by colonial rule and writing, so that for all their voicelessness they can in some way be known, understood and heard. The viewpoint of the colonized in literary texts is brought to the fore and the denial of space, subjectivity and essential importance to them is explained and highlighted. Reading texts from a postcolonial standpoint has also focussed attention on the fact of the resistance to colonialism, whether outrightly physical or in other, less overt, forms, a resistance generally written out or rewritten by the colonizers.

It is important to note that postcolonial theory is a contested field, one point of disagreement being whether its role in literary studies and more widely has been restricted by lacking adequate historical specificity and by too theoretical an approach.[4] And the field has also been criticized for being too Anglocentric. Some would argue that the political and social readings of postcolonialism are by definition limited and exclusive, if not totalizing, there being other aspects of representation and literary investigation than those terms, just as Leavis, in another generation, offered 'moral seriousness' as a defining category for evaluation. Readings of different kinds are always possible, having more to do with, for example, the concerns of aesthetics or genre, but readings drawing upon other fields can have their own limitations. Nevertheless, postcolonial readings have doubtless enlarged and corrected our sensibilities. What is important is that readings of whatever kind should draw as fully as possible on all that a text contains, providing an opportunity for richer, more sensitive readings and, in the case of Conrad, those of a writer whose complexity has proved to be chameleon-like in always offering fresh challenges and possibilities.

Beginnings

The broad field of postcolonialism, one that today includes such historical and social concerns as feminism, decolonization, globalization and neocolonialism, is generally regarded as having been initiated by Edward Said's influential *Orientalism* (1978).[5] However, others, such as Frantz Fanon (1925–61) and Aimé Césaire (1913–2008), as well as the liberation movements in the colonies, had been part of a growing resistance in the twentieth century to the various hegemonies imposed by colonialism. Said, in *Orientalism*, aims to demonstrate that the complex relationship between East and West is centrally concerned with power dynamics. This complexity is seen to lie in representations of the Orient, the evidence showing 'such representations as *representations*, not as "natural" depictions of the Orient', evidence found equally in factual and imaginative texts. Said attributes Orientalism's wrong to 'disregarding, essentializing, denuding the humanity of another culture, people, or geographical region' and makes the claim that 'every European, in what he could say about the Orient, was consequently a racist, an imperialist, and almost totally ethnocentric'.[6]

One of Said's examples is Flaubert's speaking for and about his Egyptian courtesan while denying her her own voice and describing her as 'typically Oriental'.[7] This looks forward to concerns, among others, with voice and subjectivity in the writings of many postcolonial cultural and literary critics. Said's book was interested in the Middle East, but later writers in the postcolonial field have tended to take a different geographical scope, often that of British colonialism in India.[8] An important development in the field, and one that gave rise to a searching examination of Conrad's attitude and the attitudes of his time to Africa and imperialism, was the lecture delivered at the University of Massachusetts in 1975 (published in 1977) by the Nigerian novelist Chinua Achebe (1930–2013). In his lecture, he notoriously accused Conrad in *Heart of Darkness* of being 'a bloody racist', continuing: 'that this simple truth is glossed over in criticism of his work is due to the fact that white racism against Africa is such a normal way of thinking that its manifestations go completely undetected', an example, in his view, of the unconscious attitudes embedded in Western thinking that were taken up by later postcolonial criticism.[9] Achebe objected to Conrad's representation of Africa as Other, to the African woman as only savage in relation to the European Intended and to the fact that the African voice is allowed only grunts or rudimentary expression. He also objected to Africa's use as a backdrop, giving no opportunity for its indigenous inhabitants to be portrayed as fully human.

Achebe's lecture continues to attract critical commentary, and some critics have sought, in response, to offer what they feel to be more nuanced and informed readings of Conrad's complex novella. An early example was Cedric Watts (1983), to which his later (1996) essay can usefully be added, in which he argues that 'the tale repeatedly implies an irreducible excess that eludes summary. It may thus warn commentators that they, confined to the limited discourse of rational non-fictional prose, are likely to be outdistanced by the multiple resources of the fictional text'.[10] One concern has been that Achebe was insufficiently alert to literary procedures, particularly the text's two narrators, neither of whom is Joseph Conrad. Achebe anticipated this response, arguing that the separation of the narrator from Conrad himself was unconvincing because the author gave 'no alternative frame of reference by which we may judge the character and opinions of his characters', an assertion various critics have judged inadequate.[11]

Still others have objected to his failure to recognize the novella's generic allegiances, with social realism but one of the categories, and in some views not the most important, to which it appeals. Collits, for example, while believing that Achebe was not 'simply wrong', concludes that his 'error' was 'to misread *Heart of Darkness* as a stable embodiment of Conrad's political beliefs and attitude towards blacks' and that the novella is 'too slippery to be pinned down in this way', adding that critics tend, on the whole, to believe that Achebe's polemic was unjustified.[12] According to Collits, the novella 'contains, but is not contained by, Marlow's limited and prejudice-ridden liberalism', part of the ideology supporting European imperialism at the time with its notions of the 'civilizing mission, the work ethic, and the superiority of civilized man'.[13]

Case Study: 'Karain: A Memory'

The way in which Conrad's writings disturb Western ideas of empire anticipates postcolonial concerns, even though he wrote regarding the British Empire to his relative Aniela Zagórska of 'the idea of liberty, which can only be found under the English flag all over the world' (25 December 1899, *Letters*, II, 230). Conrad was by no means alone in his time in expressing doubts about the imperial enterprise, nor in recognizing that, for all the claims often made for it as a means of advancing civilization, material gain lay at its foundation, an idea sharply voiced by a contemporary anonymous reviewer of *Almayer's Folly* in Singapore's *Straits Times*:

> The power of the European has substituted a sullen peace for the open war of the past. It has done so in the interest of trade, not of civilisation, however much we may disguise the fact. Civilisation seeks no proselytes; it indeed repels them with its barrier of racial prejudice. Left to themselves the natives are forced to judge civilisation and Christianity by the Europeans with whom they are brought most in contact, by the ethics of the trader and the manners of the beach-comber. The result is deplorable but it has none the less to be faced.
>
> *Straits Times*, 16 January 1896, p. 3[14]

Conrad's short story 'Karain: A Memory' (1898) can serve to illustrate how postcolonialist concerns can be brought to bear in literary analysis. The story centres on the friendship of three British gun-runners – Hollis, Jackson and the unnamed narrator – with Karain, a local chieftain. The sister of Karain's best friend brings dishonour on her house when she goes to live with a Dutch trader, having been promised in marriage to a Malay. For safety, the couple leave for Sumatra, where Karain and his friend, Matara, eventually track them in order to kill them to avenge the dishonour. But Karain, entranced by the woman, at the crucial moment cannot shoot her, and shoots his friend instead. The friend's ghost haunts Karain until a pious old man provides a charm to protect him. On the old man's death, the charm ceases, and Karain's peace of mind is only restored by his receiving a substitute charm from the gun-runners – a sixpence struck to celebrate Queen Victoria's golden jubilee.

Postcolonial theory encourages seeing the story as a pointed interrogation of the colonial enterprise. In such a light it might be read as a tale infused with European assumptions and descriptions of the East that are totalizing and erroneous, opinions that are then undermined by irony or by the narrator's contrasting descriptions of Karain and his people. For example, despite the evidence of their bravery and nobility, Hollis declares that Malays are 'all nerves' and 'easily impressed' (*TU*, 43.19). Such stereotyping by a European (although stereotyping comments are also made by Karain about the Dutch) is evident again when the narrator observes that Karain is 'plotting and preparing a war with patience, with foresight – with a fidelity to his purpose and with a steadfastness of which I would have thought him racially incapable' (23.7–10). The Europeans are unsuccessful in dissuading Karain from trying to stop 'the irresistible nature' of European encroachment and are only capable of seeing his vision of leadership and independence as 'primitive ideas' (23.13, 23.15).

These examples show the relevance of Said's principle of the West's construct of the East, one created despite evidence to the contrary. For the postcolonial critic, Karain's silent sword-bearer – the pious old man – could be seen as a symbol of contemplative fidelity, the unseeing Europeans viewing him only as 'something inanimate' (24.18–19); for these Westerners silence and immobility are typecast as absence. Similarly, for all Karain's nobility, he can qualify only as 'a gentleman in his way' (43.17). And when, wanting to flee his ghost by leaving with the Europeans, he characterizes them as a race who 'understand all things seen and despise all else' (40.38–39), the reader senses, for all that Karain's viewpoint is limited, the description's irony, suggesting reservations – perhaps akin to the 'cracks in the edifice' mentioned by Collits – about the culture underlying the European colonial intrusion.

A postcolonial critic might also focus on the foregrounding of the fine qualities of Malay culture. At the tale's beginning, there is a paean by the narrator to the nobility of Karain and his followers, a character-trait that ironically seems to resemble ideal British notions of good manners. The narrator's description is of people seen in their own right, with their own subjectivity, who have 'an independent bearing, resolute eyes, a restrained manner' (13.28); they boast 'with composure' and their 'murmurs' are 'well-bred' (13.30, 13.3). The embroidery on their clothes is twice mentioned, the implication being one of leisure and sophisticated and civilized taste. Relaxed but orderly, friendly and courteous, such qualities speak for themselves. Karain dispenses not only justice but also wisdom and is both practical and statesmanlike as well as excelling in physical accomplishments. Nevertheless, he is also a man who has betrayed his best friend because of his attraction to his friend's sister and his desire for power suggests uncomfortable parallels with European intrusion and conquest, underlining the impossibility of any simple view of cultural differences in Conrad's representation.[15]

Conrad's according of importance and value to the indigenous people is also generated, it could be argued, by contrast with the Europeans. Although three gun-runners cannot be seen as fully representing 'Europe', their illegal trade emanates from the interests of 'very respectable people sitting safely in counting-houses' (24.6–7), no doubt in British Singapore, 'very respectable' ironizing higher imperial claims and reminding the reader of the anonymous reviewer's 'ethics of the trader'. Similarly with the Dutch, Karain relates their threatening behaviour and how they 'watched our coast greedily' (31.14–15), hardly a term for a civilizing mission. To the Malays, the Dutch trader is a particularly offensive representative of his nation. Suggesting European colonizing attitudes at the everyday level, his behaviour is unrestrained, both sexually (with Matara's betrothed sister) and culturally more broadly (he is too familiar, laughs foolishly, despises the Malays and so on). His careful examination of the land indicates his rapacious intentions. The description of him contrasts with that of Karain and also contrasts with an important statement of counter-colonialism, a deeply felt assertion by the narrator both of the equality of races and of right-minded relations that looks beyond imperial ways of seeing:

> There are those who say that a native will not speak to a white man. Error. No man will speak to his master; but to a wanderer and a friend, to him who does not come to teach or to rule, to him who asks for nothing and accepts all things, words are spoken by the camp fires, in the shared solitude of the sea, in riverside villages, in resting-places surrounded by forests – words are spoken that take no account of race or colour. One heart speaks – another one listens; and the earth, the sea, the sky, the passing wind and the stirring leaf, hear also the futile tale of the burden of life.
>
> (29.2–11)

Much of the story's most acute criticism of colonialism is in Karain's narration of his years of wandering with Matara, an example of Conrad's giving a degree of agency and voice to indigenous subjects in a way often felt by postcolonial critics to be absent in the Western literature of empire. Karain and Matara work at many different jobs and, when sweeping the decks of 'big ships' – no doubt European ones – only have 'curses heaped upon our heads' (33.38, 33.38–39). Of Java, the core colonial possession of the Dutch, Karain can only ask: 'Is there anything good in that country?' (32.17). Through Karain we see the Dutch East Indies from the point of view of the colonized, the subaltern. Karain continues: 'The paths run straight and hard and dusty. Stone campongs, full of white faces, are surrounded by fertile fields, but every man you meet is a slave. The rulers live under the edge of a foreign sword' (32.17–20). Signs of this violent enforcement of colonial rule run like a thread throughout the story.

A ruler who 'knew native Courts, European Settlements, the forests, the sea and, as he said himself, had spoken in his time to many great men' (20.11–13), Karain has a broad view of the human condition, his privileged engagement distancing him somewhat from the experiences of the mass of the colonized. His search for Matara's sister removes that distance, and he is made to see and to suffer under the heel of colonial rule. He stands in for, and becomes one with, the ordinary colonized subject, although his journey is also concerned with other experiences, such as desire, betrayal and guilt. The pair's quest is a journey of the common man through the very heart of colonialism. It is thus not surprising that Karain can say 'those Dutchmen are all alike' (33.21), their similar appearance suggesting a like culpability, an indistinguishability because all represent the colonial common denominator. While it is too early historically for Karain's account to be postcolonial literature, it is an example of Conrad's enabling the empire to 'write back', a concept that a now well-known study explores.[16] Nevertheless, we should also note that Karain's comment mirrors the totalizing nature of Hollis's about Malays and that Karain and Matara are also cursed by the Javanese. Both these caution the reader that Conrad's tale refuses to offer simple oppositions between cultures.

Similarly, a postcolonial approach might well object to any reading of Karain's drawing comfort from the Jubilee sixpence that made it of a piece with the Western totalizing comments on natives being 'all nerves' and as weakly susceptible to 'primitive ideas'. It might be pointed out that the circumstances surrounding the European charm are presented differently from those surrounding the sorcerer's charm, albeit both show Karain reliant upon what Europeans regard as illusion. That charm came from a man steeped in the culture and religion of the people, 'a pilgrim serene and pious' (39.24–25). Furthermore, the postcolonial critic might observe that the supposed superiority of Europeans' not believing in such charms is ironically undercut by the narrator's finding 'a protection and a relief' in the ship's chronometers' 'ticking off steadily the seconds of Greenwich Time' (38.10–11, 38.9–10), merely mechanical though these timepieces are, as it is by Hollis's smiling 'capital description' (41.1) in response to Karain's claim that Europeans live in a 'land of unbelief, where the dead do not speak, where every man is wise, and alone – and at peace' (40.39–40). The reader senses a weighting against European life in the narrator's reflection on it as 'an inconceivable life of stress, of power, of endeavour, of unbelief', one that 'rolls on irresistible and hard on the edge of outer darkness' (28.35–36, 28.37).

'Karain' presents the implications of imperialism across a broad front that embraces British and Spanish imperial interests as well as Dutch in what in postcolonial terms amounts to a general interrogation of imperialism. Criticism of Britain's civilizing mission could be said to be evident, as we have seen, in gun-running as part of the business of 'respectable' (24.6) firms. There may even be a thinly disguised reference to the British Straits Settlements in the fact that the 'European Settlements' (20.12) that Karain knew are not simply European *settlements* (emphasis added), a reference that further draws Britain into the field of criticism as a power with South-East Asian possessions. And when describing the 'spirit' of Queen Victoria's nation, Hollis can only hesitatingly and with qualification say that it is 'a masterful, conscientious, unscrupulous, unconquerable devil ... that does a lot of good – incidentally ... a lot of good ... at times' (44.35–37). His words all have to do with power, irresistible purpose, violence and questionable ends, the word 'masterful' carrying an ironic relation back to the narrator's repudiation of the 'master' as one of those who 'come to teach or to rule'.

The empire of a third European power, Spain, enters the story as its main setting, a secluded bay of Mindanao, a southern island in the Philippines. This was part of a sovereign sultanate ended in 1887 by the Spanish, who had been colonizing the Philippines since the sixteenth century and whose activities in the last quarter of the nineteenth, when they were subduing the Sultanate of Sulu to the south-west, were particularly violent. It is Spanish gun-boats that the English gun-runners look out for, to avoid the possibility of 'being quietly hanged somewhere out of the way of diplomatic remonstrance' (16.4–5) for arming indigenous resistance. In addition to these European powers, there is also a broader sense in the text of empire and power in general as passing, be they Karain's or the vestiges of the former Hindu empire seen by Karain and Matara on their journey, making the story of wider application than that of European colonialism alone, just as *Heart of Darkness* reminds the contemporary reader of the Roman empire that once held sway over Britain.

Notably both beginning and ending with reports of uprisings and resistance, 'Karain' gives space to postcolonialism's concern with indigenous resistance to colonization, albeit fictionalized. The theme is introduced pointedly in the second sentence when, musing on what has become of those adventurers like himself, the narrator says: 'I am sure that the few who survive are not yet so dim-eyed as to miss in the befogged respectability of their newspapers the intelligence of various native uprisings in the Eastern Archipelago' (13.6–9). The Eastern Archipelago was generally taken to signify present-day Malaysia, the Philippines and Indonesia, and the suggestion is therefore of widespread resistance. The narrator's deeply felt memories of those times and places are then invoked as arising from within those newspaper reports that frame the narrative: 'Sunshine gleams between the lines of those short paragraphs' (13.9–10), as if the memories and resistance are inseparable. Newspaper reports also frame the end of the story when they reappear through Jackson's words: 'I saw a paper this morning; they are fighting over there again. He's sure to be in it. He will make it hot for the *caballeros*' (47.35–37).

References throughout keep resistance prominent in the background. It is earlier mentioned that Karain was 'plotting and preparing a war', and although the reader is not told against whom, it is no doubt against the Spanish colonizers seeking to extend their influence over the Philippines. As an independent chief, Karain evidences agency in this activity, a power denied to the colonized. Resistance against Spanish intrusion is mentioned again when Karain declares that he and Matara 'served the Sultan of Sulu. We fought the Spaniards' (39.35–36). Resistance to the Dutch is evident in the two references to war in Atjeh (present-day Aceh). Karain relates that he and Matara travelled to Atjeh where they fought in the war. The choice of this conflict is important (and occurs elsewhere in Conrad's Asian fiction), for this fiercely independent sultanate began by inflicting defeat on the Dutch, and the war was to last from 1873 to 1914, with isolated resistance continuing until the Second World War, a sign of the unending spirit of resistance. The great cost of this war to the Dutch government in lives and money marks it out as a landmark in the worldwide struggle against colonialism. By the time of the publication of 'Karain', the war had already lasted twenty-five years, with the Dutch using brutal military action against the Acehnese fighters and population. Conrad incorporates into the story a range of resistance, a portrayal not of the permanence and peace of colonization but of a region afire.

The end of the story sees London, where the narrator and Jackson have unexpectedly met, dissolve in a surreal representation in which colour, sound and movement overwhelm order and meaning, disturbing ironically through this representation what might be imagined to be the rationality and appeal of the empire's capital. The sense of disturbance is increased by small scenes being merely sketched and rapidly and successively invoked. Images of degradation and hopelessness abound: an old man's 'face of despair'; 'queer wreckage adrift'; 'monstrous'; 'soiled'; 'sullen' (48.40–41, 48.34, 48.37–38, 48.23, 48.15). This could be read as an anti-paean to the description of Karain and his people with which the story began. Jackson wonders whether Karain's experience of being haunted was true. The narrator in response offers the scene around them as evidence of what is real, a scene in which they are standing in front of a gun-seller's shop, a location that perhaps represents the violence implicit in the human condition. Jackson, hesitant and doubtful, concludes: 'I'll be hanged if it is yet as real to me as … as the other thing … say, Karain's story' (49.8–9). It is a statement that, however tentatively, underlines the cultural limitations of a colonizing culture.

There are, of course, important elements in the story that a postcolonial approach is unable to bring out. For example, the story is also concerned with the nature of memory, illusion and belief as well as the means (illusion, show) by which power is maintained in any culture. The narrator asks: 'I wonder what they thought; what he thought … what the reader thinks?' (46.33–34). 'What the reader thinks' can stand for an invitation to engage with the widest of enquiries into the text.

Other Histories of the Colonized

A good deal of postcolonial Conrad criticism, particularly in connection with *Heart of Darkness*, focusses on the occluding of the indigenous voice and presence, but examples to the contrary can be read in many of the writer's works in addition to 'Karain'. For example, Robert Hampson points out that in *Lord Jim*, Marlow's account of Patusan 'colonises and then empties out the category of the Other', but argues that there is 'a larger world of stories which exists beyond the limits of the novel', so that a story such as that of Jewel's mother, despite its missing details, can be important. Such incomplete stories can be observed elsewhere in Conrad's writing about colonized places. Hampson also comments regarding *Lord Jim* and *Almayer's Folly* that 'while the foreground is occupied by the problems of the Europeans, the background is full of the political life of the Bugis and the Malays'.[17] Both of these observations are indicative of how the non-European presence, even if present only as background, or limited through Europeans' narrative, can be powerfully felt and given space.

In 'Because of the Dollars' (1915), the mysterious 'Javanese plutocrat' (*WT*, 145.29) causes an unscheduled port of call. Opposing the narrator's playfully ironic description of the individual is the powerful marking out of the presence and importance of a whole world not available to the narrator, in exactly the same way that he cannot tell what version of events will be circulated in 'Malay town' (165.30–31), rendering the events and their narration matters beyond and lost to Western forms of knowing and telling. Similarly, unions between European and non-European can also suggest that Europeans are made subject to the non-European story, through which the reader is made to accept this non-European story as having its own integrity and, potentially, primacy.[18] This is certainly not because the European thus endorses the indigenous but because the European has evidently been made the subject of a transition that, although itself not necessarily made available to the reader, commands a presence in the narrative. In *Lord Jim*, Stein, married to a Malay princess and evidently still mourning her and their lost child, suggests such a possibility of cross-cultural transformation, as may do Jewel's grandparents. So too in *The Rescue* do Jörgenson and 'the girl' (103), 'a native woman' with whom 'he lived in the native quarter … in a native house' (90) and to whom he owes his life, their fidelity and protection of each other signs of what may be possible between European and non-European. Their marriage by the missionary affirms their relationship and yet can be read as ironizing the relevance to their fidelity of a European religious ceremony carried out by a 'young missionary' characterized with a slight suggestion of reservation as 'enterprising' (105). Jörgenson can affirm that 'I never broke my word to white or native' (103), and his record of assistance to the Malays against the Dutch, whom he 'saw run' and against whom he 'advised the chiefs of Manangkabo' (102), is a European's anti-colonial declaration of faith, a siding with non-European rights. In 'Falk', the former ship's captain Johnson and 'Mrs Johnson', the native woman to whom he is 'now spliced' may, for all Johnson's careless tossing of coins to his wife, suggest union and understanding (*Ty*, 191, 190). Johnson's 'white nakedness', visible through the seams of his European coat that is, significantly, falling apart, suggests the superficial nature of the differentiation assumed by Europeans to exist between native and European, and the couple reside in 'a very clean native compound' (192, 191), a description that undercuts European assumptions. In the apparently quasi-colonial circumstances of a Bangkok in which the consulate's constable can knock Johnson down and paralyze Mrs Johnson 'with extreme terror' (193), European life shows itself only as an uncivilized intrusion into this compound.

Such comparisons between European and indigenous behaviour often see the European less well regarded, even though Conrad's representation of Malay and other cultures does not mask their imperfections. One such comparison is evident in *Almayer's Folly* in Nina's decision to leave her European background for a Malay life, although, as Robert Hampson points out, this is not the simple one it might appear. But many other elements, such as the discourteously lounging Dutch officers, or Lingard's imperialist behaviour or Babalatchi's bizarre and silly 'patent leather belt bearing a brass plate with the arms of Netherlands under the inscription "Sultan of Sambir"' (71.32–33) combine to weight the case against the European. And the indigenous voices, with their frequent resistance to European hegemonic political traditions, are clearly heard in their own right in the long conversations in Sulu between Mrs Almayer and Babalatchi, including Babalatchi's purposeful and mature wisdom with regard to the Dutch colonizers: 'But I shall live to deceive them. A man knows when to fight and when to tell peaceful lies' (117.14–16). In all these examples it is as if, in an implied court of judgement, there is never any doubt in Conrad of the *locus standi* of the non-European.

Conrad, Postcolonial Writing and Looking to the Future

Collits argues for Conrad's formative place in interpreting and representing the postcolonial, an area that now contains experiences such as 'decolonization, uprootedness, migration and neo-colonialism', declaring that Conrad 'enabled Said and others to "see" their world differently, and by doing so helped to create new ways of knowing the world that would require the invention of new heuristic tools'. Summarizing an important aspect of Conrad's achievement as being a combination of early Modernist fictional experiment together with a colonial revisioning, Collits concludes that this combination 'makes his writing not just experimentalist but truly revolutionary'.[19]

If further evidence were required of Conrad's centrality to postcolonialism, it can be found in his powerful influence on writers from formerly colonized nations who have acknowledged and drawn upon his writing for its humanity and reservations about empire.[20] Collits observes the possibilities for such future postcolonial writing in Heyst's unobtrusive Chinese servant Wang in *Victory*, who up to then has been seen solely from a limited European viewpoint but who 'suddenly emerges as a person in his own right, with a consciousness whose history is non-European'. For Collits the opportunities we are then given to see into Wang's own, non-European, world look forward to 'new opportunities for English-language fiction in a postcolonial world'.[21] This, for all that he shared in the attitudes of his own time, is part of Conrad's legacy in preparing the ground for the postcolonial field, a writer highly conscious of any particular culture's limits who sought assiduously to look beyond them.

NOTES

1 Studies that deal *inter alia* with Conrad's portrayal of imperialism and the colonized include Benita Parry, *Conrad and Imperialism: Ideological Boundaries and Visionary Frontiers* (London: Macmillan, 1983); Andrea White, *Joseph Conrad and the Adventure Tradition: Constructing and Deconstructing the Imperial Subject* (Cambridge: Cambridge University Press, 1993); Robert Hampson, *Cross-Cultural Encounters in Joseph Conrad's Malay Fiction* (Basingstoke: Palgrave, 2000); and Linda Dryden, *Joseph Conrad and the Imperial Romance* (Basingstoke: Macmillan, 2008).

2 *Postcolonial Conrad: Paradoxes of Empire* (Abingdon: Routledge, 2005), p. 13. Collits points out that Leavis hardly considered race and imperialism in his reading of Conrad, political and ideological elements that are central to current critical interest, earlier criticism having focussed on narratology and aesthetic concerns.
3 Ibid., p. 43.
4 Concerning historical specificity in particular, see, for example, Benita Parry, *Postcolonial Studies: A Materialist Critique* (London: Routledge, 2004).
5 Edward W. Said, *Orientalism* (Harmondsworth: Penguin, 1985).
6 Ibid., pp. 21, 108, 204.
7 Ibid., p. 6.
8 See, for example, Gayatri Chakravorty Spivak, *In Other Worlds* (London: Routledge, 1987), and Homi Bhabha, *The Location of Culture* (London: Routledge, 1994).
9 Chinua Achebe, 'An Image of Africa', *The Massachusetts Review* 18 (1977), 782–94 (788).
10 Cedric Watts, '"A Bloody Racist": About Achebe's View of Conrad', *The Yearbook of English Studies* 13 (1983), 196–209; '*Heart of Darkness*' in *The Cambridge Companion to Joseph Conrad*, ed. J. H. Stape (Cambridge: Cambridge University Press, 1996), pp. 45–62 (58–9). A more recent example of the continuing debate over Achebe's reading is Nidesh Lawtoo, who argues for certain 'continuities' between Conrad and Achebe rather than the received notions of opposition; see 'A Picture of Africa: Frenzy, Counternarrative, Mimesis', *Modern Fiction Studies* 59, no. 1 (2013), 26–52 (27).
11 Achebe, p. 787.
12 Collits, pp. 99, 98.
13 Ibid., p. 99.
14 For a discussion, see Hans van Marle, 'Jumble of Facts and Fiction: The First Singapore Reaction to *Almayer's Folly*', *Conradiana* 10 (1978), 161–6.
15 J. H. Stape argues the importance of the 'commonalities' Conrad portrays across cultures in the story; see 'Mixing Memory and Desire: The Subtle Subversiveness of Conrad's "Karain: A Memory"', *L'Époque Conradienne* 31 (2005), 57–67 (64).
16 Bill Ashcroft, Gareth Griffiths and Helen Tynan, *The Empire Writes Back: Theory and Practice in Post-Colonial Literatures* (London: Routledge, 1989).
17 *Cross-Cultural Encounters*, pp. 142, 133, 142–3.
18 A reading of the woman in such relationships as colonized woman, a concept influenced by postcolonialism, can blur the complexity of Conrad's text; see Andrew Francis, '"You always leave us for your own ends": Marriage and Concubinage in Joseph Conrad's Asian Fiction', *The Conradian* 35, no. 2 (2010), 46–62.
19 Collits, pp. 35, 40.
20 See, for example, Andrea White, 'Conrad's Legacy in Postcolonial Literature', *Under Postcolonial Eyes: Joseph Conrad after Empire*, ed. Gail Fincham and Myrtle Hooper (Rondenbosch, South Africa: UCT Press, 1996), pp. 195–208.
21 Collits, pp. 171, 173.

12

DAVID MILLER

Conrad and Contemporary Writers

At the beginning of the twenty-first century, the Norwegian playwright Henrik Ibsen's works were the most performed in theatres worldwide, after Shakespeare. His last play, *Når vi døde vaagner* (*When We Dead Awaken*), was first performed at the Theatre Royal Haymarket, on 16 December 1899, in front of an audience of – probably – almost nobody. The morning after that performance, Joseph Conrad wrote to David Meldrum,[1] a writer who acted as our man in London for the Edinburgh firm William Blackwood, sending him a chunk of *Lord Jim*, then appearing in monthly instalments in *Blackwood's Edinburgh Magazine*. Ibsen was the European rage, his reputation built upon the predominant Germanic flavour of the age. Although Conrad wrote in his third language, his influences and experiences were dramatically more international than anyone else then writing in English. (James Joyce was yet to come, although he never budged from Europe in his life and did so little in his art.) Perhaps this international character is why Conrad's wider reputation was slightly slower in growing than other authors writing at this time – Conrad sometimes saw himself as an intruder, an exile, an outcast and once dismissed himself as 'an amazing bloody foreigner' (*Letters*, III, 488). Despite widespread serialization of Conrad in England and America, the audience that actually bought his books at the shops – up to his bestseller *Chance* (1914) – was composed mainly of a cultured elite.

Whilst Ibsen's increasing popularity remains obvious, Conrad's is arguably as pervasive today amongst readers and writers. Virginia Woolf in her obituary appreciation, published anonymously in the *Times Literary Supplement*, waspishly referred to him as 'our guest'.[2] A careful reader of her contemporaries, having once met the older writer, she wondered 'what of Conrad will survive and where in the ranks of novelists we are to place him'. Ninety years after his death, we can answer her question and take stock of the way in which both his life and work echo with those writing today, over the decade and some since the survey of contemporary writers in the *Oxford Reader's Companion to Conrad* and of those writers not mentioned there.[3]

The *Oxford Reader's Companion* entry on this topic surveys those who have been influenced by Conrad, beginning with T. S. Eliot, whose epigraph to 'The Hollow Men' (1925) famously quotes from *Heart of Darkness*. Since 1980, the American novelist Robert Stone, the American fantasy writer Terry Brooks and the Indo-American novelist and literary journalist Siddhartha Deb have quoted from the novella, as has John le Carré in *The Mission Song* (2006). Eliot's use of a quotation must have helped spread Conrad's name in certain circles, but Conrad's influence, of course, was not limited merely to quotation, and it might well be appropriate that a writer who himself borrowed so much, even to the point of inserting lines from other writers into his own texts, found himself, in turn, appropriated, and transformed, in the works of his admirers.

To read *Heart of Darkness* immediately before reading F. Scott Fitzgerald's *The Great Gatsby* (1925) is a fascinating experience – the same mood hovers over Nick Caraway's narration as it does with Marlow, but the two books share a similar texture – the arrival of Jay Gatz's father at the end of Fitzgerald's elegiac romance is surely similar to the appearance of the Intended in Conrad's novella. (There are, as well, numerous resonant echoes from *Victory* in *The Great Gatsby* from Lena's voice to the enigmatic sign that haunts West Egg.)[4] Sixty years later, the Irish-Canadian novelist Brian Moore (1921–99) published *Black Robe* (1985), a short and powerful novel about a Jesuit missionary among the Huron of seventeenth-century Canada. He wrote: 'I wanted to write this as a tale. I thought of it in terms of authors I admire, like Conrad. I thought of *Heart of Darkness*, a tale, a journey into an unknown destination, to an unknown ending'.[5] Setting a man of faith in a savage wilderness has become a trope in modern fiction, even as traditional faith has diminished, as the transplanted New York writer Hanya Yanagihara's *The People in the Trees* (2013), widely noted as 'Conradian', shows.[6] And the descent into troubled psychological territory impelled Canadian novelist and playwright Timothy Findley (1930–2002) to make Kurtz, for the schizophrenic librarian protagonist of *Headhunter* (1993), literally jump out of the novel – whose epigraph comes from *Heart of Darkness* – to plague her and the streets of modern-day Toronto until Marlow forces him back into fiction:

> Kurtz came forward – did he come through the water? – and stood beside her. She could smell him – the smell of old, dried paper was on him – and the smell of printer's ink and binding glue. He wore a pale grey suit, as pale and grey as his skin, and the shapes of his knees and elbows could be seen beneath the cloth. *Heart of Darkness* lay in Lilah's lap, open where Kurtz had been

> emancipated. She raised it up and snapped it shut in his face, as she might if trying to kill a fly. When she opened her eyes, he was buzzing still and wiping the palms of his hands with the handkerchief.
>
> 'Go back in!' she said to him. 'They don't allow people out of books in here.'[7]

Other Conradian titles provide less apparent inspiration either as epigraphs or in titles. Peter Nichols' *Voyage to the North Star* (1999) quotes *The Nigger of the 'Narcissus'*; Howard Norman uses a line from *The Secret Agent* in *The Haunting of L.* (2003); the Turkish Nobel prize winner Orhan Pamuk's *Snow* (2002) quotes 'The Westerner in me was discomposed' from *Under Western Eyes* (*UWE*, 242.32); Anthony Powell (1905–2000) appropriates a phrase from *Chance* (perhaps recalling the surname he shares with one of that novel's characters) as the collective title to his memoirs, *To Keep the Ball Rolling* (1983); and Philip Hensher's *The Fit* (2004) invokes 'The pluck of women! The optimism of the dear creatures!' from the same novel (*Ch*, 136). British travel-writer Jonathan Raban creatively misquotes *The Shadow-Line* in his *Passage to Juneau: A Sea and its Meanings* (1999): '"That's a funny piece of water," said Captain Hamilton,'[8] a tacit acknowledgement that Conrad's sea-fiction provides a touchstone for anyone writing about the complex effects of experience at sea.

Much more rarely used epigraphically are Conrad's letters, although the German novelist W. G. Sebald quoted a letter of Conrad's written in French from the Ukraine to his marriage relation the Franco-Belgian novelist Marguerite Poradowska of 23 March 1890 in his *Die Ringe des Saturn: Eine englische Wallfahrt* (*The Rings of Saturn: An English Pilgrimage*, translated by Michael Hamburger, 1995): 'Il faut surtout pardonner ces âmes malheureuses qui ont élu de faire le pèlerinage à pied, qui côtoient le rivage et regardent sans comprendre l'horreur de la lutte, la joie de vaincre ni le profonde désespoir des vaincus' (*Letters*, I, 42).[9]

Novelists are by no means the only writers who quote or allude to Conrad. Harvard historian Richard Pipes's study of terror and treason in pre-revolutionary Russia, *The Degaev Affair: Terror and Treason* in *Tsarist Russia* (2005), calls upon *Under Western Eyes* for the unchanging political truism: 'For who with us, in Russia, is to tell a scoundrel from an exceptionally able man?' (275.4–6), and the British historian Niall Ferguson (another Harvard professor) in *Empire: How Britain Made the Modern World* (2003), appropriately, uses *Heart of Darkness*. In his analysis of modern terrorism and the Al-Qaeda phenomenon, *On the Road to Khandahar: Travels through Conflict in the Islamic World* (2006),[10] journalist Jason Burke uses *The Secret Agent* epigraphically. The events in New York of September 2001 and terrorist atrocities since have often inspired journalists to recall *The*

Secret Agent, a novel that Burke has recommended as essential reading on the terrorist mindset: 'Basically, anything you want to know about how terrorism works you can find in this book.'[11] The best-selling novelist Robert Harris evoked the novel's arch-terrorist and psychotic Comrade Ossipon in the *Daily Telegraph* in October 2001 to come to terms with his contemporary equivalent Osama bin Laden, and journalist Francis Wheen found the novel 'more resonant than ever' in light of the psychopathology displayed by Al-Qaeda's adherents.[12] At the end of 'The Age of Horrorism', Martin Amis invoked Conrad when suggesting:

> Opposition to religion already occupies the high ground, intellectually and morally. People of independent mind should now start to claim the spiritual high ground, too. We should be with Joseph Conrad:
>
> 'The world of the living contains enough marvels and mysteries as it is – marvels and mysteries acting upon our emotions and intelligence in ways so inexplicable that it would almost justify the conception of life as an enchanted state. No, I am too firm in my consciousness of the marvellous to be ever fascinated by the mere supernatural, which (take it any way you like) is but a manufactured article, the fabrication of minds insensitive to the intimate delicacies of our relation to the dead and to the living, in their countless multitudes; a desecration of our tenderest memories; an outrage on our dignity. Whatever my native modesty may be it will never condescend to seek help for my imagination within those vain imaginings common to all ages and that in themselves are enough to fill all lovers of mankind with unutterable sadness'
> (Author's Note to *The Shadow-Line*, 1920).[13]

Conradian echoes are heard elsewhere – one is tempted almost to say everywhere in writing about certain contemporary themes and topics, with Conrad's 'influence', broadly interpreted, as a supreme commentator on the modern condition and the problems of contemporary life. Simon Raven's *Alms for Oblivion* series (1964–76) features Fielding Gray writing a commercially successful study of Conrad and later winning the Joseph Conrad Prize for Fiction. The traveller writer Paul Theroux's novel *Saint Jack* (1973), set in Singapore, has more than a hint of *Lord Jim* about it, and that novel's evocative phrase 'one of us' haunts histories of the administrations of Margaret Thatcher. According to Theroux, Conrad also flavoured V. S. Naipaul's teaching practice in the United States, as well as his later romantic life.[14] Francis King's *Act of Darkness* (1983), Margaret Drabble's *The Gates of Ivory* (1992) and the investigative journalist Nick Davies's commentary on poverty in the United Kingdom *Dark Heart: The Shocking Truth About Hidden Britain* (1998) all nod, with varying layers of complexity and implication, to Conrad's most famous novella, as do the Swedish essayist and journalist Sven Lindquist's *Exterminate All the Brutes* (1992), the British journalist Michaela Wrong's *In the Footsteps of Mr Kurtz* (2001) and, almost inevitably, Tim Butcher's vivid account of his journey to the Congo *Blood River: A Journey to Africa's Broken Heart* (2007), which returns to the scenes of Conrad's own transformative experience. Sebastian Hope's story of life with the Bajau Laut on Sulawesi's east coast, *The Outcasts of the Islands: The Sea Gypsies of South East Asia* (2001) alludes to the title of Conrad's second novel, *An Outcast of the Islands*. The South African novelist J. M. Coetzee did the same with the title of his autobiographical novel *Youth*, (although it is likely that the title is also meant literally, being more in tune with Ford Madox Ford than Conrad). In 2007, the year marking the 150th anniversary of Conrad's birth in the Ukraine, two British novelists arguably echoed Conradian titles: Graham Swift with *Tomorrow*, and the best-selling novelist Victoria Hislop with *The Return*.

Robert Edric's *The Book of the Heathen* (2000), set in the Belgian Congo of 1897, has obvious affinities with *Heart of Darkness*, immediately noticed by reviewers, as does the Northern Irish novelist Ronan Bennett's *The Catastrophist* (1998), while Siddhartha Deb's second novel, *Surface* (2005), at once a thriller and a coming-of-age story set in contemporary North East India, playfully echoes Conrad in several ways, from the title of a book within the novel – *Eastern Eyes* – and most obviously in a verbal echo that suggests the continued power of the short phrase Eliot had recalled decades earlier:

> On our return from the aunt's house, Meghen and I found out that Malik's absence was likely to a permanent, final one. We watched Malik's wife being moved out of the hotel. Sanat came up to my room and joined us, peering out from the window every now and then and he told us the news we had missed.
>
> Mr Malik? He's dead.[15]

Argentine writer Carlos María Domínguez's *The Paper House* (2005), which is dedicated to Conrad – 'In memory of the great Joseph', meditates on the same passage from *The Shadow-Line* quoted earlier, with one reviewer going so far as to claim that the novella itself is the 'true protagonist in this tale'.[16] *The Other Side of You* (2007) by psychotherapist-turned-novelist Salley Vickers has a distinctly Marlovian narrative structure, its awareness of Conrad forming part of the subconscious of the text. Martin Amis's *House of Meetings* (2006) again plays with Conradian themes, although often in a rather forced manner: 'My eyes, in a Conradian sense, have stopped being Western and started being Eastern', 'Now, pluck out your Western eyes.'[17] Writing in *The Guardian* about American writer Cormac McCarthy's *The*

Road (2006), a vision of a post-apocalyptic United States, the novelist Alan Warner noted its 'complete Conradian savagery'.[18]

Conrad's influence on writers might not always be immediately apparent, and only so when writers talk about him. Gabriel García Márquez, for instance, once admitted: 'I would have liked to translate Conrad.'[19] The Spanish writer Javier Marías actually has, turning his admiration for his writing into a translation of *The Mirror of the Sea* (*El espejo del mar: Recuerdos e impresiones*, 2005) and his fascination with Conrad's life experience into a biographical sketch in *Vidas escritas* (1992).[20] The American Joan Didion 'often reread[s] *Victory* which is maybe my favorite book in the world. ... It's incredibly skilful. I have never written a novel without re-reading *Victory*. It opens up the possibilities of a novel. It makes it seem worth doing.'[21] This is an opinion shared by the Australian novelist Shirley Hazzard, whose fascination with Conrad began as early as the age of 8,[22] who revealed in an interview that 'I always have a copy around me of *Victory*.'[23] The literary critic and journalist James Campbell, who interviewed Hazzard in *The Guardian* in July 2006, noted 'a reader might glimpse the shadow of Joseph Conrad, a writer preoccupied not so much with war as with the savagery beneath the civilised skin' in Hazzard's novels. 'Hazzard was re-reading Conrad's *Victory* in the Capri cafes this spring. She is curious as to why this affinity has been overlooked, in favour of another, with Henry James, which doesn't exist. "There is this myth that I was formed on Henry James," she says. "I had hardly read anything of him when I started to write. It must be because I take more trouble, perhaps, with words than authors usually do these days. James is a consummate writer, but you do feel it's like the needle on the old gramophone, that it's got stuck and you want to move it on. Also, I have to say, I think I'm funnier than Henry James."'[24] More flippantly, Conrad appeared as the sixth seed in Australian John Clarke's tennis satire *The Tournament* (2002) defeating Robert Graves 6–2, 6–4, 6–2 in the first round only to fall to William Faulkner 6–3, 5–7, 6–4, 6–2 in the second (2002: 61, 129, 267, 270).

In 2004, something strange occurred; by an odd and sudden turn of some screw, at least three novelists turned to Henry James. James suffused Alan Hollinghurst's Booker Prize-winning *The Line of Beauty* while both Colm Toíbín, in *The Master*, and David Lodge, in *Author! Author!*, resurrected James in more overt fictional form. Since the 150th anniversary of Conrad's birth in 2007, Conrad has made similar reappearances in the fiction of others. The Brazilian writer Bernardo Carvalho's *Nove noites* (2002), published in English that year as *Nine Nights*, is saturated in Conrad, with its echoes of *Lord Jim* and mirroring of both 'The Secret Sharer' and *Heart of Darkness* in its plotting and storyline. The heroine of Australian writer Gail

Jones's fourth novel *Sorry* (2007), set in Western Australia's outback during the Second World War, Perdita comes to Conrad:

> There were three novels by Joseph Conrad which she avidly read. ... At the beginning of *Heart of Darkness* she came across a passage. ... Although, in truth, she did not understand the novel at all, Perdita loved this paragraph. It gave her such dreamy pleasure that she put the book down, keeping the page, and allowed herself slowly to absorb the words.[25]

In an interview accompanying the audio edition of his novella *On Chesil Beach* (2007), Ian McEwan states: 'I suppose I take always as my motto Conrad's "Preface" to *The Nigger of the Narcissus*, "to make you see"',[26] the same line quoted by Craig Raine in his allusive long poem *À la recherche du temps perdu* (2000). The Nobel prize-winning Peruvian author Mario Vargas Llosa published in English an essay, 'The Roots of Humankind', about *Heart of Darkness*.[27] Reviewing the collection of that writer's essays in May 2007, Ian Thomson acknowledged Conrad as one of Vargas Llosa's 'literary idols':

> Conrad's conviction that society is everywhere a rotten fabric appears to chime with Vargas Llosa's own avowed pessimism and reflections on the cruelty of revolution, the abuse of human rights and the evil of material acquisitiveness. Even Conrad's slightly exaggerated rhetoric is music to the Peruvian author, who has a taste for sonorous, operatic gesture. In some ways Conrad introduced to English an epic or ceremonial ring more proper to French prose (Claude Debussy was among the earliest to remark on the meditative music of Conrad's prose).[28]

Three years later, Conrad had considerably more than a walk-on role in Vargas Llosa's novel about the Irish patriot Roger Casement, *El sueño del celta* (2010), translated by Edith Grossman as *The Dream of the Celt*.

Conrad's only command whilst at sea, the *Otago*, appears in Nicholas Shakespeare's novel *Secrets of the Sea* (2007), set in Tasmania, which is also haunted, perhaps not surprisingly by *The Shadow-Line*. Nathan Zuckerman, in Philip Roth's *Exit Ghost* (2007), confesses, 'Lately I've been rereading Conrad for the first time in fifty years, most recently *The Shadow-Line*.'[29] Conrad himself also appears in the fiction of American writers; Cynthia Ozick in her short story 'Dictation' (2007) brought to life his family and, in particular, his unsung secretary, Lilian M. Hallowes,[30] and he also makes a guest appearance in Edmund White's *Hotel de Dream* (2007), a novel about the last months of Conrad's only American friend, Stephen Crane:

> Conrad came to visit him in the late afternoon. As it happened Stevie had dictated to Cora, just before leaving Brede Place, a letter to Arnold Bennett,

> asking him to get Conrad a pension on the civil list: 'He is poor and a gentleman and proud.' Crane might have been describing himself. Crane added that he feared no one might ever like Conrad's books beyond a cult of other writers. Stevie was deeply embarrassed when he discovered that Lady Churchill was circulating a letter asking 'the friends of Stephen Crane' to contribute to an emergency fund. In any event, Lady Churchill was unable to raise any money for him.
>
> Conrad was as small as Stevie but he bristled with energy. His eyes were pinpoints of trouble, his mouth a flat line of pain, his shoulders so strong and high that he appeared to have no neck at all. He entered the room as if he'd just been asked to ascend a throne and, after an initial reluctance, now meant to show just how decisive he could be. The tips of his waxed, black mustaches and spade-shaped black beard preceded him. His skin was sallow and the lines in his face spoke of long night watches on the ship of art.
>
> He sat beside Stevie and planted both hands on the sick man's shoulders. 'My dear friend,' he said, his breath smelling of tobacco and sardines, 'I can see you're about to leave this world.'
> Crane smiled at his frankness.

The writer of the present chapter has also made Conrad's life a subject of fiction for his short novel *Today* (2011), set on three days in August 1924 in the immediate aftermath of Conrad's death, drawing on close friends and immediate family to evoke that transitional moment.

In the last thirty years, Conrad's reach has been wider, stepping outside of the classroom and the purview of academic criticism. The true spirit of Woolf's 'guest' resembles more Conrad's own creation, Mr Jones, when he says 'I am the world itself, come to pay you a visit' (*V*, 379). Conrad was the first true novelist of globalization, and the survey here shows how his writing and vision has inflected the writings of those writing almost a century after his death on several continents and in a wide variety of genres.

Perhaps two writers show this more than most. The Colombian novelist Juan Gabriel Vásquez's *Historia secreta de Costaguana* (2007) is obviously coloured by Conrad's *Nostromo*. Opening in London in 1903, it centres on José Altamirano, recently arrived from the newly established Republic of Panama, who meets Conrad, then working on *Nostromo*. Altamirano tells the novelist – who feels his own memories of the region are dimmed, falling short of a man intent on recreating the memories of his own experiences in the Caribbean – the story of his life and, in the process, the turbulent history of his native Colombia, an account of endless wars and revolutions that culminates in one of the most bitter conflicts of the early twentieth century: the secession of Panama. In doing so, he reveals the 'Secret History of Costaguana'.

Vásquez's first novel, *Los informantes* (2004), is likewise pervaded by Conrad, with *The Secret Agent* and *Under Western Eyes* the very vivid ghosts haunting a thriller set in 1940s Colombia.[31] Vásquez observed that Conrad's writing was key to him, particularly 'his obsessive idea that novels go into dark places and come back with the news. It's not necessarily geographical, but shedding light on dark places of the soul'.[32] Some could posit that *Nostromo* is the first Latin American novel; Garcia Márquez plays with this by calling his novel *One Hundred Years of Solitude*, surely smiling at the title of *Fifty Years of Misrule*, the book by Don José Avellanos that Conrad says he used when researching his own novel, and it is fascinating to see one the best of the young generation of novelists from that continent so illuminated by Conrad's vision.

The other author is John le Carré. As long ago as 1977, a *New York Times* reviewer noted that 'Le Carré seems to have gotten tired of being compared to Graham Greene, and decided to be instead Joseph Conrad'.[33] Philip French observed the same: he 'set aside the terse style of Greene and Eric Ambler and brought together the dense, probing moral inquiry of Joseph Conrad'.[34] In a special preface to his twenty-third novel, *A Delicate Truth* (2013), Le Carré once again adapted the quotation from *The Nigger of the 'Narcissus'* and alluded to the fact that he sees his own work drawing upon Conrad's legacy. In his most recent four novels, Conrad has been quoted, alluded to or mentioned by characters; but in a less superficial way, le Carré's moral vision seems to mirror Conrad's own. Le Carré is one of the few authors who could be said to be truly global in his view of the world. In May 2013, it was reported in a number of newspapers that his next novel is 'loosely based on a story by Joseph Conrad, which he wants to translate into espionage terms'.[35]

Conrad is not about to leave this world. As John Burnside puts it in his poem 'Joseph Conrad's Last Day' (2007), 'if we die of anything, we die of distance',[36] and Conrad's work and concerns are not distant but, indeed, still near to us. The best thing that has happened to Conrad is distance. With time comes forgetting – and ignorance. Today's younger readers are sometimes amazed to discover that Conrad was not an 'English gentleman'. It is safe to say he will be read more widely at the end of this century than he was at its beginning, reaching audiences in developing countries and taking his vision to them, both in his own work and in his influence on other writers.

Almost twenty years ago, Peter Nazareth, a Ugandan-turned-American writer and academic, reviewing his experience of teaching Conrad to university students stated 'Conrad lives',[37] and today Conrad's spirit moves upon the waters still. He is more visible today than even the most ardent Conradian might at first imagine, no longer a 'guest', outcast or intruder, but an integral part of literary culture and even of contemporary culture more generally.[38] Robert Stone commented in a 1985 interview: 'He [Conrad] saw things as they are without wanting to reduce them to theory. In that respect he's closer to the temper of our own time and certainly closer to my own ideas about reality and about how to explore it in fiction'.[39] Conrad phrased it differently in *The Mirror of the Sea*: 'In his own time a man is always very modern' (*MS*, 72). Virginia Woolf might well be chastened by the reality that this most modern of writers is ranked by contemporary novelists – and will be by those yet to pick up a pen – as one of them. Indeed, he's in their blood.

NOTES

1 See *Letters*, II, 227.
2 'Joseph Conrad', *Times Literary Supplement*, 14 August 1924, p. 493; rpt. *The Common Reader* (1925).
3 'Influences on Other Writers' in Owen Knowles and Gene M. Moore, *Oxford Reader's Companion to Conrad* (Oxford: Oxford University Press, 2000), pp. 168–71. For a slightly earlier survey, see Gene M. Moore, 'Conrad's Influence', *The Cambridge Companion to Joseph Conrad*, ed. J. H. Stape (1996), pp. 223–41.
4 The echoes are explored in the introduction and notes of Peter Lancelot Mallios's reading edition of *Victory, An Island Tale* (New York: The Modern Library, 2003), pp. xi–xliv, 323–44.
5 Liam Lacey, 'Less is Moore for Brian', *The Globe and Mail* (Toronto), 20 October 1987, p. D5; quoted in Colm Tóibín, 'Introduction', *Black Robe* (Toronto: Penguin Canada, 2006), p. xi.
6 For instance, Fiona Wilson characterized it as 'a *National Geographic* story by way of Conrad's *Heart of Darkness*', *The Times*, 18 January 2014, p. 16.
7 Timothy Findley, *Headhunter* (Toronto: HarperCollins, 1993), pp. 4–5.
8 Cf. '"A funny piece of water – that," said Captain Giles' (*SL*, 41.28–29).
9 'Above all, we must forgive the unhappy souls who have elected to make the pilgrimage on foot, who skirt the shore and look uncomprehendingly upon the horror of the struggle, the joy of victory, the profound hopelessness of the vanquished' (*Letters*, I, 43).
10 *Five Books*, 'An interview with Jason Burke on Islamic Militancy', 22 August 2011 (http://fivebooks.com/interviews/jason-burke-on-islamic-militancy). Accessed: January 2014.
11 Jason Burke, 'The Key Books on Muslim Extremism', *The Guardian*, 7 November 2012.
12 Robert Harris, 'Forget Islam: Bin Laden is No More than a Spoilt Rich Kid', *The Daily Telegraph*, 9 October 2001, p. 26; Francis Wheen, 'A Lust for Killing That Defies All Our Reason', *Evening Standard*, 15 August 2006, p. 12.
13 'The Age of Horrorism, Faith and the Dependent Mind: Part 3', *The Observer*, 10 September 2006.
14 Paul Theroux, *Sir Vidia's Shadow: A Friendship across Five Continents* (1998), pp. 259, 333.

15 Siddartha Deb, *Surface* (London: Picador, 2005), pp. 45, 211–12.
16 Carlos María Domínguez, *The Paper House* (London: Harvill Secker, 2005), p. 31; review by Janelle Martin, 6 July 2006 (readysteadybook.com/BookReview.aspx?isbn=1843432080): Accessed: January 2014.
17 Martin Amis, *House of Meetings* (London: Cape, 2006), pp. 11, 84.
18 Alan Warner, 'The Road to Hell', *The Guardian*, 4 November 2006, p. 7.
19 Peter H. Stone, '*Paris Review* Interview, No. 69: Gabriel García Márquez', *The Paris Review* 82 (1981), 333.
20 Javier Marías, *Written Lives*, trans. Margaret Jull Costa (New York: New Directions, 2006).
21 Hilton Als, 'Joan Didion: The Art of Nonfiction, No. 1', *The Paris Review* 176 (2006), 481.
22 J. D. McClatchy, 'Shirley Hazzard: The Art of Fiction, No. 185', *The Paris Review* 173 (2005).
23 Marianne Macdonald, 'A Writer's Life: Shirley Hazzard', *The Daily Telegraph*, 6 December 2003, p. 12.
24 James Campbell, 'Notes from a Small Island', *The Guardian*, 8 July 2006, p. 19.
25 Gail Jones, *Sorry* (London: Harvill Secker 2007), pp. 144–6.
26 CD-Audio, *On Chesil Beach* (Random House Audio, 2007), 4A: 3: 40–44: 58.
27 Mario Vargas Llosa, *Touchstones: Essays in Literature, Art and Politics*, ed. and trans. John King (London: Faber & Faber, 2007), pp. 32–42.
28 Ian Thomson, 'No Difference between Politics and Art', *The Sunday Telegraph*, 31 May 2007.
29 Philip Roth, *Exit Ghost* (New York: Houghton Mifflin, 2007), pp. 3–4.
30 Collected in her *Dictation: A Quartet* (New York: Houghton Mifflin Harcourt, 2008). The story was first published in 'Conrad: A 150th Birthday Celebration', ed. Allan H. Simmons and David Miller, *The Conradian* 32, no. 2 (2007), 76–109.
31 *The Informer*, trans. Anne McLean (London: Bloomsbury UK, 2009).
32 Maya Jaggi, 'A Life in Writing: Juan Gabriel Vásquez', *The Guardian*, 26 June 2010, p. 12.
33 John Leonard, 'Books of the Times': Review of John le Carré's *The Honourable Schoolboy*, *New York Times*, 22 September 1977, www.nytimes.com/books/99/03/21/specials/lecarre-school.html. Accessed January 2014.
34 Philip French, '*Tinker Tailor Soldier Spy* – Review', *The Observer*, 18 September 2011, p. 26.
35 See, for example, 'Le Carre Set to Rework Joseph Conrad Story', *The Australian* (Sydney), 4 May 2013 (theaustralian.com.au/news/latest-news/le-carre-set-to-rework-joseph-conrad-story/story-fn3dxix6-1226635239396): Accessed January 2014.
36 *Times Literary Supplement*, 7 September 2007, p. 4.
37 Peter Nazareth, 'Conrad's Descendants', *Conradiana* 22 (1990), 109.
38 On this topic, see Richard J. Hand's chapter on adaptation in the present volume.
39 William Crawford Woods, 'Robert Stone: The Art of Fiction, No. 90', *The Paris Review* 98 (1985), 51.

13

RICHARD J. HAND

Conrad Adapted

Adaptation – whereby a source text is translated into a different form – has not only been common practice for centuries but is also arguably a central process in Western culture. To this end, we might consider the use of the oral tradition in the formation of Classical Greek dramatic texts or the dramatization of scripture into mediaeval miracle and mystery plays. Shakespeare, English literature's pre-eminent figurehead, was an adapter *par excellence*, taking history books, Italian novels and pre-existing plays and reworking these materials to create 'new' dramatic works. In turn, his plays have been adapted into a countless number of reinterpretations, appropriations and intertextual allusions. Adaptive processes, therefore, lie at the very heart of English literary culture. The rise of new art forms and media from the late nineteenth century onwards has done nothing to diminish adaptation, and our own time has seen an exponential proliferation of adaptations across the widest range of contemporary culture.

When adaptation is mentioned, the usual assumption is that one is discussing the conversion of fictional narrative into film. The reflex association of adaptation with the cinema is not arbitrary; film and television have, for several reasons, made adaptation a central enterprise. On one level, it reflects a cautious screen industry reluctant to take chances on original, 'untested' storylines. A published source text that has been a commercial, popular or critical success might seem to offer a ready-made 'story worth telling' and may promise a head-start towards box office success. Certainly, in pursuing this dream Hollywood continually buys the rights to works of popular fiction.

In defining adaptation as an act that signals 'a relationship with an informing source text or original',[1] Julie Sanders reveals just how all-encompassing the adaptation process can be. Although the immediate connotation of adaptation is probably cinema, it is an equally important practice in the worlds of theatre, radio, graphic art and digital games. When it comes to Conrad, his works have been transformed into all types of media in adaptive relationships that have been hidden as much as overt. This chapter explores the adaptation of Conrad's work in the widest range of media since the mid-1990s, beginning with examples of cinema and television.[2]

Conrad on Screen

Conrad's position as a major author in the canon of English literature would lead us to expect that he would be unproblematically a most 'visible' of sources, to be embraced by adaptors and emblazoned on the credits of any adaptation. Certainly, during his lifetime the nascent Hollywood industry keenly bought the rights to Conrad's fiction, produced Maurice Tourneur's high-profile feature film of *Victory* (1919) and even paid Conrad an advance to write screenplays himself. In the decades after his death, other films would appear, above all that most cinematically melodramatic of all his works: *Victory*. However, in more recent years what is distinctive about the adaptation of Conrad in a broadly 'postmodern' context is how it appears in both *overt* and *invisible* ways. Just as in the adaptation industries surrounding Charles Dickens and Jane Austen, for example, most often dramatizations will draw attention to the author of the source text, in some cases a similar decision to foreground the name of 'Joseph Conrad' is evident. For example, all posters and subsequent home release formats of Christopher Hampton's 1996 screen adaptation of *The Secret Agent* present the film as *Joseph Conrad's The Secret Agent*. Similarly, the international co-production of *Nostromo* that adapted the novel into a television mini-series was presented as *Joseph Conrad's Nostromo*. At the same time, Conrad can be an invisible or 'hidden' source. Perhaps the most famous Conrad adaptation of all – Francis Ford Coppola's *Apocalypse Now* (1979) – keeps Conrad and *Heart of Darkness* uncredited.

The irony of the invisible Conrad in *Apocalypse Now* reverberates in different ways with examples of loudly heralded Conrad adaptations that proved problematic or unmade. That Orson Welles's first film project for Hollywood was an adaptation of *Heart of Darkness* that he instead abandoned for *Citizen Kane* (1941) has become something of a popular culture legend and taken on its own curious journey of adaptation and inspiration. Similarly unmade was David Lean's *Nostromo*, the director dying just before filming was due to start in 1991. Proud of his adaptation of *Victory*, Harold Pinter published it (2000), although Richard Lester's film was never produced.

Over the decades, when 'overt' film adaptations of Conrad have been produced they have sometimes been less than successful. It is fair to say that Alfred Hitchcock's *Sabotage* (1936) and Richard Brooks's *Lord Jim*

(1965) are not the directors' finest works, and the tradition continued for similarly talented directors since in the 1990s. For example, a major *auteur* of British film, Nicolas Roeg, directed a feature film of *Heart of Darkness* (1993) for U.S. television (TNT). The film was made in Guyana (but still set in Africa) and starred celebrated actors Tim Roth (as Marlow) and John Malkovich (Kurtz). Despite the superficial realism (indeed, perhaps because of it), the resulting film was surprisingly cliché-ridden and anticlimactic compared to other adaptations of Conrad's most famous novella and, it must be said, many of Roeg's other films. Also produced in the mid-1990s, one of the most ambitious Conrad adaptations for the screen is Christopher Hampton's *Joseph Conrad's The Secret Agent* (1996).

The popular British screen actor Bob Hoskins had long harboured a desire to play Verloc in a big-screen adaptation of *The Secret Agent* and in 1991 liaised with the screenwriter Christopher Hampton, a notable figure in film adaptation with credits such as Stephen Frears's *Dangerous Liaisons* (1988). Hampton and Hoskins met with difficulty as 'several potential investors reeled back, appalled at the darkness of the story'.[3] Ultimately, Hampton directed the screenplay himself, and the movie opened in the United States in 1996. A box office flop, in the UK it went straight to video. Hoskins and Hampton managed to command an impressive cast of established and rising international actors including Gérard Depardieu (Ossipon), Patricia Arquette (Winnie) and Christian Bale (Stevie). The adaptation also used performers more usually associated with comedy: Eddie Izzard (Mr Vladimir), Jim Broadbent (Inspector Heat) and Robin Williams (the Professor), a decision that captures the grotesque humour in Conrad's original where the consistently ironic treatment of characters makes them frequently ridiculous.

The individual performances are strong, the casting generally proves apt (although Arquette as Winnie is never quite convincing), and American composer Philip Glass's soundtrack is excellent. The film disappoints, however, in its construction of the Victorian city context. *The Secret Agent* is a great urban novel, about a city as much as the individual characters who inhabit it. Hitchcock could capture the dynamism and experience of London in films as far apart as *The Lodger* (1927) and *Frenzy* (1972), and his own adaptation of Conrad's *The Secret Agent – Sabotage* (1936) – is convincing on an urban level, even if his cast and adaptive decisions (the Verlocs run a cinema) disappoint. As director, Hampton faced a problem in filming a Victorian city tale in the 1990s. Britain's 'heritage film' industry can draw on a choice of ideal locations when making an Austen adaptation, but creating the teeming city of *The Secret Agent* is more difficult as the filmmakers had to create the interior and exterior of Victorian London in Ealing Studios. As a result, the film unfurls like a sequence of *tableaux* with a bleak and superficial realism, a film of condensed interiority rather than Conrad's part-realist, part-abstract metropolis. The exception perhaps is the closing sequence in which the eerily convincing Robin Williams (who chose to play the Professor uncredited) walks in horror through a bustling London street before squeezing his hand on the detonator strapped to his body.

Not simply the failure to capture the scale of the novel's urban world made the film a box office disaster. Like potential backers, the few spectators who saw it in the cinema probably baulked at the depressing storyline. The novel is bleak and the absence of the narrator who navigates the plot with ironic humour and humanity is acutely felt. This problem confronted Conrad himself when he wrote his own stage adaptation of the novel in 1919 and found that the cross-media process of adaptation revealed the novel's 'grisly skeleton' (*SA*, 8.30). An additional reason that the film made little impact in the UK was that it was released not long after David Drury's three-part BBC television series of the same story (1992), scripted by Dusty Hughes and featuring David Suchet as Verloc. The mini-series had a luxury of duration compared to Hampton's feature film, and the 'cliff hanger' technique enforced by television episodes worked admirably when interpreting Conrad's anti-chronological plot. In addition, the BBC could take its 'classic serial' approach with a design, cast and *mise-en-scène* highly suitable for the adaptation of a major literary work. Arguably, the dramatization locates Verloc at the story's tragic heart, and David Suchet interprets the role with nuanced, psychological depth. As a result, the BBC Verloc is a tragic figure not without pathos compared to the novel's uncharismatic, frequently absurd figure, with the adaptation effective but transforming Conrad's novel into a psychological drama.

The BBC itself has taken a different approach in dramatizing the same novel; in David Napthine's two-part BBC radio adaptation of *The Secret Agent* (2006), the play opens with the bomb attack at Greenwich – a loud explosion and a richly realized soundscape (splintering trees, screams and neighing horses which merge into the cries of newspaper vendors) and then continues with Inspector Heat (Ron Cook) 'on the case'. The effect of this is to emulate the novel's fractured time structure (albeit ordering the plot differently), but it also makes the work allusive to the detective or whodunit genre that has had immense significance in the history of radio drama. True to genre, the play begins with a gruesome crime, and we follow the investigation as the culprits are identified and the motives unravelled through flashbacks, interviews and dramatic action. The drama is two hours in duration. Napthine's dialogue for the large cast succeeds in developing the exposition of the plot with generally strong characterization, and Jessica Drongoole's production constructs a convincing auditory sense of this Victorian story and its multiple locations.

In the same year as Christopher Hampton's version of *The Secret Agent*, the BBC led an international television co-production of *Joseph Conrad's Nostromo* (Alastair Reid, 1996). The lavish four-part serialization, adapted by John Hale, was filmed in Colombia and boasted a high-profile, international cast. The adaptation strove to realize the story comparatively fully, using the luxury of its five-hour duration and big budget. However, like the contemporaneous big-screen Conrad adaptation, *Joseph Conrad's Nostromo* met with disappointing audience figures and lukewarm reviews. The problems with the series reveal issues with the processes of adaptation as a whole. In other words, although Conrad's longest novel has narrative coherence, this becomes sprawling when translated to the screen; the integrity of characterization on the page becomes fractured on television, and Conrad's exploration of enigma and irony can become confusing when dramatized.

The fact that *Joseph Conrad's Nostromo* was a global co-production reveals that Conrad has acquired an appeal for international filmmakers and their audiences. Several film adaptations have emerged out of France since the 1990s. *Pour Demain* (Fabrice Cazeneuve, 1992) is a feature-length television adaptation of Conrad's story 'To-morrow' (1902), a tale inherently dramatic enough to form the basis of Conrad's own first stage play *One Day More* (1907). Similarly, French television viewers could mark the centenary of 'The End of the Tether' (1902) by watching Thierry Binisti's feature-length adaptation *Au bout du rouleau* (2002), which contemporized Conrad's short story. As well as television, French cinema has produced Conrad adaptations. Patrice Chéreau's *Gabrielle* (2005) – an adaptation of 'The Return' (1914) – sets Conrad's domestic short story in Paris prior to the First World War. The eponymous character is played by Isabelle Huppert who, in partnership with Pascal Greggory as her husband, locates an emotional range and intensity befitting the Conrad original in the interpretation of a flawed bourgeois marriage. The acclaimed Belgian director Chantal Akerman's Franco-Belgian co-production of *La Folie Almayer* (2011) updated *Almayer's Folly* (1895) to the 1950s in a languid but passionate vision using a soundtrack featuring Wagner's *Tristan und Isolde* and Dean Martin.

The financial imperative of global co-production has seen a British, German and French co-production of the most adapted Conrad novel: Mark Peploe's *Victory* (1995), featuring prominent actors including the American Willem Dafoe (as Heyst), the British Rufus Sewell (Ricardo), the Australian Sam Neill (Jones) and the French Irène Jacob (Alma). The film follows Conrad's plot more closely than some earlier adaptations; by retaining Lena's death, it avoids some of the more sugar-coated finales of other versions. Although Heyst is permitted to survive and make a 'new start', this offers viewers something fragilely 'hopeful' rather than unambiguously 'happy'. Similarly international is Beeban Kidron's *Swept from the Sea* (1997), a Canadian, British and U.S. co-produced film based on 'Amy Foster' (1903). Kidron creates an epic, historical love story out of the short story, charting the illicit romance of the servant Amy (Rachel Weisz) and shipwrecked Yanko (Vincent Perez) in a scenic Cornwall. The passionate but doomed love of Amy and Yanko is starkly contrasted by the conformist presence of Dr Kennedy (Ian McKellen) and Miss Swaffer (Kathy Bates).

The increasing international interest in recent years in adapting Conrad to film has not been restricted to Western filmmakers. The Malaysian filmmaker U-Wei Haji Saari's adaptation of *Almayer's Folly* as *Hanyut* (2012) is a richly detailed historical drama set in late nineteenth-century Malaya, capturing the tensions of its dynamically cosmopolitan culture. The film explains to its audience that the Malay word *hanyut* means 'drifting off into ominous peril without any real way of getting back'. The word, which lacks a direct English equivalent, is particularly resonant in a Conradian context.

Conrad on Stage

Although Conrad did experiment in screenplay writing (the unproduced film scenario *Gaspar the Strong Man* being based on 'Gaspar Ruiz'), his most concerted efforts in adaptation were in the area of theatre. His own plays did not enjoy much success – his *Laughing Anne* was not staged until 2000[4] (see Hand 2001 and 2002) – even if *One Day More* (1907) and *The Secret Agent* (1922) did enjoy a degree of public profile in their own time with London productions. Since then, festivals and academic gatherings have witnessed revivals of Conrad's own plays, most notably *One Day More* at, for example, a Conrad conference in Colgate University, New York (1999), in Swansea's Dylan Thomas Centre (2012) and in several other locations. The one-act, small cast concision of Conrad's first play lends itself to production fairly easily, its tragic absurdity somewhat allusive to the plays of Eugene O'Neill or Samuel Beckett, making it an interesting experience for some audiences. In contrast, the demands of Conrad's dramatization of *The Secret Agent* in terms of set and cast have made it rarely revived, although it has been staged in fringe and amateur productions and in Italian translation (Genoa, 2008). Christopher Hampton cites seeing a London fringe production in the 1980s.[5]

Despite the difficulties of realizing Conrad on stage, there has been increased interest in his work for live adaptation in recent years, especially in opera. Conrad was an opera aficionado and the medium permeates his work,[6] and he confessed that *Victory* could 'make a libretto for a Puccini opera' (*Letters*, V, 452). The novel was eventually adapted into an opera by Richard Rodney Bennett in 1970, one of several operas based on Conrad's works. Most recently, there have been attempts to adapt *Under Western Eyes*, *The Secret Agent* and *Heart of Darkness*.

Greg Bartholomew's *Razumov*, a three-act chamber opera, is based on *Under Western Eyes* (1911). Although there is yet to be a full production of *Razumov*, various scenes and suites from the opera have been regularly performed from 2002 onwards, including a notable CD recording of the First Suite from *Razumov* by the Kiev Philharmonic in 2005. In recounting the genesis of the composition, Bartholomew explains that he first read *Under Western Eyes* in the 1980s and began to adapt it into a screenplay, 'without much hope that it would lead to a movie being made, but more out of an expectation that by pulling the story apart and putting it back together again I would gain a better sense of how Conrad so brilliantly developed his plot'.[7] Having started work on the screenplay, Bartholomew saw a production of Claude-Michel Schönberg's *Les Misérables*, the musical based on Victor Hugo's 1862 novel. The experience was inspiring enough to make Bartholomew shift media and 'decide to convert the screenplay project into an opera project'.[8] Bartholomew immersed himself in writings about Conrad and his historical context.

Bartholomew found two key aspects of *Under Western Eyes* particularly compelling when creating his opera. First, he was struck by 'the nature of Razumov as someone totally misunderstood by everyone around him, with his life so dramatically affected by other people's misunderstandings and incorrect assumptions about him'.[9] Secondly, he was 'intrigued by Conrad's focus on the personal psychology of the revolutionaries, and the ironies deriving from that'.[10] These two factors – the alienated individual and the inner workings and world-views of the story's ideologues – gave the composer powerful dramatic material to underpin and infuse his chamber opera, while Bartholomew admits that he had to streamline and simplify Conrad's complex novel. (Some years after he decided to call his adaptation *Razumov*, he learned, with 'great pleasure', that Conrad's first draft bore that title, a discovery that made Bartholomew feel 'in sync' with Conrad.[11])

British composer Simon Wills adapted *The Secret Agent* into a chamber opera that premiered at Germany's 2006 Feldkirch Festival. Wills's work can be interpreted, to a certain degree, as following in the traditions of nineteenth-century music-drama associated with Wagner and the use of *leitmotiv*. In particular, Wills acknowledges the influence of Alban Berg's 1925 adaptation of *Wozzeck* (as the modern apotheosis of *leitmotiv*) in creating *The Secret Agent*. At the same time, Wills uses Victorian popular song – namely, 'Love's Old Sweet Song' (1884) – as an offstage chorus in ironic juxtaposition to the unfurling horrors. These compositional decisions are reminiscent of Conrad's own richly intertextual strategies. Although nearly three hours long, Wills distils Conrad's novel into four sung roles: Verloc (bass-baritone), Winnie (soprano), Inspector Heat (tenor) and the Professor (countertenor). Of equal importance is the mute Stevie for whom Wills composes an 'aria-in-mime'.[12] Wills deliberately develops Conrad's Stevie so that he becomes evidently 'the character with most insight' in the opera (Wills 2013b). Poignantly and potently, Stevie is denied a literal voice, but as Wills states in his programme note for the premiere, 'the loudest sound in music is a sudden silence'.[13]

As Wills playfully reveals, his opera 'holds the world record for fatalities in an opera, since the audience dies as well: the Professor (in a suicide waistcoat) performs the peroration then in the last bar steps into the auditorium and presses the detonator'.[14] The arbitrary horror of terrorist slaughter (whatever the asserted 'ideology' might be) emphasizes the broadly political impetus to the opera; years before its composition, Wills was nearby an Irish Republican Army bomb attack in which two terrorists accidentally blew themselves up. With hideous irony, Wills was composing the Professor's aria about bomb-making while the 7 July 2005 terrorist attacks on London were happening. When he had completed writing the score and libretto for the opera, Wills reveals: 'I have a keener sense of the pity of our brutalities to each other, but am no nearer to grasping why our political generals, our latter-day Mr Vladimirs, should wish so fervently to convince us that we are at war with such a chimerical creature as terrorism.'[15]

Despite this, Wills follows Conrad's line in insisting that *The Secret Agent* is 'a domestic tragedy' and further argues that the characters are just ordinary people who are 'destroyed by their failure to imagine, failure to communicate, failure to love'.

In a statement that is a curious echo of Conrad's own difficult experience of dramatizing *The Secret Agent* in 1919, for Wills, the process of adapting the novel proved a challenge that became 'a personal heart of darkness that messed with my head quite badly' and prevented him composing for some time.[16] In many respects, Wills's version captures the grotesque humour and sheer horror of *The Secret Agent* in his intensely focussed and experimental production. Other operatic interpretations of the same text have been larger in scale (but not duration), using full casts and more traditional structures and music to animate Conrad's panoramic vision of London.

In 2011, a two-act opera based on *The Secret Agent* with score by Michael Dellaira and libretto by J. D. McClatchy premiered at New York's Center for Contemporary Opera, with a subsequent premiere at Hungary's Armel Festival. In developing the opera, Dellaira and McClatchy decided to use Conrad's own adaptation of *The Secret Agent*. As a result, some of the novel's isolated and fragmented scenes are consolidated into more dramatically epic scenes. For example, the opera opens with a ball at the German (*sic*) Embassy with a uniformed Ambassador in a duet with Lady Mabel (the novel's unnamed patroness, called Mabel in Conrad's stage play) that subsequently merges into Verloc's arrival. The long duet between the Ambassador and Verloc distils the exchange between the two as the Ambassador compels the attack on Greenwich Observatory. The scene ends – structurally echoing the opening duet with the patroness – with a short encounter with the British Prime Minister in which the Ambassador condemns the government's lack of vigilance. Subsequent scenes take us to Verloc's home life with Winnie and her beloved Stevie flowing into the meeting of the anarchists (in this interpretation, the trio of Ossipon, Michaelis and the Professor). A bold ellipsis finds Ossipon and the Professor at a café where they discuss the Greenwich outrage and assume Verloc its victim, a scene powerfully juxtaposed with a forensic sequence with the police attempting to piece together the crime, as well as the victim's body.

The second act opens with another ball, this time Lady Mabel's *soirée*. News of the bomb attack is interpolated with the music of Schubert's lieder version of Goethe's '*Erlkönig*' creating, as in Wills's opera (and Conrad's novel), a deliberately intertextual mechanism. The same dramatic expediency that locates Verloc in the embassy during an elite party brings, as in Conrad's play, the Professor to the Verloc house at the end of the opera so that he can cast judgement and draw a perverse moral. Hence, the operatic Winnie does not drown herself but, as in the stage play, loses her mind and can utter nothing but 'Blood and dirt!' in manic despair. Where Conrad's novel is fractured and anti-chronological with isolated characters and episodes, the opera finds an epic sweep with longer, structurally developed scenes. In the review of its premiere in *Operaticus* (18 March 2011), Dellaira and McClatchy's *The Secret Agent* proves 'timely for post–9/11 America, both relevant and yet removed enough so as not to be too uncomfortable, playing as *film noir* or Dickensian fiction, instead of reality'.

Remarkably soon after Dellaira and McClatchy's work, a completely separate two-act opera, Curtis Bryant's *The Secret Agent*, to a libretto by Allen Reichman, premiered at Atlanta's Capitol City Opera in 2013. Reichman had originally showed Bryant his libretto in 2004 and the composer explains why it appealed to the librettist: Reichman 'saw all of the makings of grand

Italian opera: a wrongful death, a murder, and a suicide. It was these features, along with the psychological complexity of the characters that first appealed to him, notwithstanding the more obvious fascination in a drama that had a renewed relevance in the wake of the terrorist events of the recent past.'[17]

Bryant and Reichman relocate the action to 1930s London in what could be seen as a tacit homage to Hitchcock's *Sabotage*. Bold decisions are taken in the adaptation; once again the narrative is straightened into a chronological exposition, and the Professor disappears and is merged into the aged radical Karl Yundt, the bomb-maker. A decision is made to keep more on stage. For example, the final scene of the first act is set in Greenwich Park, in which Verloc sends Stevie off with the bomb. In an aria, Verloc witnesses the clumsy Stevie die (complete with the sound effect of an explosion) after which an apparition of Vladimir appears berating Verloc for his incompetence. Later, Winnie murders Verloc with the pair of compasses from Stevie's art set. The opera, which also opts to interpret Winnie's elopement with Ossipon, who abandons the sleeping woman as the train departs from Southampton, concludes in a thunderously melodramatic finale as Winnie throws herself from the speeding train.

In November 2011, *Heart of Darkness*, a one-act opera by the young British composer Tarik O'Regan to a libretto by Tom Phillips premiered at London's Royal Opera House. In the short opera (seventy-five minutes), Marlow is played by a tenor, Kurtz is a bass, and a soprano plays the Intended and her ironic *Doppelgänger* (in the opera, the 'River Woman'). Several other characters from the source text feature in the adaptation (such as the Company Secretary, the Harlequin, the Accountant, the Manager and the Helmsman), often functioning as dialogic foils for Marlow, giving clues and insight into the enigmatic Kurtz. The opera breaks the novella's structure inasmuch as it begins with two short sequences of an aged Marlow recollecting his journey to find Kurtz and his encounter with Kurtz's Intended. After this, the narrative moves swiftly, with Marlow aboard ship on the Thames as he takes the audience from his medical check-up in Europe to his journey deeper and deeper down the African river, reaching a climax with the encounter with Kurtz, who dies uttering 'The horror, the horror' on board the steamer as it leaves the Inner Station.

The librettist Tom Phillips, a visual artist best known for his art book *A Humument: a treated Victorian novel* (1970 with subsequent revisions), created *A Humument* from a junkshop copy of W. H. Mallock's forgotten novel *A Human Document* (1892), and turned each page into an artistic palimpsest: through painting, drawing, erasing and framing the text, Phillips locates seemingly hidden narratives and ironic meanings, adapting Mallock's antiquated, banal story into a beautifully abstract work of lyricism and irony. A postmodern artist with a particular interest in late-Victorian culture, Phillips was an inspired choice as O'Regan's librettist. He used text from Conrad's *Congo Diary* as well as *Heart of Darkness* to create the libretto and adapts the Victorian narrative into an intense and economical drama. The *Observer* review of the premiere found that 'Phillips's gloriously spare libretto ... hacks through the dense jungle of the author's prose and elevates it to the status of the finest poetry'.[18] In contrast, the *Daily Telegraph* review (2 November 2011) felt that 'Conrad's classic novel isn't easily packaged' with the result that the adaptation feels 'eviscerated'.[19] Nevertheless, the same review believed that O'Regan's 'magical and haunting sound-world' of the opera – partly recreated in the composer's 'Suite for *Heart of Darkness*' (2013) – is clearly a 'landmark' by a major new talent. The *Observer* concurs, regarding O'Regan and Phillips's *Heart of Darkness* as a work of 'brilliance' with a score of 'startling beauty'. As a whole, the opera captures the original's nightmarish and symbolic power, not least in Robert Innes Hopkins's stage design for the first production in which the central ship literally became awash with water.

The decision to shift away from the realism that has arguably dogged screen interpretations of Conrad is not only an option for opera. In recent years, Conrad has found a similar lease of life in *avant-garde* theatre. In 2010, for example, the Give It A Name Theatre Company created an immersive, site-specific version of *Heart of Darkness* in Cardiff's Ten Feet Tall nightclub. Directed by James Williams, the production used various spaces in the building, allowing the narrative to unfold in diverse ways as the audience made literal choices as to which door they would pass through or whose story they would listen to. The innovative adaptation therefore took its audience through multiple layers of history and narrative as well as architectural space in a version that arguably challenged the hypnotic compulsion of Marlow's story and transformed it into an environment of conflicting accounts.

In their collaborative development of *The Secret Agent* (2013), playwright Matthew Hurt and Theatre O stripped down the action to locate the core plot of this 'simple tale' and its motifs. Some surprising production choices were made in the doubling of roles: the actor playing Winnie's mother also played the Professor, Inspector Heat also played Comrade Ossipon, and Mr Vladimir played Stevie. On UK tour, *The Secret Agent* was a physical theatre production that choreographed action with deliberate eclecticism; for example, at one point footlights illuminated Verloc as he delivered a jolly music hall rendition of 'I Don't Want to Set the World on Fire'. Interestingly, the published script of the adaptation features more 'showman' features such as a 'Cabinet of Desires', which displayed characters from the story as Victorian carnival freaks. This device was abandoned as the production evolved, and the play opened and closed with the *tableau* of the Verloc family, like an image from a Victorian family album. Conrad is the last writer one would consider to have the potential for audience participation, but in the production Mr Vladimir recruited audience members for a pantomimic and deeply satirical 'committee' meeting, the engineered 'unanimous' consensus of which was the need for a terrorist attack on the Greenwich Observatory. Elsewhere in the production some surprising and effective moments of theatre craft were used, such as a mimed *tableau* of Winnie drowning with hideous gracefulness in the twilight waters of the English Channel.

The production used certain motifs in the novel dramatically. For example, in the scene in which Winnie learns of Stevie's fate we find her, as Conrad says, with her hands 'pressed convulsively to her face, with the tips of the fingers contracted against the forehead, as though the skin had been a mask which she was ready to tear off violently' (*SA*, 160.35–38). Theatre O turned this into a grotesque and elaborate dance with Verloc attempting to coax, encourage and prise her hands away. Likewise, Stevie's mad circles become a long speech as he describes the place of circles in the universe as he recreates, with furniture, the pathetic horse and the 'Cab of Death' (131.25). Overall, Hurt's adaptation can surprise Conrad aficionados while adhering to a pared-down narrative of the novel. The script and production capture the novel's satirical, absurdist and abstract qualities rather than opting for a televisual 'classic serial' realism. All the same, in the radical fracturing of its source text, certain lines end up rather contentiously redeployed, such as when the Professor uses the novel's final line – 'like a pest in the street full of men' (231.38–39) – to describe Verloc's heading off with the bomb.

From Conrad to the Conradesque

As mentioned, Conrad goes uncredited in the greatest of all Vietnam movies: Coppola's *Apocalypse Now* (1979). This was redressed in the documentary film *Hearts of Darkness: A Filmmaker's Apocalypse* (Fax Bahr, George Hickenlooper, Eleanor Coppola, 1991), when Eleanor Coppola describes her husband's film as being 'loosely based' on *Heart of Darkness*. The status and popularity of *Apocalypse Now* has led to its own domino-chain of adaptation. In the late 1980s, J. F. Lawton made Kurtz a female scientist who disappears in the jungle and when found has established her own empire among a tribe of women: *Cannibal Women in the Avocado Jungle of Death* (1989). In this comedy spoof of *Apocalypse Now* Conrad is once again invisible in the credits. More interesting is Cineclash's *Apocalypse*

Oz (Ewan Telford, 2006), a short film that 'remixes' *Apocalypse Now* with Victor Fleming's *Wizard of Oz* (1939) adhering to a strict manifesto, including the rule that 'There is no original dialogue in the film at all. All lines come strictly from one or the other of the "parent" films. Most lines "sample" or re-arrange dialogue from both films'.[20] Consequently, the film offers lines of dialogue like: 'There's no horror like home'. Interestingly, in the credits, one finds: 'APOCALYPSE OZ – screenplay by Ewan Telford, adapted from works by: Joseph Conrad, L. Frank Baum, Noel Langley, Florence Ryerson, Edgar Allan Woolf, John Millius, Francis Ford Coppola and Michael Herr.' Conrad is instated as the first named source. The Cineclash team that made *Apocalypse Oz* quote Coppola on their website: 'our work is here for all of you young writers: please steal from it, that's good, that's what it's supposed to be, that's the cultural transfer that happens from generation to generation'.[21] Adaptation, it would seem, can be or should be theft.

The screenplay of Orson Welles's abandoned *Heart of Darkness* film project is extant and in circulation, albeit never officially published let alone produced. Welles's two different radio adaptations of 1938 and 1945 give clues as to the performance style that Welles might have opted to use on screen. The unfulfilled link between Welles and Conrad found a curious consummation in the summer of 2012 in a project developed by the artist Fiona Banner, with British actor Brian Cox reading out the entire film-script of Welles's *Heart of Darkness* from 'A Room For London', a small studio space designed to resemble the *Roi des Belges* (the riverboat Conrad navigated up the Congo) erected atop the South Bank Centre. The four-and-a-half hour reading was relayed online and on a cinema screen in the South Bank Centre itself.

Another example of the posthumous realization of Wells's Conrad work came in the form of an experiment in animation by Gerald Conn, an award-winning filmmaker specializing in the technique of sand-on-glass animation. Conn describes his *Heart of Darkness* project thus:

> Adapted from Joseph Conrad's novel, this film will bring Marlow's quest for the enigmatic Kurtz to a new audience using sand animation and a 3D stereoscopic treatment to capture the brooding atmosphere inherent in this classic story. *Heart of Darkness* is a unique animated production using a combination of sand animation and 2D animation directed by Gerald Conn and designed by artist Derek Mawudoku.[22]

Designed to be a full feature, the shorter pilot versions of the film used extracts from Orson Welles's radio recordings. Conn and Mawudoku's visualisation of *Heart of Darkness* is rich in texture and depth and reveals an influence of African art. In this regard, their adaptation is not dissimilar to

David Zane Mairowitz and Catherine Anyango's 2010 graphic novel adaptation of *Heart of Darkness* although Conn insists that his film is a more thoroughly 'expressionistic' visualization of Conrad.[23] A *Guardian* review believed the novel might 'have worked better as a wordless collection of tableaux' feeling that Anyango's detailed and immersive art succeeds better than Mairowitz's radical pruning of Conrad's text.[24] This statement reveals the considerable achievement of Anyango in finding an authentic equivalent to Conrad's prose in an altogether different medium.

Heart of Darkness continues to be a key and frequently referenced work in contemporary culture, perhaps all the more exciting for its Achebe controversy and provocation.[25] Conrad's *Heart of Darkness* is – like Mary Shelley's *Frankenstein* (1818) – one of the most convincing examples whereby nineteenth-century English literature has produced works that have become modern myths. In Conrad's case, *Heart of Darkness*, with its journey that leads not into religious salvation or humanistic enlightenment but into total horror, has become an apt myth for modern and postmodern times.

The *Heart of Darkness* 'myth' can be found in numerous examples of 'hidden' Conrad or what might be called the 'Conradesque'. The *Heart of Darkness* paradigm can be detected again and again in contemporary performance cultures. Major cinema *auteurs*, such as Werner Herzog, seem to be drawn recurrently to the 'Conradian journey' in their fictional, fact-based and documentary films.[26] *Heart of Darkness* is the source that underpins the Canadian Robert Morin's film *Windigo* (1994) in which government representatives and a television crew venture to a remote region of Canada where the indigenous community strive for independence under the leadership of the enigmatic Eddy Laroche (played by Donald Morin). Other recent 'Conradesque' films include Fabrice Du Welz's *Vinyan: Lost Souls* (2008) – co-written by Du Welz, Oliver Blackburn and the playwright David Greig, a narrative about a European couple's increasingly desperate soul-searching journey through Thailand and Burma as they look for their child who disappeared during the Asian Tsunami of December 2004.

The Conradesque can even be found in the world of digital gaming. In the late 1990s, *Heart of Darkness* emerged as the title of a game on the Sony Playstation (1998) although it had no connection to Conrad beyond a broad narrative parallel that could be drawn between an isolated avatar and his perilous journey. However, more recent videogames have developed Conradian links. In Ubisoft's *Far Cry 2* (2008) the central mission is to track down an insane, Nietzsche-reading arms-dealer in the fictional civil-war-torn African country of 'Leboa-Sako'. At the end of the game, the player finally encounters the arms-dealer face-to-face in a hut called 'The Heart of Darkness'. Arguably, another game, *Spec Ops: The Line* (2K

Games, 2012), develops the Conradian influence more profoundly. In it, three American soldiers search a devastated Dubai for the missing Captain John Konrad. What seems a generic 'shoot 'em up' is increasingly filled with moral complexities as a review of the game reveals. The reviewer is discussing a sequence in which a mission is (mandatorily) mismanaged and innocent non-combatants are killed:

> But the unimaginably horrible death of civilians alone wasn't what made it get to me so much. ... No, the most horrifying part of it was remembering what had been going through my mind at the time. Seeing all those white blobs and thinking 'Oh boy! ... Bombs away! I'm the best at shooters!' When the truth about what I'd done became clear, that was what made me feel sick. Not the gore, not the darkness in Walker, but the darkness in *me*.[27]

Just as Conrad took the adventure genre and created a work that questions the practices and morality of empire, the Conrad-influenced creators of *Spec Ops: The Line* exploit and transgress generic conventions and challenge their audience with a similar journey into self-interrogation.

In the ever-proliferating culture of adaptation, Conrad is a particularly interesting case. Since the 1990s, the *œuvre* has provided dynamic source texts for the widest range of media, including opera, historical films and digital games. Two texts in particular – *The Secret Agent* and *Heart of Darkness* – seem to have become increasingly important in (and for) the postmodern era. Well over a century after they were first published, the stories, settings and language (including key phrases) of these fictions have inspired a diverse range of contemporary work, evidently capable of creating compelling narratives and eliciting a pertinent commentary on our time.

NOTES

1 Julie Sanders, *Adaptation and Appropriation* (London: Routledge, 2005), p. 26.
2 See also Richard J. Hand, 'Dramatic and Other Adaptations' in *Conrad in Context*, ed. Allan H. Simmons (Cambridge: Cambridge University Press, 2009), pp. 91–8. For detailed discussion of film adaptations, see Gene M. Moore, ed., *Conrad on Film* (Cambridge: Cambridge University Press, 1997).
3 Christopher Hampton, *The Secret Agent and Nostromo* (London: Faber & Faber, 1996), p. ix.
4 Richard J. Hand, 'Staging an "Unbearable Spectacle": The World Premiere of Joseph Conrad's *Laughing Anne*', *Studies in Theatre and Performance* 21, no. 2 (2001), 109–17, and 'Producing *Laughing Anne*', *Conradiana* 34, no. 1–2 (2002), 43–62.
5 Letter from Christopher Hampton to Richard J. Hand, 17 July 1991.
6 For a discussion, see Laurence Davies, 'Conrad in the Operatic Mode', *Joseph Conrad and the Performing Arts*, ed. Katherine Isobel Baxter and Richard J. Hand (London: Ashgate, 2009), pp. 127–45.

7 Letter from Greg Bartholomew to Richard J. Hand, 10 December 2013.
8 Ibid.
9 Ibid.
10 Ibid.
11 Ibid.
12 Letter from Simon Wills to Richard J. Hand, 1 September 2013.
13 Simon Wills, 'Programme Note: *The Secret Agent*' (2006). simon-wills.co.uk/pages/Compositions/Secret%20Agent%202.html. Accessed: August 2013.
14 Letter from Simon Wills to Richard J. Hand, 31 August 2013.
15 Wills, 'Programme Note' (2006).
16 Simon Wills, 'Compositions: *The Secret Agent*' (2010). simon-wills.co.uk/pages/Compositions/Secret%20Agent.html. Accessed: August 2013.
17 Letter from Curtis Bryant to Richard J. Hand, 2 September 2013.
18 Stephen Pritchard, 'Heart of Darkness; *Duke Bluebeard's Castle*; *La sonnambula* – Review', *The Observer*, 6 November 2011, p. 31.
19 Rupert Christiansen, 'Heart of Darkness, Royal Opera House, Review', *The Daily Telegraph*, 2 November 2011. telegraph.co.uk/culture/music/opera/8868031/Heart-of-Darkness-Royal-Opera-House-review.html. Accessed: December 2013.
20 *Apocalypse Oz*, apocalypseoz.com/About.aspx. Accessed: July 2010.
21 Ibid.
22 Letter from Gerald Conn to Richard J. Hand, 15 October 2013.
23 Letter from Gerald Conn to Richard J. Hand, 9 September 2013.
24 Michel Faber, 'Heart of Darkness by Joseph Conrad, adapted by Catherine Anyango and David Zane Mairowitz – Review', *The Guardian*, 25 September 2010, p. 10.
25 On this topic, see the chapters on 'Reception' and 'Postcolonial Conrad' in the present volume.
26 Hand, 'Dramatic and Other Adaptations', p. 97.
27 Ben 'Yahtzee' Croshaw, 'Extra Punctuation: Crossing *Spec Ops: The Line*'. *The Escapist*, 17 July 2012. escapistmagazine.com/articles/view/columns/extra-punctuation/9810-Crossing-Spec-Ops-The-Line. Accessed: December 2013.

FURTHER READING

Dauntingly varied in their range and quality, books, articles and notes about Conrad's life and work have appeared regularly since the 1940s when he was discovered by academe. The bibliographies listed here provide guidance about an ever-growing body of writing, which invariably reflects the critical trends and fashions of a given moment. In addition to listing basic reference sources, the following list offers a selective chronological guide to the major criticism and scholarship. Emphasis falls on full-length studies written or published in English dealing with Conrad's achievement as a whole or with selected aspects of it. The notes to the chapters of the present volume refer to studies of particular relevance to the works they consider or to the broader topics in their purview.

Texts

Dent's Collected Edition of the Works of Joseph Conrad. London: Dent, 1946–55. A complete edition but lacking the dramatizations and *The Nature of a Crime* (written with Ford). A re-issue of Dent's Uniform Edition of 1923–8, this edition's pagination is identical to it and to that of the numerous collected 'editions' (in fact, issues) published in the United States throughout the 1920s. The texts are mostly those of the first editions, but have no special authority and their usefulness lies only in their wide availability.

Opere. Ed. Ugo Mursia. 5 vols. Milan: Mursia, 1967–82. Thematic arrangement of the complete works, with erudite commentaries and useful explanatory notes. In Italian.

Oeuvres. Ed. Sylvère Monod. Pléiade edition. 5 vols. Paris: Gallimard, 1982–92. Monod's general introductions offer valuable critical perspectives, while frequently illuminating 'Notices' appear on individual works by their translators or other critics. The informative explanatory notes are authoritative on Conrad's Gallicisms, French borrowings and French literary connections. In French.

Oxford World's Classics. Oxford: Oxford University Press, 2000s. Photo-offset reprintings, purged of the printer's errors of many of the volumes of Dent's Collected Edition, first produced in the 1980s. These were replaced in the 2000s by re-set texts augmented by critical introductions, a chronology of Conrad's life, a selected bibliography, a note on the text, maps and explanatory notes.

Penguin Twentieth-Century Classics. Harmondsworth: Penguin Books, 1990s–. Using various copy-texts, this collection presents most of Conrad's fiction in a format similar to that of Oxford's World's Classics series. In 2007, several volumes were issued with fresh introductions and notes, giving a random publishing venture a coherence not previously an aim in this series.

The Cambridge Edition of the Works of Joseph Conrad. Cambridge: Cambridge University Press, 1990–. A critical edition of the canon providing a detailed discussion of sources, a history of composition, revision, publication and reception. Textual variants and extensive explanatory and textual notes give the scholar and advanced student a full view of a particular work in context.

Conrad First: The Joseph Conrad Periodical Archive (conrad.net), comp. Stephen Donovan. A comprehensive digitized collection of Conrad's works in serial form. An invaluable resource for the study of the various markets in which many of the novels and short fiction first appeared. The print collection itself, housed at St Mary's University, Twickenham, London, may be consulted by contacting its Centre for the Study of Joseph Conrad (smuc.ac.uk/joseph-conrad-studies/index.htm).

The standard canon is supplemented by:

'Congo Diary' and Other Uncollected Pieces. Ed. Zdzisław Najder. Garden City, NY: Doubleday, 1978. Includes the Congo notebooks, the unfinished novel *The Sisters*, *The Nature of a Crime* and uncollected minor pieces. Now largely surpassed by the critical edition of *Last Essays* in the Cambridge Edition.

Of the many paperback and separate re-issues of Conrad's work a few merit special mention:

The Portable Conrad. Ed. Michael Gorra. Harmondsworth: Penguin Books, 2007. The latest incarnation of this handy compendium for the general reader beginning to explore Conrad includes *The Secret Agent*, selections of short fiction and letters as well as some occasional prose. It first appeared edited by Morton Dauwen Zabel (New York: Viking, 1947), and a revised edition appeared edited by Frederick R. Karl in 1969. Classic introduction by Zabel.

Norton Critical Editions. New York: Norton. *Heart of Darkness*, ed. Robert Kimbrough, 1963; 3rd edn. 1988; *Lord Jim*, ed. Thomas Moser, 1968; 2nd edn. 1996; *The Nigger of the 'Narcissus'*, ed. Robert Kimbrough, 1970. While boasting 'authoritative texts', the series reprints the corrupt Heinemann Collected Edition texts of 1920–21. (*Lord Jim*'s 2nd edn. reprints the first English.) The volumes offer selections of criticism reflecting trends of their moment and background materials on Conrad's sources.

Selected Literary Criticism and 'The Shadow-Line'. Ed. Allan Ingram. London: Methuen, 1986. Provides a setting for the novella in extracts from Conrad's letters and Author's Notes.

'Heart of Darkness': A Case Study in Contemporary Criticism. Ed. Ross C. Murfin. New York: Bedford Books of St Martin's Press, 1989. Reprints the Heinemann Edition's defective text without explanatory notes, but offers a kaleidoscopic view of critical trends in five essays covering the psychoanalytic, reader-response, feminist, deconstructive and New Historicist perspectives.

Correspondence

Conrad's wife and friends saw into print collections of his letters as early as the 1920s, but all are casual in their textual transcriptions and overly protective. (Sensitive topics such as his finances and allusions to persons then living occasioned editorial deletions.) Collections based on scholarly principles were published beginning in the late 1950s and in the wake of Jocelyn Baines's 1960 biography. The earliest collections have now been superseded by the *Collected Letters*.

The Collected Letters of Joseph Conrad. General editors Frederick R. Karl and Laurence Davies, with Owen Knowles, J. H. Stape and Gene M. Moore. 9 vols. Cambridge: Cambridge University Press, 1983–2007. Presents reliable texts of the some 5,000 extant letters, including those in French and translations of those in Polish. Each volume provides a detailed chronology of the years covered, an introduction, short biographies of Conrad's correspondents, a description of editorial procedures, illustrations, annotations and indices. The final volume includes a cumulative index and extensive corrigenda and addenda. Letters discovered after the publication of the last volume appear, by arrangement with the Conrad Estate, in *The Conradian* (see Journals).

Of the separately published volumes of letters, the following remain important:

Joseph Conrad: Life and Letters, edited by G. Jean-Aubry (London: William Heinemann; Garden City, NY: Doubleday, Page, 1927). Now of interest only as the first attempt to present and contextualize Conrad's correspondence.

Joseph Conrad: Letters to William Blackwood and David S. Meldrum. Ed. William Blackburn. Durham, NC: Duke University Press, 1958. Supplements Conrad's letters of the period of the *Youth* volume and *Lord Jim* with correspondence from the files of the Blackwood firm.

Conrad's Polish Background: Letters to and from Polish Friends. Ed. Zdzisław Najder. Trans. Halina Carroll. London: Oxford University Press, 1964. Presents translations of the letters Conrad's uncle and guardian Tadeusz Bobrowski addressed to him as well as other correspondence translated from Polish. An invaluable biographical source.

Joseph Conrad's Letters to R. B. Cunninghame Graham. Ed. C. T. Watts. Cambridge: Cambrige University Press, 1969. The texts have been replaced by *Collected Letters*, but a solid introduction and informative notes situate an important friendship.

Conrad's correspondence is supplemented by two selections of letters addressed to or principally about Conrad:

A Portrait in Letters: Correspondence to and about Conrad. Ed. J. H. Stape and Owen Knowles. Amsterdam: Rodopi, 1996.

'My Dear Friend': Further Letters to and about Joseph Conrad. Ed. Owen Knowles. Amsterdam: Rodopi, 2008.

Reviews

Joseph Conrad: Contemporary Reviews. 4 vols. General editors: Allan H. Simmons, John G. Peters, J. H. Stape, with Richard Niland, Mary Burgoyne and Katherine Isobel Baxter. Cambridge: Cambridge University Press, 2012. The contemporary reviews of the novels, short story collections and non-fiction in the English, American and colonial press. Replaces *Conrad: The Critical Heritage*, ed. Norman Sherry (London: Routledge & Kegan Paul, 1973) and allows for a comprehensive view of Conrad's work as seen by his contemporaries.

Biographies

As early as the 1920s, Conrad's extraordinary life attracted the attention of biographers. His friend Jean-Aubry preserved material that might otherwise have been lost, but he produced a poor and sometimes unreliable life. A genuinely scholarly approach to Conrad's biography was essayed only some three decades after his death.

The unusual shape of his life and career has demanded research into his Polish background, acquaintances and fellow writers in England. Documentary materials are scattered in public archives and private collections in Europe, North America, Asia and Australia. The biographer must also cope with lacunae caused by the depredations of time, in particular, the destruction of records and crucial collections of letters during the Russian Revolution and the Second World War. Archival work undertaken during the past two decades has now securely established the main outline of Conrad's life, although the challenging conditions mentioned do not disallow further discoveries.

Baines, Jocelyn. *Joseph Conrad: A Critical Biography.* London: Weidenfeld & Nicolson; New York: McGraw-Hill, 1960. Rpt. Penguin Books, 1971. First significant full-length biography based on scholarly research. Repays reading despite its now very outdated discussion of the fiction. Later scholarship has fully pursued Baines's major revelations.

Sherry, Norman. *Conrad's Eastern World.* Cambridge: Cambridge University Press, 1966. Traces models and sources for Conrad's Eastern fiction in his actual experience and wide reading. Influential in showing how Conrad altered his sources and in having stimulated further biographical research.

Conrad's Western World. Cambridge: Cambridge University Press, 1971. Continues the approach of Sherry's first volume, covering *Heart of Darkness*, *Nostromo* and *The Secret Agent.*

Conrad and His World. London: Thames and Hudson, 1972, rpt. 1988; New York: Scribner's, 1977. Handsomely illustrated and well-informed brief summary of the main events of Conrad's life and literary career. Excellent starting-point for the student new to Conrad.

Karl, Frederick R. *Joseph Conrad: The Three Lives – A Biography.* New York: Farrar, Straus and Giroux; London: Faber & Faber, 1979. An ungainly organization and factual inaccuracies mar this volume which none the less contains information about Conrad's career and finances that at the time of writing was otherwise unprinted.

Najder, Zdzisław. *Joseph Conrad: A Life.* Trans. Halina Carroll-Najder. Rochester, New York: Camden House, 2007. (A revised and updated version of *Joseph Conrad: A Chronicle.* New Brunswick, NJ: Rutgers University Press; Cambridge: Cambridge University Press, 1983.) Renamed to take advantage of interest in the 150th anniversary of Conrad's birth, a reliable and painstaking account of the facts of Conrad's life based on ardent archival research. If not especially readable, it is unlikely to be surpassed on Conrad's Polish context.

Batchelor, John. *The Life of Joseph Conrad: A Critical Biography.* Oxford: Blackwell, 1994. Traverses highly familiar biographical territory but sensitively relates Conrad's writings to his life in balanced readings of the major fiction and short stories.

Fletcher, Chris. *Joseph Conrad*. The British Library Writers' Lives series. London: The British Library, 1999. A richly illustrated and genially written brief life, supplementing Sherry's *Conrad and His World* (1972).

Stape, J. H. *The Several Lives of Joseph Conrad*. London: Heinemann, 2007; New York: Knopf, 2007. Attempts in a brief compass to recuperate neglected aspects of Conrad's life – going beyond the tripartite division of Pole, writer and seaman – and to de-mythify aspects of it. Presents much new information about his wife's family and his two sons.

Specialized biographical works concentrate on selected aspects of or particular approaches to Conrad's life:

Allen, Jerry. *The Sea Years of Joseph Conrad*. Garden City, NY: Doubleday, 1965; London: Methuen, 1967. Pioneering study of Conrad's maritime career, seriously marred by relying upon the fiction as a biographical source.

Meyer, Bernard C. *Joseph Conrad: A Psychoanalytical Biography*. Princeton, NJ: Princeton University Press, 1967. Discusses Conrad's psychology and writings from a Freudian perspective but occasionally eludes its orientation's straitjacket.

Villiers, Peter. *Joseph Conrad, Master Mariner*. Dobbs Ferry, NY, 2006. An account of Conrad's maritime career and of his ships, focussing also on the conditions of late nineteenth-century shipping.

Watts, Cedric. *Joseph Conrad: A Literary Life*. London: Macmillan, 1989. Foreshortened account of the historical and economic circumstances of the writing career, covering such topics as serialization and Conrad's relations with his agent and publishers. Suggests some of the formal consequences of marketplace pressures but is marred and incomplete by its neglect of unpublished materials and archival sources.

The following works complement the scholarly biographies:

Najder, Zdzisław, ed. *Conrad under Familial Eyes*. Trans. Halina Carroll-Najder. Cambridge: Cambridge University Press, 1983. Presents documents and letters related to Conrad's family and early years as well as reminiscences by Polish relatives and friends.

Knowles, Owen. *A Conrad Chronology*. London: Macmillan; Boston: Hall, 1989. Highly readable annual and sometimes day-by-day account of Conrad's life and writing career in the form of crisply written diary entries.

Ray, Martin, ed. *Joseph Conrad: Interviews and Recollections*. London: Macmillan, 1990. A wide-ranging and generously annotated selection of reminiscences by family, friends, acquaintances and fellow writers.

Moore, Gene M., Allan H. Simmons and J. H. Stape, eds. *Conrad between the Lines: Documents in a Life*. Amsterdam: Rodopi: 2000. Collection of documents related to Conrad's life and career.

Ray, Martin, ed. *Joseph Conrad: Memories and Impressions – An Annotated Bibliography*. Amsterdam: Rodopi, 2007. Canvasses and engagingly describes widely scattered recollections of the writer by family and friends, colleagues and acquaintances.

Bibliographies

William R. Cagle's scholarly primary bibliography of Conrad's *œuvre*, begun in the 1960s, remains unpublished. (Photocopies may be obtained at cost from: The Institute of Bibliography and Editing, Kent State University, Kent, Ohio, 44242–0001 USA). A number of descriptions of major collections and more wide-ranging compilations serve advanced researchers.

Wise, T. J., ed. *A Bibliography of Joseph Conrad*. 2nd edn. London: Richard Clay & Sons, 1921. Describes Wise's large personal collection of manuscripts, typescripts, limited-edition pamphlets and signed first editions, now mostly in the British Library's Ashley Collection.

Keating, George T., ed. *A Conrad Memorial Library: The Collection of George T. Keating*. Garden City, NY: Doubleday, Doran, 1929. Catalogues the largest single collection of original materials and other Conradiana, now in Yale University's Beinecke Rare Book and Manuscript Library.

Ehrsam, Theodore G., comp. *A Bibliography of Joseph Conrad*. Metuchen, NJ: Scarecrow Press, 1969. A comprehensive, if flawed, listing of first editions, contemporary reviews, translations and miscellanea including obituaries, memoirs and early auction records.

Fagnani, Flavio, comp. *Catalogo della collezione Conradiana di Ugo Mursia*. Milan: Mursia, 1984. Lists holdings of the Ugo Mursia Memorial Collection at the Universitá di Pisa (see Study Centres).

Moore, Gene M., comp. 'A Descriptive Location Register of Conrad's Literary Manuscripts'. *The Conradian* 27, no. 2 (2002), 1–93. Building upon the foundational work of Gordon Lindstrand ('A bibliographical survey of manuscripts of Joseph Conrad'. *Conradiana* 2.1 (1969–70), 23–32; 2.2 (1969–70), 105–14; 2.3 (1969–70), 153–62) and other scholars offers a comprehensive listing of extant holographs and typescripts. Updated and amended version housed on the website of The Joseph Conrad Society (UK).

Criticism and scholarship in English and other major languages has been carefully recorded and/or evaluated in a number of bibliographical surveys:

Teets, Bruce E., and Helmut E. Gerber, comp. *Joseph Conrad: An Annotated Bibliography of Writings about Him*. DeKalb: Northern Illinois University Press, 1971. A guide up to 1966 of reviews, criticism, scholarship and doctoral theses.

Secor, Robert and Debra Moddelmog, comp. *Joseph Conrad and American Writers: A Bibliographical Study of Affinities, Influences, and Relations*. Westport, CT: Greenwood Press, 1985. A useful listing of comparative and influence studies, but making somewhat exaggerated claims for affinity.

Teets, Bruce E., comp. *Joseph Conrad: An Annotated Bibliography*. New York and London: Garland Publishing, 1990. An updating of and supplement through 1975 to Teets and Gerber's earlier volume.

Knowles, Owen, comp. *An Annotated Critical Bibliography of Joseph Conrad*. Hemel Hempstead: Harvester Wheatsheaf; New York: St Martin's Press, 1992. A critically sophisticated and judiciously selective guide to criticism from 1914 to 1990. The main emphasis is on books and articles published from 1975 to 1990.

Perczak, Wanda, comp. *Polska Bibliografia Conradowska, 1896–1992*. Toruń: Wydawnictwo Universytetu Mikołaj Kopernika, 1993. A comprehensive listing of translations and of books and articles in Polish. Also lists works in English about Conrad's Polish experience, influence and reception.

Peters, John G. 'A Bibliography of Books, Pamphlets, and Broadsides about Joseph Conrad'. Part 1: 1910–79; Part 2: 1980–2010. *The Conradian* 36, no. 1 (2011), 98–118 and 37, no. 1 (2012), 84–106. A useful listing of criticism and scholarship, covered chronologically and by topic, for the years covered.

Peters, John G. *Joseph Conrad's Critical Reception*. Cambridge: Cambridge University Press, 2013. A chronologically organized description of the reception of Conrad's work from his own day through to modern scholarly appraisals. Useful for anyone wishing to make a judicious overview of the large body of critical writings.

Introductions

Daleski, H. M. *Joseph Conrad: The Way of Dispossession*. London: Faber & Faber; New York: Holmes & Meier, 1977. A discriminating and subtle account of philosophical issues in the major fiction. For the advanced student.

Berthoud, Jacques. *Joseph Conrad: The Major Phase*. Cambridge: Cambridge University Press, 1978. Offers nuanced and informed discussions of the fiction from *The Nigger of the 'Narcissus'* to *Under Western Eyes* that remain valuable despite advances in theory.

Watts, Cedric. *A Preface to Conrad*. London: Longman, 1982; rev. edn. 1993. A brief treatment of Conrad's biographical and cultural circumstances and of Conradian narrative techniques with particular attention given to *Nostromo*.

Middleton, Tim. *Joseph Conrad*. London: Routledge, 2006. Offers for the beginning student an orientation to Conrad's life and canon and surveys contemporary criticism.

Peters, John G. *The Cambridge Introduction to Joseph Conrad*. Cambridge: Cambridge University Press, 2006. Covers much of the same terrain as the previously listed title and as the next entry, Simmons, with all three works appearing in the same year and addressed to the same market.

Simmons, Allan H. *Joseph Conrad*. Critical Issues Series. London: Palgrave Macmillan, 2006. Critically informed and engagingly written in-context discussion ranging over the canon. Offers sound guidance to the major works and short fiction.

Joseph Conrad in Context, ed. Allan H. Simmons. Cambridge: Cambridge University Press, 2009. Offers thirty-two brief essays about facets of Conrad's writings and life, offering further detail and updating some of the angles covered in the *Oxford Reader's Companion* (2000). An excellent starting-point for the scholar and advanced student.

Reference

Tutein, David W. *Joseph Conrad's Reading: An Annotated Bibliography*. West Cornwall, CT: Locust Hill Press, 1990. An alphabetical list of titles. Surveys an important and previously neglected subject but suffers from inadequate documentation. For more on the topic of Conrad's reading, see The Open University's website *UK Red: The Experience of Reading in Britain from 1450 to 1945* (open.ac.uk/Arts/reading/UK/ index.php)

Marle, Hans van. 'A novelist's dukedom: from Conrad's library'. *The Conradian* 16, no. 1 (1991), 55–78. Adds numerous additional titles to Tutein's census and establishes a scholarly approach to researching Conrad's reading.

Knowles, Owen, and Gene M. Moore. *Oxford Reader's Companion to Joseph Conrad*. Oxford: Oxford University Press, 2000. A vividly written essential source for all topics of Conradian interest, ranging over the writer's canon, life, literary and intellectual contexts and circle. A 'must' for any Conrad library and a highly recommended starting-point for students at all levels of expertise.

Criticism

Following Conrad's death, his reputation suffered a decline. In the 1940s, in both England and America a revival of interest consolidated his reputation as a major writer and roughly coincided with the decline of the impressionistic essay and the rise of academic criticism. The major fiction has now been subjected to intense investigation for several decades, and even some of his minor writings have been extensively, possibly exhaustively, analyzed. Criticism of Conrad's work has invariably reflected critical fashions. (These are ably surveyed in Knowles's bibliography listed above.) Only essential work can be mentioned here for the earlier decades, while an attempt has been made to suggest the range and diversity for more recent criticism.

The 1930s to the 1950s

The recovery of Conrad's reputation in England began with general surveys by Edward Crankshaw and Muriel Bradbrook, and gained momentum and sophistication under the impetus of F. R. Leavis. At the same time, in America, John Dozier Gordan and Morton Dauwen Zaubel were laying the foundations for an increasingly nuanced perception of Conrad's achievement by closely examining its sources. Influenced by post-war preoccupations and urged on by the expansion of post-secondary education, a new professionalism among university teachers, and the then-emergent New Criticism, the serious academic revaluation and interpretation of Conrad's writings was underway during the 1950s.

Crankshaw, Edward. *Joseph Conrad: Some Aspects of the Art of the Novel*. London: John Lane, 1936; rpt. New York: Russell & Russell, 1963. An appreciative treatment by a friend of Ford Madox Ford. Mainly of historical interest.

Gordan, John Dozier. *Joseph Conrad: The Making of a Novelist*. Cambridge, MA: Harvard University Press, 1940. Pace-setting study of documentary sources and composition history. The foundation for much subsequent scholarly work.

Bradbrook, M. C. *Joseph Conrad: England's Polish Genius*. Cambridge: Cambridge University Press; New York: Macmillan, 1941; rpt. New York: Russell & Russell, 1965. General overview. Mainly of historical interest.

Leavis, F. R. 'Revaluations: Joseph Conrad'. *Scrutiny* 10.1 (1941), 22–50 and 10.2 (1941), 157–81. Reprinted in *The Great Tradition: George Eliot, Henry James, Joseph Conrad*. London: Chatto & Windus; New York: G. W. Stewart, 1948. An enormously influential revisionist essay placing Conrad in the line of the major English realists.

Hewitt, Douglas. *Conrad: A Reassessment*. Cambridge: Bowes & Bowes, 1952; 3rd edn. Bowes & Bowes and Totowa, NJ: Rowman & Littlefield, 1975. A brief but perceptive discussion consolidating the upward movement of Conrad's reputation.

Moser, Thomas C. *Joseph Conrad: Achievement and Decline*. Cambridge, MA: Harvard University Press, 1957; rpt. Hamden, CT: Archon Books, 1996. Long influential in its negative assessment of the late fiction and for its thesis that Conrad could not treat sexual psychology convincingly. Considerably challenged by revisionist trends after the 1980s, now mainly of historical interest.

Guerard, Albert J. *Conrad the Novelist*. Cambridge, MA: Harvard University Press, 1958. rpt. 1979. An influential psychological and myth-oriented study that, despite its occasional reductiveness, provides stimulating readings of individual works.

The 1960s and 1970s

The criticism of the 1960s pursued the arguments suggested by Moser and Guerard and was influenced by the archetypal approach generated by Northrop Frye's *Anatomy of Criticism* (1957). Likely the more lasting critical achievements of this period were original discussions of Conrad's philosophical orientations and politics and his relationship to dominant nineteenth-century ideologies. His continental context also became an area of interest. The 1960s, particularly in doctoral theses in the United States, also witnessed a dawning awareness of the deficiencies of Conrad's received texts and the beginnings of serious textual scholarship. Conferences held in Texas, Miami, Canterbury and San Diego to observe the fiftieth anniversary of Conrad's death marked a watershed in Conrad studies, confirming Conrad's status as a writer of world stature diversely investigated by a far-flung community of scholar-critics. In addition to refining the insights of the previous two decades of criticism, they announced an interest in rhetoric and narratology.

Hay, Eloise Knapp. *The Political Novels of Joseph Conrad: A Critical Study*. Chicago: University of Chicago Press, 1963; rev. edn. 1981. A detailed treatment of selected fiction with an emphasis on Conrad's emerging political viewpoints.

Watt, Ian. 'Joseph Conrad: alienation and commitment'. *The English Mind: Studies in the English Moralists Presented to Basil Willey*. Ed. Hugh Sykes Davies and George Watson. Cambridge: Cambridge University Press, 1964, pp. 257–78. A seminal essay brilliantly situating Conrad's response to philosophical and political ideas, including conservatism, existentialism and Marxism.

Busza, Andrzej. 'Conrad's Polish literary background and some illustrations of Polish literature on his work'. *Antemurale* 10 (1966), 109–255. Identifies Conrad's debts to the Polish literary tradition, traces sources and sensitively treats the inter-cultural dimensions of his aesthetics.

Miller, J. Hillis. *Poets of Reality: Six Twentieth-Century Writers*. Cambridge, MA: Harvard University Press, 1966. Highly influential phenomenological approach to Conrad, highlighting *The Secret Agent*.

Fleishman, Avrom. *Conrad's Politics: Community and Anarchy in the Fiction of Joseph Conrad*. Baltimore, MD: Johns Hopkins University Press, 1967. Traces Conrad's political thought in his familial and cultural circumstances and analyzes his publicistic writings.

Kirschner, Paul. *Conrad: The Psychologist as Artist*. Edinburgh: Oliver & Boyd, 1968. Pioneers the exploration of Conrad's continental influences in studying his borrowings from Maupassant and Anatole France. Offers suggestive close readings of individual works focussing on the self and society.

Graver, Lawrence. *Conrad's Shorter Fiction*. Berkeley: University of California Press, 1969. The first full-length study of the short fiction, presenting some individually illuminating insights and a useful overview of Conrad as a writer of short stories and novellas. Now mostly superseded.

Thorborn, David. *Conrad's Romanticism*. New Haven, CT: Yale University Press, 1974. Intelligently places Conrad in the context of English literary Romanticism.

Sherry, Norman, ed. *Joseph Conrad: A Commemoration*. London: Macmillan; New York: Barnes and Noble, 1976. A richly varied and stimulating selection of papers from the 1974 Canterbury Conference.

Hawthorn, Jeremy. *Joseph Conrad: Language and Fictional Self-Consciousness*. London: Arnold; Lincoln: University of Nebraska Press, 1979. Explores relationships between narrative technique, language and ideology from a Marxist perspective.

Watt, Ian. *Conrad in the Nineteenth Century*. Berkeley: University of California Press, 1979; London: Chatto & Windus, 1980. Gathers up and considerably extends Watt's substantial work on Conrad's literary and intellectual contexts and offers an original study of his methods. Widely regarded as the most important full-length critical study of the early fiction.

The 1980s

In addition to assimilating the work of the previous decade, including major biographies, increasingly refined textual studies and much original criticism, recent students of Conrad have had to take into account newly emergent critical trends, including post-structuralism, New Historicism and feminism, which emphasize extrinsic approaches to the study of literature. While scholarship continued to pursue traditional interests – aesthetics, contextualization, the discovery and preservation of documents – recent criticism has inevitably reflected the crosscurrents of interpretive debates. A number of recent studies often explicitly or implicitly attempt revaluations of a given work or of the canon.

Senn, Werner. *Conrad's Narrative Voice: Stylistic Aspects of his Fiction*. Berne: Francke Verlag, 1980. A detailed study of Conrad's style and its relationship to his aesthetic and philosophical positions.

Hunter, Jefferson. *Edwardian Fiction*. Cambridge, MA: Harvard University Press, 1982. Contains an important chapter situating Conrad in his Edwardian context and dealing with his responses to adventure fiction and imperialism.

Hunter, Allan. *Joseph Conrad and the Ethics of Darwinism: The Challenges of Science*. London: Croom Helm, 1983. Addresses an important subject but unconvincingly asserts specific debts.

Berthoud, Jacques. *Introductions to The Nigger of the 'Narcissus'* and *Almayer's Folly*. Oxford: Oxford University Press, 1984, 1992. Introductions to *The Shadow-Line* and *Chance*. Harmondsworth: Penguin Books. 1986, 1996. Critically ambitious and stimulating essays that, as a group, represent an acute and impressive understanding of Conrad's literary and historical contexts, the discussion of which informs an analysis of the formal aspects of individual works.

O'Hanlon, Redmond. *Joseph Conrad and Charles Darwin: The Influence of Scientific Thought on Conrad's Fiction*. Edinburgh: Salamander Press; Atlantic Highlands,

NJ: Humanities Press, 1984. Despite its title, concentrates only on *Lord Jim*, and, like Hunter, over-eagerly assigns specific influences.

Parry, Benita. *Conrad and Imperialism: Ideological Boundaries and Visionary Frontiers*. London: Macmillan; Topsfield, MA: Salem Academy/Merrimack Publishing, 1984. Drawing on modern ideological criticism, eschews historical and contextual perspectives for a critically eclectic and comprehensive reading of the colonial fiction.

Purdy, Dwight H. *Joseph Conrad's Bible*. Norman: University of Oklahoma Press, 1984. Identifies and analyzes the rhetorical and ideological consequences of Conrad's extensive use of biblical allusion.

Watts, Cedric. *The Deceptive Text: An Introduction to Covert Plots*. Brighton: Harvester; Totowa, NJ: Barnes & Noble, 1984. Concentrates on Conrad's fiction in investigating narratorial duplicity and ambiguous plotting.

Conroy, Mark. *Modernism and Authority: Strategies of Legitimation in Flaubert and Conrad*. Baltimore, MD: Johns Hopkins University Press, 1985. Informed by Jameson's Marxism and influenced by Foucault, takes on the Modernist writer's legitimation of his work for a bourgeois capitalist audience.

Fogel, Aaron. *Coercion to Speak: Conrad's Poetics of Dialogue*. Cambridge, MA: Harvard University Press, 1985. Draws on Bakhtinian discourse theory to analyze the functions of dialogue.

Murfin, Ross C., ed. *Conrad Revisited: Essays for the Eighties*. University: University of Alabama Press, 1985. Selected conference papers on, among other topics, colonialism and the late fiction, both typical concerns of recent criticism.

Bloom, Harold, ed. *Joseph Conrad: Modern Critical Views*. New York: Chelsea House, 1986. Reprints classic essays and includes feminist and post-structural studies. Seriously fails to represent the range and quality of contemporary criticism in limiting itself to work published in the United States. Similar volumes are available for *Heart of Darkness*, *Lord Jim* and *Nostromo* (all 1987). *Marlow* (1982), in Chelsea House's Major Literary Characters series, ranges more widely in its choice of critics.

Raval, Suresh. *The Art of Failure: Conrad's Fiction*. London: Allen & Unwin, 1986. Analyzes and pursues the implications of the radical scepticism informing Conrad's major fiction.

Billy, Ted, ed. *Critical Essays on Joseph Conrad*. Boston: Hall, 1987. Useful compendium of trends, reprinting articles published during 1971–84.

The 1990s

Hamner, Robert D., ed. *Joseph Conrad: Third World Perspectives*. Washington, DC: Three Continents Press, 1990. Conveniently reprints articles dealing with Conrad's African, Asian and South American worlds and includes evaluations from non-Western viewpoints.

Hawthorn, Jeremy. *Joseph Conrad: Narrative Technique and Ideological Commitment*. London: Arnold, 1990. Extends the implications of Hawthorn's earlier volume and offers a detailed and nuanced analysis of free indirect style.

Erdinast-Vulcan, Daphna. *Joseph Conrad and the Modern Temper*. Oxford: Oxford University Press, 1991. Informed by Bakhtinian discourse theory, targets fissures and ambiguities, focussing on Conrad's notorious unevenness.

Hervouet, Yves. *The French Face of Joseph Conrad*. Cambridge: Cambridge University Press, 1991. Illuminates Conrad's position in the history of the aesthetics of the novel through abundant evidence of his extensive borrowings from French authors. Discusses the influence of Flaubert, Anatole France and Maupassant.

Nadelhaft, Ruth L. *Joseph Conrad*. Atlantic Highlands, NJ: Humanities Press; Hemel Hempstead: Harvester Wheatsheaf, 1991. A reductively partisan feminist study, unconvincing and now looking very dated in its revisionist programme.

Smith, David R., ed. *Joseph Conrad's 'Under Western Eyes': Beginnings, Revisions, Final Forms – Five Essays*. Hamden, CT: Archon Books, 1991. A well-edited cluster of essays focussing on the composition and personal and cultural sources of a novel that moved to the centre of the Conrad canon during and in the wake of the Cold War.

Henricksen, Bruce. *Nomadic Voices: Conrad and the Subject of Narrative*. Urbana: University of Illinois Press, 1992. A deconstructionist study of narrative technique in the major works.

Moore, Gene M., ed. *Conrad's Cities: Essays for Hans van Marle*. Amsterdam: Rodopi, 1992. Well-edited and wide-ranging gathering of biographical, historical and interpretive essays exploring the several influences on Conrad's fiction of the various cities he knew.

Harpham, Geoffrey Galt. *One of Us: The Mastery of Joseph Conrad*. Chicago: University of Chicago Press, 1996. A stimulating reading of Conrad's ideological concerns through a distinctly contemporary prism but, ultimately, more about 'us' than about a late-Victorian/early Modernist writer.

Moore, Gene M., ed. *Conrad on Film*. Cambridge: Cambridge University Press, 1997. A baker's dozen of critical essays survey the some eighty films, from the first to the 1990s, based on or inspired by Conrad's fiction, with a valuable filmography and film bibliography.

The 2000s

The criticism of the early twenty-first century follows what became fairly well-established trends and tends to view Conrad's works through the prism of various theories, several influenced by philosophy, sociology, linguistics and the postcolonial, gender and popular culture approaches to literature. The decline of publishers' interest in producing volumes collecting conference papers means that, unlike the 1960s and 1970s, most papers of this kind have found their way into the journals devoted to the writer. Areas previously neglected – Conrad's forays into the drama and the complexity and diversity of his early reception – garnered attention.

Watt, Ian. *Essays on Conrad*. Cambridge: Cambridge University Press, 2000. Brings together the scattered writings of one of the major modern critics of the novel and of one of Conrad's most probing, balanced and engaging commentators.

Bock, Martin. *Conrad and Psychological Medicine*. Lubbock: Texas Tech University Press, 2002. An innovative and thoroughly researched study of Conrad's medical conditions, particularly his neurasthenia and the ways in which illness affected his life and is portrayed in his work.

Kaplan, Carola M., Peter Lancelot Mallios and Andrea White, ed. *Conrad in the Twenty-First Century: Contemporary*. New York: Routledge, 2005. A collection of sixteen essays by scholars alert to trends announced during the previous decade, particularly colonialism, feminism, globalization and textuality. Includes an interview with Edward Said by Peter Mallios.

Hand, Richard J. *The Theatre of Joseph Conrad*. Palgrave Macmillan, 2005. A thorough, lovingly detailed and carefully researched account of the genesis and production of Conrad's plays.

Donovan, Stephen. *Conrad and Popular Culture*. Palgrave Macmillan, 2005. Traces the presence in and influence of various aspects of popular culture on Conrad's writings.

Fothergill, Anthony. *Secret Sharers: Joseph Conrad's Reception in Germany*. Bern: Peter Lang, 2006. Covers German literary and popular responses to Conrad, including those of Thomas Mann and the work in Nazi-dominated Germany. A stimulating viewpoint, marred by some organizational issues, with the book coming off more as a collection of individual essays and losing some coherence thereby.

Lothe, Jakob, Jeremy Hawthorn and James Phelan, eds. *Joseph Conrad: Voice, Sequence, History, Genre*. Columbus: Ohio State University Press, 2008. A finely edited and strong collection of twelve stimulating essays on narrative issues, bringing together papers delivered at a colloquium held in Oslo in 2005.

Goonetilleke, D. C. R. A. *Joseph Conrad's 'Heart of Darkness'*. London: Routledge, 2007. Focussed on contexts, the contemporary and critical reception, and offering reliable guidance for further reading, an engaging and useful guide to the novella for students.

Ruppel, Richard. *Homosexuality in the Life and Work of Joseph Conrad: Love between the Lines*. New York: Routledge Press, 2008. A product of gender and queer theory examining homoeroticism in Conrad's work and (not convincingly) in his life.

Baxter, Katharine Isobel, and Richard J. Hand, eds., *Joseph Conrad and the Peforming Arts*. Farnham, Surrey: Ashgate, 2009. Engaging collection of eight essays surveying facets of the theatrical, including Shakespeare, film and opera, in and around Conrad's writings.

Mallios, Peter. *Our Conrad: Constituting American Modernity*. Stanford, CA: Stanford University Press, 2010. An original, wide-ranging discussion of Conrad's critical fortunes in the United States in the early twentieth century that established him as a major writer, with particular attention to important commentators such as H. L. Mencken.

Hampson, Robert. *Conrad's Secrets*. Basingstoke: Palgrave Macmillan, 2012. Canvasses areas of Conrad's life – his sexual experience and finances, for instance – about which fact is frustratingly absent and traverses selected works to bear upon this exploration.

Study Centres

The Center for Conrad Studies. Institute for Bibliographical and Editing, Kent State University. The centre holds a wide variety of primary and secondary materials (in both print and digital forms) amassed to support the editing of the Cambridge Edition of the Works of Joseph Conrad originally housed in it (and now at St Mary's University, Twickenham, London). Scholars desiring to consult the collection should contact The Director, The Institute for Bibliography and Editing, Kent State University, The Library, Kent, Ohio 44242–0001, USA.

The Ugo Mursia Memorial Collection. Università di Pisa, Pisa, Italy. Extensive non-lending collection of first editions and later states of Conrad's texts. Large holdings of standard critical monographs and also of Conrad criticism in Italian. (For the collection's catalogue, see Bibliographies). Scholars desiring to consult the collection should contact the University's Department of English.

Journals

Articles on Conrad are to be found in a number of academic journals. The four specialist journals listed publish scholarship and criticism concerned with all aspects of his life and work and provide information about regular and occasional conferences.

The Conradian: Journal of The Joseph Conrad Society (UK), issued twice yearly, publishes essays and notes on all aspects of Conrad and, by arrangement with the Conrad Estate, is the journal of record for unpublished letters. Reviews appear on the society's website (josephconradsociety.org). Subscriptions are available from: The Honorary Secretary, The Joseph Conrad Society (United Kingdom), c/o The Polish Social and Cultural Association, 238–246 King Street, London W6 0RF, UK. Also available through JSTOR: http://about.jstor.org/content/conradian

Conradiana: A Journal of Joseph Conrad Studies, issued twice yearly, publishes articles, notes, reviews. Subscriptions are available from: Texas Tech Press, Sales Office, Texas Tech University, Lubbock, TX 79409–1037, USA. Also available through Project Muse: http://muse.jhu.edu/journals/conradiana

Joseph Conrad Today: The Newsletter of the Joseph Conrad Society of America, issued twice yearly, publishes brief notes and reviews, announcements about and reports on the Society's sessions at the annual convention of the Modern Language Association of America and other news of interest to Conradians. Includes news about other scholarly conferences. Subscriptions are available from: josephconradtoday.org.

L'Époque Conradienne, issued annually, publishes articles, conference proceedings and reviews mainly in English. Subscriptions are available from: Société Conradienne Française, Faculté des Lettres et des Sciences Humaines, Campus Universitaire de Limoges-Vanteaux, 39E rue Camille-Guérin, 87036 Limoges, France.

INDEX

Cambridge Companions to...

AUTHORS

Edward Albee edited by Stephen J. Bottoms
Margaret Atwood edited by Coral Ann Howells
W. H. Auden edited by Stan Smith
Jane Austen edited by Edward Copeland and Juliet McMaster (second edition)
Beckett edited by John Pilling
Bede edited by Scott DeGregorio
Aphra Behn edited by Derek Hughes and Janet Todd
Walter Benjamin edited by David S. Ferris
William Blake edited by Morris Eaves
Brecht edited by Peter Thomson and Glendyr Sacks (second edition)
The Brontës edited by Heather Glen
Bunyan edited by Anne Dunan-Page
Frances Burney edited by Peter Sabor
Byron edited by Drummond Bone
Albert Camus edited by Edward J. Hughes
Willa Cather edited by Marilee Lindemann
Cervantes edited by Anthony J. Cascardi
Chaucer edited by Piero Boitani and Jill Mann (second edition)
Chekhov edited by Vera Gottlieb and Paul Allain
Kate Chopin edited by Janet Beer
Caryl Churchill edited by Elaine Aston and Elin Diamond
Coleridge edited by Lucy Newlyn
Wilkie Collins edited by Jenny Bourne Taylor
Joseph Conrad edited by J. H. Stape
H. D. edited by Nephie J. Christodoulides and Polina Mackay
Dante edited by Rachel Jacoff (second edition)
Daniel Defoe edited by John Richetti
Don DeLillo edited by John N. Duvall
Charles Dickens edited by John O. Jordan
Emily Dickinson edited by Wendy Martin
John Donne edited by Achsah Guibbory
Dostoevskii edited by W. J. Leatherbarrow
Theodore Dreiser edited by Leonard Cassuto and Claire Virginia Eby
John Dryden edited by Steven N. Zwicker
W. E. B. Du Bois edited by Shamoon Zamir
George Eliot edited by George Levine
T. S. Eliot edited by A. David Moody
Ralph Ellison edited by Ross Posnock
Ralph Waldo Emerson edited by Joel Porte and Saundra Morris
William Faulkner edited by Philip M. Weinstein
Henry Fielding edited by Claude Rawson
F. Scott Fitzgerald edited by Ruth Prigozy
Flaubert edited by Timothy Unwin
E. M. Forster edited by David Bradshaw
Benjamin Franklin edited by Carla Mulford
Brian Friel edited by Anthony Roche
Robert Frost edited by Robert Faggen
Gabriel García Márquez edited by Philip Swanson
Elizabeth Gaskell edited by Jill L. Matus
Goethe edited by Lesley Sharpe
Günter Grass edited by Stuart Taberner
Thomas Hardy edited by Dale Kramer
David Hare edited by Richard Boon
Nathaniel Hawthorne edited by Richard Millington
Seamus Heaney edited by Bernard O'Donoghue
Ernest Hemingway edited by Scott Donaldson
Homer edited by Robert Fowler
Horace edited by Stephen Harrison
Ted Hughes edited by Terry Gifford
Ibsen edited by James McFarlane
Henry James edited by Jonathan Freedman
Samuel Johnson edited by Greg Clingham
Ben Jonson edited by Richard Harp and Stanley Stewart
James Joyce edited by Derek Attridge (second edition)
Kafka edited by Julian Preece
Keats edited by Susan J. Wolfson
Rudyard Kipling edited by Howard J. Booth
Lacan edited by Jean-Michel Rabaté
D. H. Lawrence edited by Anne Fernihough
Primo Levi edited by Robert Gordon

Lucretius edited by Stuart Gillespie and Philip Hardie

Machiavelli edited by John M. Najemy

David Mamet edited by Christopher Bigsby

Thomas Mann edited by Ritchie Robertson

Christopher Marlowe edited by Patrick Cheney

Andrew Marvell edited by Derek Hirst and Steven N. Zwicker

Herman Melville edited by Robert S. Levine

Arthur Miller edited by Christopher Bigsby (second edition)

Milton edited by Dennis Danielson (second edition)

Molière edited by David Bradby and Andrew Calder

Toni Morrison edited by Justine Tally

Nabokov edited by Julian W. Connolly

Eugene O'Neill edited by Michael Manheim

George Orwell edited by John Rodden

Ovid edited by Philip Hardie

Harold Pinter edited by Peter Raby (second edition)

Sylvia Plath edited by Jo Gill

Edgar Allan Poe edited by Kevin J. Hayes

Alexander Pope edited by Pat Rogers

Ezra Pound edited by Ira B. Nadel

Proust edited by Richard Bales

Pushkin edited by Andrew Kahn

Rabelais edited by John O'Brien

Rilke edited by Karen Leeder and Robert Vilain

Philip Roth edited by Timothy Parrish

Salman Rushdie edited by Abdulrazak Gurnah

Shakespeare edited by Margareta de Grazia and Stanley Wells (second edition)

Shakespeare on Film edited by Russell Jackson (second edition)

Shakespeare and Popular Culture edited by Robert Shaughnessy

Shakespeare on Stage edited by Stanley Wells and Sarah Stanton

Shakespearean Comedy edited by Alexander Leggatt

Shakespearean Tragedy edited by Claire McEachern

Shakespeare's History Plays edited by Michael Hattaway

Shakespeare's Last Plays edited by Catherine M. S. Alexander

Shakespeare's Poetry edited by Patrick Cheney

George Bernard Shaw edited by Christopher Innes

Shelley edited by Timothy Morton

Mary Shelley edited by Esther Schor

Sam Shepard edited by Matthew C. Roudané

Spenser edited by Andrew Hadfield

Laurence Sterne edited by Thomas Keymer

Wallace Stevens edited by John N. Serio

Tom Stoppard edited by Katherine E. Kelly

Harriet Beecher Stowe edited by Cindy Weinstein

August Strindberg edited by Michael Robinson

Jonathan Swift edited by Christopher Fox

J. M. Synge edited by P. J. Mathews

Tacitus edited by A. J. Woodman

Henry David Thoreau edited by Joel Myerson

Tolstoy edited by Donna Tussing Orwin

Anthony Trollope edited by Carolyn Dever and Lisa Niles

Mark Twain edited by Forrest G. Robinson

John Updike edited by Stacey Olster

Mario Vargas Llosa edited by Efrain Kristal and John King

Virgil edited by Charles Martindale

Voltaire edited by Nicholas Cronk

Edith Wharton edited by Millicent Bell

Walt Whitman edited by Ezra Greenspan

Oscar Wilde edited by Peter Raby

Tennessee Williams edited by Matthew C. Roudané

August Wilson edited by Christopher Bigsby

Mary Wollstonecraft edited by Claudia L. Johnson

Virginia Woolf edited by Susan Sellers (second edition)

Wordsworth edited by Stephen Gill

W. B. Yeats edited by Marjorie Howes and John Kelly

Zola edited by Brian Nelson

TOPICS

The Actress edited by Maggie B. Gale and John Stokes

The African American Novel edited by Maryemma Graham

The African American Slave Narrative edited by Audrey A. Fisch

Allegory edited by Rita Copeland and Peter Struck

American Crime Fiction edited by Catherine Ross Nickerson

American Modernism edited by Walter Kalaidjian

American Realism and Naturalism edited by Donald Pizer

American Travel Writing edited by Alfred Bendixen and Judith Hamera

American Women Playwrights edited by Brenda Murphy

Ancient Rhetoric edited by Erik Gunderson

Arthurian Legend edited by Elizabeth Archibald and Ad Putter

Australian Literature edited by Elizabeth Webby

British Literature of the French Revolution edited by Pamela Clemit

British Romantic Poetry edited by James Chandler and Maureen N. McLane

British Romanticism edited by Stuart Curran (second edition)

British Theatre, 1730–1830, edited by Jane Moody and Daniel O'Quinn

Canadian Literature edited by Eva-Marie Kröller

Children's Literature edited by M. O. Grenby and Andrea Immel

The Classic Russian Novel edited by Malcolm V. Jones and Robin Feuer Miller

Contemporary Irish Poetry edited by Matthew Campbell

Creative Writing edited by David Morley and Philip Neilsen

Crime Fiction edited by Martin Priestman

Early Modern Women's Writing edited by Laura Lunger Knoppers

The Eighteenth-Century Novel edited by John Richetti

Eighteenth-Century Poetry edited by John Sitter

English Literature, 1500–1600 edited by Arthur F. Kinney

English Literature, 1650–1740 edited by Steven N. Zwicker

English Literature, 1740–1830 edited by Thomas Keymer and Jon Mee

English Literature, 1830–1914 edited by Joanne Shattock

English Novelists edited by Adrian Poole

English Poetry, Donne to Marvell edited by Thomas N. Corns

English Poets edited by Claude Rawson

English Renaissance Drama edited by A. R. Braunmuller and Michael Hattaway (second edition)

English Renaissance Tragedy edited by Emma Smith and Garrett A. Sullivan Jr.

English Restoration Theatre edited by Deborah C. Payne Fisk

The Epic edited by Catherine Bates

European Modernism edited by Pericles Lewis

European Novelists edited by Michael Bell

Fantasy Literature edited by Edward James and Farah Mendlesohn

Feminist Literary Theory edited by Ellen Rooney

Fiction in the Romantic Period edited by Richard Maxwell and Katie Trumpener

The Fin de Siècle edited by Gail Marshall

The French Novel: From 1800 to the Present edited by Timothy Unwin

Gay and Lesbian Writing edited by Hugh Stevens

German Romanticism edited by Nicholas Saul

Gothic Fiction edited by Jerrold E. Hogle

The Greek and Roman Novel edited by Tim Whitmarsh

Greek and Roman Theatre edited by Marianne McDonald and J. Michael Walton

Greek Lyric edited by Felix Budelmann

Greek Mythology edited by Roger D. Woodard

Greek Tragedy edited by P. E. Easterling

The Harlem Renaissance edited by George Hutchinson

The Irish Novel edited by John Wilson Foster

The Italian Novel edited by Peter Bondanella and Andrea Ciccarelli

Jewish American Literature edited by Hana Wirth-Nesher and Michael P. Kramer

The Latin American Novel edited by Efraín Kristal

The Literature of the First World War edited by Vincent Sherry

The Literature of London edited by Lawrence Manley

The Literature of Los Angeles edited by Kevin R. McNamara

The Literature of New York edited by Cyrus Patell and Bryan Waterman

Literature on Screen edited by Deborah Cartmell and Imelda Whelehan

The Literature of World War II edited by Marina MacKay

Medieval English Culture edited by Andrew Galloway

Medieval English Literature edited by Larry Scanlon

Medieval English Mysticism edited by Samuel Fanous and Vincent Gillespie

Medieval English Theatre edited by Richard Beadle and Alan J. Fletcher (second edition)

Medieval French Literature edited by Simon Gaunt and Sarah Kay

Medieval Romance edited by Roberta L. Krueger

Medieval Women's Writing edited by Carolyn Dinshaw and David Wallace

Modern American Culture edited by Christopher Bigsby

Modern British Women Playwrights edited by Elaine Aston and Janelle Reinelt

Modern French Culture edited by Nicholas Hewitt

Modern German Culture edited by Eva Kolinsky and Wilfried van der Will

The Modern German Novel edited by Graham Bartram

Modern Irish Culture edited by Joe Cleary and Claire Connolly

Modern Italian Culture edited by Zygmunt G. Baranski and Rebecca J. West

Modern Latin American Culture edited by John King

Modern Russian Culture edited by Nicholas Rzhevsky

Modern Spanish Culture edited by David T. Gies

Modernism edited by Michael Levenson (second edition)

The Modernist Novel edited by Morag Shiach

Modernist Poetry edited by Alex Davis and Lee M. Jenkins

Modernist Women Writers edited by Maren Tova Linett

Narrative edited by David Herman

Native American Literature edited by Joy Porter and Kenneth M. Roemer

Nineteenth-Century American Women's Writing edited by Dale M. Bauer and Philip Gould

Old English Literature edited by Malcolm Godden and Michael Lapidge

Performance Studies edited by Tracy C. Davis

Popular Fiction edited by David Glover and Scott McCracken

Postcolonial Literary Studies edited by Neil Lazarus

Postmodernism edited by Steven Connor

The Pre-Raphaelites edited by Elizabeth Prettejohn

Renaissance Humanism edited by Jill Kraye

The Roman Historians edited by Andrew Feldherr

Roman Satire edited by Kirk Freudenburg

Science Fiction edited by Edward James and Farah Mendlesohn

Scottish Literature edited by Gerald Carruthers and Liam McIlvanney

The Sonnet edited by A. D. Cousins and Peter Howarth

The Spanish Novel: From 1600 to the Present edited by Harriet Turner and Adelaida López de Martínez

Travel Writing edited by Peter Hulme and Tim Youngs

Twentieth-Century British and Irish Women's Poetry edited by Jane Dowson

The Twentieth-Century English Novel edited by Robert L. Caserio

Twentieth-Century English Poetry edited by Neil Corcoran

Twentieth-Century Irish Drama edited by Shaun Richards

Twentieth-Century Russian Literature edited by Marina Balina and Evgeny Dobrenko

Utopian Literature edited by Gregory Claeys

Victorian and Edwardian Theatre edited by Kerry Powell

The Victorian Novel edited by Deirdre David

Victorian Poetry edited by Joseph Bristow

War Writing edited by Kate McLoughlin

Writing of the English Revolution edited by N. H. Keeble

20376006R00130

Printed in Great Britain
by Amazon